BRIGHT SIGNALS

SIGN | STORAGE | TRANSMISSION

A series edited by Jonathan Sterne and Lisa Gitelman

BRIGHT

SIGNALS

A HISTORY *of* COLOR TELEVISION

SUSAN MURRAY

DUKE UNIVERSITY PRESS *Durham and London* 2018

Printed in the United States of America on
acid-free paper ∞
Designed by Matthew Tauch
Typeset in Scala Pro by Copperline Books

Library of Congress Cataloging-in-Publication Data
Names: Murray, Susan, [date] author.
Title: Bright signals : a history of color television /
Susan Murray.
Description: Durham : Duke University Press, 2018. |
Series: Sign, storage, transmission |
Includes bibliographical references and index.
Identifiers: LCCN 2017051308 (print)
LCCN 2017054717 (ebook)
ISBN 9780822371700 (ebook)
ISBN 9780822371212 (hardcover : alk. paper)
ISBN 9780822371304 (pbk. : alk. paper)
Subjects: LCSH: Color television—History. | Television
broadcasting—Technological innovations—United States. |
Television broadcasting—United States—History. |
Television broadcasting—Social aspects—United States.
Classification: LCC PN1992.3.U5 (ebook) |
LCC PN1992.3.U5 M86 2018 (print) | DDC 621.388/04—dc23
LC record available at https://lccn.loc.gov/2017051308

Cover art: GE 950 colour wheel television receiver.
Courtesy the National Museums Scotland.

DUKE UNIVERSITY PRESS GRATEFULLY ACKNOWLEDGES THE
SUPPORT OF THE NYU HUMANITIES INITIATIVE GRANTS-
IN-AID, NEW YORK UNIVERSITY, WHICH PROVIDED FUNDS
TOWARD THE PUBLICATION OF THIS BOOK, AND THE LEBOFF
FACULTY GRANT, NEW YORK UNIVERSITY, WHICH PROVIDED
FUNDING TOWARD THE PUBLICATION OF THIS BOOK.

FOR MUNRO & QUINN

CONTENTS

ACKNOWLEDGMENTS | ix

INTRODUCTION | 1

1 ▸ "AND NOW—COLOR" | 11
Early Color Systems

2 ▸ NATURAL VISION VERSUS "TELE-VISION" | 34
Defining and Standardizing Color

3 ▸ COLOR ADJUSTMENTS | 86
Experiments, Calibrations, and Color Training, 1950–1955

4 ▸ COLORTOWN, USA | 127
Expansion, Stabilization, and Promotion, 1955–1959

5 ▸ THE WONDERFUL WORLD OF COLOR | 176
Network Programming and the Spectacular Real, 1960–1965

6 ▸ AT THE END OF THE RAINBOW | 217
Global Expansion, the Space Race, and the Cold War

CONCLUSION | 251

NOTES 259 | BIBLIOGRAPHY 293 | INDEX 303

ACKNOWLEDGMENTS

I have been extremely fortunate to receive significant funding for this project. In 2012 the Hagley Museum and Library awarded me an exploratory grant to work in the still unprocessed David Sarnoff and RCA collections. During the 2013–2014 academic year, I was a recipient of both an American Council of Learned Societies (ACLS) fellowship and an NYU Center for the Humanities Fellowship, enabling me to take time away from teaching and administration and to concentrate on writing. That same year, I received three grants supporting a publication subvention for the production and inclusion of the book's color images: an NYU Center for the Humanities Grant-in-Aid, an NYU Steinhardt Professional Development Award, and an NYU Media, Culture, and Communication Leboff Faculty Grant. Finally, I received a National Endowment for the Humanities (NEH) Faculty Fellowship for 2015–2016, which enabled me to finish the manuscript over the period of a full-year sabbatical. Any views, findings, conclusions, or recommendations expressed in this book do not necessarily reflect those of the National Endowment for the Humanities.

Of course, support comes in many forms, and I am tremendously grateful for the encouragement and assistance of so many friends, family, and colleagues. Courtney Berger, Sandra Korn, Jessica Ryan, and the reviewers at Duke University Press and series editors Lisa Gitelman and Jonathan Sterne have been enormously helpful and supportive. My research assistants, Shane Brennan and Kamilla Pollock, and indexer Jason Begy were efficient, creative, and proactive and this project would have surely taken me much longer to finish had it not been for their efforts. Anna McCarthy, Aurora Wallace, Dana Polan, Marita Sturken, and Jonathan Sterne read chapters at various stages and gave me invaluable feedback. Dana and Jonathan also generously wrote letters in support of this project for my multiple fellowship applications and were undoubtedly a primary factor of my success in that area. Sarah Street and the anonymous readers at *Screen* gave productive comments on the article that formed the basis for, and which is reprinted in part within, chapter 3.

My colleagues in Media, Culture, and Communication at NYU inspired me to reconsider my approach to the histories of television technology. I am especially indebted to Carolyn Kane, who, while an MCC PhD student researching the dissertation that would eventually become her book *Chromatic Algorithms,* asked me if I had ever come across any histories of color television. It was in trying to answer her query that I first became interested in this project. Alison Garforth and Jamie Schuler, MCC grants managers, along with administrative director Melissa Lucas-Ludwig, operations administrator Carlisa Robinson, and department chair Lisa Gitelman, were an enormous help in acquiring and processing funding related to this project.

Peter Decherney provided me with one of the first opportunities to present my very early research on color television to the cinema studies colloquium at the University of Pennsylvania during my time as a Wolf Visiting Professor of Television Studies in 2010. I am indebted to Jane Tylus and Gwynneth Malin of the NYU Center for the Humanities, along with my extraordinary cohort of fellows (Ademide Adelusi-Adeluyi, Dwaipayan Banerjee, J. M. DeLeon, Jen Heuson, Dania Hueckmann, Thomas Looser, Eduardo Matos-Martín, Ara Merjian, Melissa Rachleff Burtt, Andrew Romig, Delia Solomons, Cara Shousterman, and Zeb Tortorici), for their support of and contributions to early drafts of this work.

The archivists, librarians, and assistants at the various institutions that I visited while researching this book were invaluable and generous with their time and expertise: George Kupczak at the AT&T archives, Lynn Catanese at the Hagley Museum, Jane Klain at the Paley Center, the archivists at the Library of Congress and at the Wisconsin Historical Society, and Timothy Horning at the university archives at the University of Pennsylvania.

I started this project in 2009, when my oldest son was three years old, and finished revisions during my second son's first year. As a single mother by choice, I would not have been able to research and write this book during these past eight years had it not been for the help and care of my community of family and friends. Sompit Oerlemans has taken care of both of my children, becoming like a second mother to them and a sister to me. Omar Amores and the Greenwich House After-School and Arts Camp provided me with a generous financial-aid package and provided a warm and loving community in which my eldest thrived for the majority of his elementary school years. My family, Donald, Dorrit, and Steve Murray, along with Aurora Wallace, John Paton, Marina and Roddy Bogawa, Anna McCarthy and Bill Vourvoulias, Paula Gardner, Amy and Adam Reyer, Alison Macor, Lauren Bowles, Patrick Fischler, Sandra Clifford, and the teachers at University Plaza Nursery School and PS3, have also loved and cared for my children in ways that have not only enabled me to work on this project, but that have also sustained us in other more meaningful ways.

This book is dedicated to Munro, my eldest, who has been incredibly patient with me when I have had to disappear behind the computer screen and into this project and whom I love more than the Empire State Building, and to his brother, Quinn, whose impending arrival motivated me to work tirelessly to finish the manuscript and who has brought us so much joy since.

FIGURE I.1 Image from a 1954 Inco Nickel TV Shadow Mask ad.

Introduction

The prevailing U.S. apathy to tinted TV was echoed last week by
an idle viewer at Rich's department store in Atlanta. "I know the
grass is green at Ebbets Field," he said. "It isn't worth $400 more
to find out *how* green."

—*Time*, 1956

Color television was a hard sell. Although the public, regulators, and
industry insiders were impressed by the relatively crude images they
saw at even the very first demonstrations of the technology in the late
1920s, and while color was generally thought to be the inevitable technological addition that would ultimately complete the sensory experience of television, it was deemed impractical from the start. At times,
color television was considered too expensive, technologically cumbersome, and challenging to stabilize and manage; it required too much
bandwidth and would set a higher bar for "true fidelity." As a result of
this demanding complexity, the technology for color television existed
for over twenty years primarily either as a novelty or as a challenge to
what the industry came to quickly accept as the speediest route to standardization and commercialization—black and white television. Even
after the color standard was adopted by the Federal Communications
Commission (FCC) in 1953, it would be more than a decade before color
television became widely available in the United States. Consequently,
the historical narrative of color television is full of false starts, failure,
negotiation, and contention. Yet it is also a narrative that reveals the

complex interconnections between the development of color television and the study of subjectivity and perception, the presumed role of video aesthetics, the psychological power of color use, the play between the spectacular and the real, the assumptions that structure the production and reception of specific genres, and the power of television's narrational and commercial agency, especially when compared to film and photography. The unique qualities of color television are both historically located in the larger context of nineteenth- and twentieth-century color media and tied to the specific discourses framing the capacities and affordances of television as a seeing device.

Surprisingly, there has been little scholarly attention paid to this fertile history. While there have been countless books and articles written about postwar U.S. television, few mention color as more than an aside, a footnote, or a singular moment in the history of broadcast regulation. These histories have ignored the many ways in which the quest for and production of color became central to the operations, finances, branding, and marketing of RCA (which owned NBC) and CBS at different moments in their maturation. Or how color was widely considered the ultimate victory in innovation for the industry and a defining factor in the modernization of the look of television and its relationship to other forms of visual media post-1960. Moreover, unlike in some recent color film scholarship, television scholars have not yet read industrial discourses around, and studies of, electronic color in relation to broader philosophical and cultural conversations about the nature of color. And even though the study of color in design and media has become a key area of research as of late in other fields, surprisingly this interest, with a few exceptions, has not extended to research on television color specifically. In the last five years or so, a number of notable books have been published on the topic of film and color (primarily in the United States and United Kingdom) that have explored production techniques, color management, technical and artistic processes and practices, and the meanings generated by color use.[1] Additional works on color and consumerism, design, and digital color released in recent years have also altered our understanding of color use and production.[2] For these authors, color represents a fresh vantage point through which to reconsider well-trodden histories, analyses, and approaches to various forms of media and consumer culture. Color also invites meditations on subjectivity and perception, which opens up new pathways for discussions of aesthetics and spectatorship.

The explanation for the oversight of color in the study of television likely involves the placement of the battle for FCC approval as the sole focus of all color television history, as well as the reluctance of many contemporary U.S. television studies scholars to engage with questions of technology, vision, and aesthetics. Television is most commonly thought about in terms of the cultural narratives and ideologies it creates and engages with, rather than as a highly complex technology of visual culture. Consequently, thinking through how technology and the processes of development and regulation shape the look of the television image is not something that has been considered until recently.

In the past, technical histories of television have primarily been left to the engineers, most notably George Shiers, Raymond Fielding, and Albert Abramson, who have written books and articles in technical journals, and Ed Reitan, who slavishly chronicled the history of color television technology and production in mostly nonnarrative form on his website before his death in 2015.[3] These technical histories are highly detailed chronicles of the processes and results of innovation in television; however, they often lack the cultural, industrial, and/or political context needed to provide a more complete picture of the various forces at work in the formulation of the idea and material object of television. This marginalization of the technical in relation to the rest of television studies scholarship has been showing signs of change in the last few years, in large part due to the growing influence of media archeology and the history of science and technology on the methods and focus of media historiography. A handful of scholars have even recently begun to engage with color television history specifically.[4] For example, Andreas Fickers has chronicled the history of color television standards in Europe, while Jonathan Sterne and Dylan Mulvin have written two articles that explore rich and intricate "perceptual histories" of the American standards period.[5]

While my analysis of the FCC color standards helps frame this book, my overall focus is more expansive. The question of color and the nature of its attendant affordances, conventions, limitations, and complications were unremitting and influenced not only the priorities and direction of the television industry but also the way that viewers understood themselves in relation to that industry and its technology. In conceptualizing the project, my aim was to locate the core period from the moment of the technology's invention to the time in which it was no longer considered novel in U.S. broadcasting. What I discovered through archival research was an extended and rigorous discussion, over more than forty years, about electronic color, occurring across commercial, regulatory, consumer, and scientific communities, that not only was one of the primary forces determining television's future but also configured the broader understanding and use of a distinctly modern form of vision.

One of the primary lines of argument threaded through all the chapters of this book is that color television, distinct from both monochrome television and other forms of color media, was imagined and sold as a new way of seeing. Color not only represented a new aesthetic for television (largely determined by FCC standards for color technology and the color management and production techniques established by networks) but also promised a peculiar viewing experience for audiences. Even though color television was not broadcast in 3D or even high-definition during the years before 1970, there was a consistent assertion made about its dimensionality and the way that it invited viewers to completely immerse themselves in the image, which is similar to the way that IMAX or 3D technologies are discussed today. Fabric textures were said to pop, the reflection on bodies of water shimmered, and dancers and their costumes revealed a new level of subtlety and expressiveness in movement—the viewer felt transported, her senses stimulated on a multitude of levels. The sense of immersion arose from the way that the electronic color images were said to overwhelm the senses, refine and enhance vision, and expand horizons. Jack Gould, television critic for the *New York Times*, made this very argument in a 1964 review of two color documentaries, stating, "The addition of color imparted a vibrancy and dimension to the superb photography that left no doubt there is virtually a new medium of TV at hand. The delicacy of the shading and greater pictorial depth stemming from the contrast offered by various hues were integral parts of a more exciting process of communication." He added that in the documentary on Rome he was reviewing, "one could almost feel the texture of the historic streets and buildings."[6] The 1952 manual for the CBS Remington Rand Vericolor TV camera chain asserted this idea even more vigorously:

Much of the significance of color in television is striking, even to the casual observer. Aside from the most obvious effect, namely, that color introduces a sense of reality and a lifelike quality into the picture, comparison of a color television picture with the corresponding black-and-white image makes it apparent that not only are small objects more perceptible, but outlines in general seem to be more clearly defined. . . . Color television also seems to introduce a certain perception of depth. This is due, in part, to the increased ability of color to reproduce the contrasts and shadows as well as highlights and reflections in different hues, while the degree of color saturation, which is a function of distance, strongly enhances the three dimensional quality.[7]

Color television's promise of an immersive and intimate level of visual proximity fostered its development in a field outside of entertainment too: medical education. Largely promoted in the late 1940s and early 1950s by investor Smith, Kline and French (SKF), a Philadelphia-based pharmaceutical company, along with I. S. Ravdin, chief of surgery at University of Pennsylvania Hospital, and Peter Goldmark, head of CBS Laboratories, color television technology modified for medical use was adopted by teaching hospitals across the nation and was demonstrated regularly at medical conventions.[8] Praised for offering the ability to virtually transport viewers to an ideal viewing position of a live surgery or other medical event, for being able to transmit live and large-scale microscopic images from one location to another for diagnostic purposes, and for enabling medical practitioners to see what they otherwise could not on a microscopic image through the manipulation of color and light, color television promised to improve upon medical vision and the traditional surgical amphitheater experience. Although there were attempts to use monochrome television for medical purposes, the technology proved insufficient. Dr. Ravdin argued that one of the unique properties of color television that made it so ideal for medical use was "a sense of depth which is necessary for the adequate teaching of surgery," noting that with color television, "the deep recesses of body cavities which ordinarily are difficult to discern can now be readily observed because of the various color gradations."[9]

Coupled with the claims about its distinctive form of vision, color television was said to have a unique psychological and emotional hold over viewers that made them more attentive, engaged, and open to the images and claims made before them. These beliefs about the power of color television were, of course, sold to advertisers and audiences by the networks and manufacturers in an effort to get them on board with the color project. Yet they also informed what genres and production techniques would be used to illuminate the purported unique qualities of the technology. Color television was positioned as the ideal form of modern American consumer vision, a discursive construct that by the 1960s had begun to intersect with Cold War rhetoric regarding surveillance and truth-telling devices and technologies. At that point, color television came to also represent American scientific prowess and the ability to withstand seeing and being seen via a technology of revelation and veracity.

The other argument underpinning this book is that color, as a concept and a phenomenon, came with a significant amount of cultural and industrial complexity and baggage and therefore brought with it tension, instability, and anxiety as it shaped the discussion about what television was ultimately supposed to do and be. In placing electronic color in relation to the aims and ideologies of American consumer culture and alongside the history of color theory and of other forms of color media (film and photography), we see how both the subjectivity and the volatility of color in general informed the way that color television was produced and received. We also come to understand how the processes and practices around electronic color and its management were simultaneously extensions of and distinct from those developed for other forms of color media.

These arguments give shape and direction to this book, which is organized chronologically, starting at the moment of invention (1928) and ending at the point at which the U.S. networks completed their conversion to color and a significant portion of the audience owned color sets (1970). This bracketing allows me to explore color television technology as a point of difference in the production and experience of television and to investigate the various ways color was, over time, integrated into the system of production and process of reception through cultural, industrial, regulatory, commercial, technological, and aesthetic negotiation. Each chapter is organized around a particular issue or stage—for example, innovation, standardization, calibration, conversion, and global expansion—that defined the industry's relationship to color at a specific moment. The first half of the book focuses more overtly on the technology of color television, while the second half brings that history and conceptual framing to bear on moments in more traditional cultural and industrial histories.

Chapter 1 examines the early experimentation in and demonstration of color television technology, focusing primarily on the mechanical systems of John Logie Baird in the United Kingdom and Herbert E. Ives at Bell Labs in the United States. In this chapter, I am decidedly not interested in any sort of "inventor as hero" narrative or making claims about who should be considered the *true* inventor or patent holder of color television. Instead, I investigate the ways the technology was conceived of in terms of its relation to vision and veracity, as well as to other image-based mediums, while also considering the specifics of the demonstrations of this new technology and how they were described and received. Because this was a period in which the various possible applications for the technology were being imagined and debated, it is a rich moment to explore in terms of what were considered to be the unique qualities of electronic color and how it was expected to alter communication, pleasure, knowledge, and access to cultural and educational experiences. I end with a brief discussion of Baird's part-electronic high-definition and stereoscopic color systems (demonstrated in the late 1930s and early 1940s) and CBS's 1940–1941 demonstrations and public relations push for Goldmark's mostly electronic field-sequential system. With these demonstrations, which were primarily to the press, retailers, and regulators, CBS was attempting to disrupt the National Television Systems Committee (NTSC)—a group formed by the Federal Communications Commission to study systems and recommend standards—and the FCC process that appeared at that time to be leading toward a 525–scan line black and white standard, which the network and others felt was too limiting for future technological advancements, such as the broadcasting of color, which, as CBS argued, required a larger bandwidth. The protracted process of setting a separate color standard for U.S. television almost a decade after the black and white standard was established is a discussion that is saved for the following chapter.

My objective in chapter 2 is to place the process of color television standardization within a larger history of color theory, measurement, and management across various disciplines and industries. In framing the chapter this way, my intention is to intervene in the typical television history narrative of the "color wars" between RCA/NBC and CBS, wherein standards are primarily a result of the moves and machinations of various governmental and broadcast industry players. This approach to the history creates the impression that the debates and discussion and ultimate outcome of this process (from 1948 to 1953) occurred in isolation and without the influence of complicated scientific, organizational, and historical precedents and entanglements. Like a number of recent books on the histories of color film, I begin the chapter outlining the philosophical and theoretical engagements with the question of color and subjectivity and then go on to explore the nineteenth-century development of color measurement systems (by scientists, artists, and philologists) that relied on studies of the nature of human vision and empirical research into the makeup of and interaction between colors. However, I then track how these systems of colorimetry made possible the standardization of color in industry and governmental institutions in the twentieth century and the role that those institutions and systems of measurement had in the formation of standards for film and then, eventually, television. The chapter concludes with an extended discussion of the approval process of the FCC and the work of the NTSC panels, detailing their psychophysical and technical tests of various color systems and the theories and cultural assumptions about color, television, and perception that structure them.

Even after the NTSC color system became the standard in 1953 and commercial broadcasting had been approved, color television remained technologically unstable and required much refinement and management at the levels of production, transmission, and reception. The first half of the decade, therefore, primarily served as an experimental and promotional period. In chapter 3, I analyze the discourses that framed the responses of critics, advertisers, network executives, and the public to the arrival of color to television in the context of both the specific value of and concerns over electronic color and the larger cultural anxieties around the potentialities and failures of color. I trace the development of color training for ad agencies, sponsors, and network employees, along with systems of calibration and color adjustment at the points of production and reception. The chapter wraps up with an examination of the earliest color programs and NBC's strategy behind its "introductory year" of color programming in 1954.

Chapter 4 moves beyond NBC's first year of color broadcasts and examines the use of color and video technology as a central component of modern design on network specials during the mid-1950s. However, before I get to the topic of network programming in this chapter, I first recount RCA/NBC's investment in local station conversion, their road-showing of color television across the nation, NBC's branding in relation to symbols of color, the building of color studios, the placement of color sets in public places, and the network's initial attempts at studying and then selling the "quality" color audience to advertisers. In covering this ground, we witness the processes of both conversion and expansion, and also the way that color had to be marketed and promoted through specific means and referring to specific rhetorical tropes and visual symbols. At a time in which color set ownership was still limited to relatively well-off early adopters, executives had to devise strategies for consumers to envision color television, whether through network identifications that announced color programs as they came on their black and white sets or through local promotional events that not only provided opportunities for people to view color television but in some instances lit up buildings and the sky in RGB color as the company worked to place electronic color into the public imagination. This was also a time in which both specific emotional and perceptual engagements with color were analyzed and then used to promote color viewing. Color use in television was said to engender a more intensive psychological and visual attentiveness in relation to the image, and that belief framed the assumed relationship between a viewer/consumer and color commercials and color programming. It also buttressed the idea that color viewing as an experience is more immersive, expansive, and both more realistic and more sensational than viewing monochrome.

I continue to delineate color media's relationship to the indexical and fantastical in chapter 5 by examining the use of color in, and marketing of, certain genres in the early to mid-1960s that were considered to be better at highlighting the features of color television viewing than others. Specifically, I spend the majority of the chapter discussing color cultural documentaries. Documentaries of this period are typically thought of as sober, highly political black and white endeavors intended as a cultural corrective to late-1950s network scandals and FCC chair Newton Minow's 1961 "vast wasteland" speech to the National Association of Broadcasters (NAB). Yet color cultural documentaries, which combined educational imperatives with visual exploration and entertainment, were also popular at this time and were considered to be an excellent form through which to sell the need for and attributes of color on television. These documentaries tended to focus on art, travel and tourism, and nature, and promised to transport or immerse viewers in another world—one that could only be fully experienced through color. Whether the topic was diving deep with Jacques Cousteau, traveling through Rome with Sophia Loren, or receiving a guided tour of the Louvre, these colorcasts encouraged viewers to linger on the spectacular and realistic image before them in order to increase their sense of "being there" and temporarily submerge themselves in another world.

This purported ability of color television to expose the spectacular "real" or "natural" as it extends human sight continues to be explored in chapter 6, but is placed in the context of color television's 1960s global expansion through international displays, satellite technology, the adoption of color systems by other nations, and eventually, the inclusion of a color TV system on Apollo missions to the moon. In this chapter, I also look at the way color television's heightened relationship to veracity was picked up by and fused with forms of Cold War rhetoric that worked to claim color television as a potential tool of surveillance and detection.

I end the book by looking ahead from the 1960s to the normalization and full dissemination of analog color television and point toward the questions that need to be raised in terms of contemporary screen color in an effort to link them up to the history explored here.

The governing idea of this book is that color television was an incredibly complex technology of visual culture that disrupted and reframed the very idea of television while also revealing deep tensions and aspirations about technology's relationship to and perspective on the "natural" world and, relatedly, our potential to extend human sight and experience. As the following pages will demonstrate, color television was considered both an assumed next step in the advancement of the technological extension and replication of human sight as well as a radical departure from the norms, procedures, and priorities set by the black and white standard.

CHAPTER ONE

"And Now—Color"

Early Color Systems

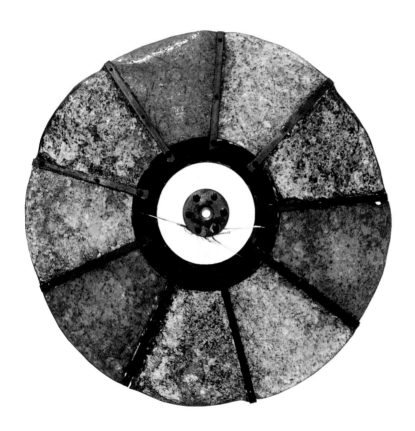

FIGURE 1.1 A color wheel from a 1946 GE 950.

As others have long argued, television is distinguished from other visual media, especially film, by its claims to *liveness, immediacy,* and *extension of vision.* The notion of "seeing at a distance"—seeing through walls, through space and time, witnessing things as they happen *elsewhere*— has been the primary promise of television since the late nineteenth century and is the frame through which early research into television is discussed. The notion of television entered the public imaginary as a possible, or even probable, form of seeing device that would add pictures to the already existing sound-based communication media of the telegraph and telephone, often retaining the point-to-point function of those parent media. Conceptualizations of technologies similar to what would come to be known as television were often represented as an improvement on or completion of the sensory experience of the telephone (in the form of what came to be called two-way television), enabling geographically distant individuals to share time and space in a state of simultaneous virtual presence. Television imagined in this manner would provide a complete replication (through sound and image) of another place or person to be experienced by a viewer. In fact, in drawings and descriptions of early models of technologies prefiguring television, it is as though the person before the camera is being transported, appearing before the viewer not within the confines of a receiving set, but existing in real space as a kind of apparition (see figure 1.2).

Even though "natural" color processes (as opposed to tinting or hand coloring) were not yet available in color photography or motion pictures, it was assumed color would eventually be a feature of a device such as television, since it would surely be essential for the realistic experience of virtual presence. While there had been conceptual proposals for color television systems as early as 1880, the first patent application describing a rudimentary system, which included the use of color filters, tubes, selenium cells, and a mirror drum, was put forth in 1902 by Otto von Bronk for Telefunken in Germany.[1] Six years later, Armenian engineer Hovannes Adamian patented his own mechanical system in Germany, Britain, and France, and then in Russia in 1910. In 1925, Vladimir Zworykin filed a patent for a television system that included a color screen; Adamian demonstrated a three-color system (an advancement on his earlier two-color model) in the United States; and Harold McCreary, an engineer for Associated Electric Laboratories in Chicago, used cathode ray tubes to design a system of simultaneous color transmission, which

FIGURE 1.2 "The reproducing apparatus at work." From "The Teleectroscope: Herr Szczepanik's Wonderful Invention Explained," *Los Angeles Times*, April 3, 1898, 3.

meant that it would transmit three colors—red, blue, and green—at the same time. Yet a working color system that was able to reproduce images with a decent level of fidelity was proving to be far more difficult to develop than a black and white system, so the race to be first in television was one that focused primarily on monochrome.

As do many discussions about the process of invention, histories of television technologies often become bogged down in descriptions of "firsts." These histories can be helpful in the construction of chronologies and in tracing the complicated path of innovation; however, they also bear the marks of what Wiebe E. Bijker refers to as "implicit assumptions of linear development" of the technology over time.[2] This type of narrative can also obscure the labor of particular individuals and the economic, political, and social structures that enable one inventor or lab to come out on top in the race to claim ownership over a particular technology. The early history of color television has been traditionally framed as such a history, and various nations have laid claim to being the site of the invention of color television, including Scotland (inventor John Logie Baird) and Mexico (inventor Guillermo González Camarena). In truth, there is in this history no singular narrative resulting in an ultimate moment of innovation. We can best understand the history of color television as an invention that came about through research into a number of various technologies, including monochrome television, color photography, telephony, radio, and telephotography (the transmission of still images via telephone wire).

During the mid-1920s, inventors such as John Logie Baird, Charles Francis Jenkins, Ernst Alexanderson, Herbert E. Ives, Ulises Armand Sanabria, Vladimir Zworykin, and Philo T. Farnsworth were experimenting with, demonstrating, and filing patents related to television. Their systems and devices were first conceptualized and then realized as both monochrome and mechanical (meaning they operated through moving parts rather than cathode ray tubes), although two of those individuals, Baird and Ives, demonstrated *color* systems at decade's close. In a 1954 presentation, Elmer Engstrom, head of research at RCA labs, claimed that "it has always been the objective of those engaged in television research to achieve television in color. . . . Color was considered as a natural step to follow black-and-white television."[3] Putting it another way, Frank Stanton, who served as president of CBS from 1946 until 1971 and was an early champion of color television, asserted in 1946 that "any discussion of television's future must be based on one incontrovertible and well-documented fact: that, at best, black and white television on the lower frequencies can constitute a temporary service."[4] This is certainly how color television is described in retrospect: an inevitable and predetermined move toward the perfection of the technology. This familiar refrain is both a result of the narrative of linear progress that underscores so much of technological innovation and a discourse specific to television that has to do with veracity and vision.

The framing of "seeing at a distance" through television acts as an analogy as well as indicating television's role as a kind of prosthesis. Those working on early models of television would describe the apparatus both in relationship to how it engages with the human eye (persistence of vision, for example) and how it mimics the eye's basic functions, including color reception. Doron Galili's research reveals that this relationship between the electronic eye and the human eye was assumed from the very earliest moments in which television entered into the "technological imaginary."[5] These nineteenth-century conceptual models for a technology that would later become television represented a unique form of electrical sight. Early experiments with selenium cells, a photoconductive chemical element that was a component of a number of early proposals for television, were especially resonant with the idea of a technological replication of the eye, as the way in which the cells responded to light and color closely aligned with contemporary beliefs about how the retina functioned. As Galili notes, this metaphorical connection was also a consequence of the way that synapses and neural pathways were already being conflated with the functions of electricity in the 1860s and '70s.[6]

An experiment by Baird—a Scottish engineer and inventor who early in his career worked on prototypes of thermal socks, rustless razors, and pneumatic shoes but who would be written into history as one of the primary inventor-founders of television (both color and monochrome)—provides an example of television as prosthetic eye that takes the analogy a step further. Working with an actual human eyeball acquired through somewhat questionable means from the chief surgeon at Charing Cross Ophthalmic Hospital, Baird later told the *New York Times* that the "eye of a London boy helped him to see across the Atlantic," as the organ was part of an experimental machine for testing television's "long-distance vision." He went on to describe his acquisition and use of the eye in detail:

> I had persuaded a surgeon to give me a human eye which he had just removed, in order that I might try by artifice to rival nature. . . . As soon as I was given the eye I hurried in a taxicab to the laboratory. Within a few minutes I had the eye in the machine. Then I turned on the current and the waves carrying television were broadcast from my aerial. The essential image for television passed through the eye within half an hour of the operation. On the following day the sensitiveness of its visual nerve was gone. The eye was dead, but it had enabled me to prove an important theory on which I had been working on for some time. I had been dissatisfied with the old-fashioned optical dodge of a selenium cell and lens, and felt that television demanded something more refined. The most sensitive optical substance known is the nerve of the eye, called the visual purple. It was essential to get some of this visual purple in the natural setting of the human eyeball in order to use it as a standard of perfection in completing the visual parts of my apparatus.[7]

Despite the probability, as many have claimed, that the "visual purple" (rhodopsin, a light-sensitive receptor protein) of the boy's eye may not have actually revealed much of anything about Baird's "Televisor," the story is a fascinating example of the way that the contemporary understanding of the human eye was built into television's very technology. Baird's tale is vivid and gruesome, but it also leaves the reader with the image of technology's ability to beat out, to extend the life of, to replicate indefinitely the fragile and ultimately mortal human sensory system. That poor eye of the London boy of Baird's retelling gave up its last bit of life for the larger project of seeing at a distance. However it's not just the way that the eye functions that helps model television, but also how its seeing is a complicated and subjective process. As Anne-Katrin Weber argues, television's reliance on persistence of vision and other forms of "trickery" of the eye, such as enabling the eye to construct a cohesive image from a collection of dots or lines, "highlighted the difficulty of conceiving vision as unmediated or direct, as an 'exterior image of the true or the right,' and revealed the subjectivity of seeing, produced not outside but within the perceiving subject."[8]

While the transmission and reception of black and white moving images was certainly a remarkable achievement, it did fall short of the ideal of replicating what one experiences in the process of seeing. Seeing in "natural color" at a distance in stereoscopic or 3D—advancements that were already in development at the time of Baird's experiment—was considered the closest one could come to replicating the human experience of seeing the world, and therefore was held up as an ideal for television.[9] However, as mentioned briefly in the introduction, even if color was considered to be an essential component of the ultimate end state of television, it was also considered expensive and troublesome. It took up far more bandwidth than monochrome; the technology and lighting required were often cumbersome; there was more potential for problems with the image (flicker rate issues, instability, etc.); and the bar for "true fidelity" (especially when it came to the representation of human flesh) was set significantly higher for color, which meant that the technology had to be at a more advanced state of development to even be considered acceptable by viewers, consumers, and regulators. Consequently, the period of the late 1920s was primarily a time of experimentation with color systems that had little hope of becoming the industry standard and going on the market. In a 1930 paper in the *Journal of the Optical Society of America*, Herbert E. Ives, the head of Bell Labs' special research department (which focused on facsimile and television research), and A. L.

Johnsrud acknowledged the expensive, complex, and often difficult nature of color television compared to monochrome, predicting that these features would mean that the technology would have to "wait much longer for its practical application."[10] They would be proven correct on this point, as the color television project would largely be abandoned for the majority of the 1930s.

In the rest of this chapter, I will briefly detail the little known period of early experimentation with and demonstration of mechanical television in the late 1920s and the work done by CBS's Peter Goldmark in the late 1930s on his mechanical field-sequential color system, which was largely considered a significant advancement on that of Baird's and Bell Labs' apparatuses. I will spend some time discussing the details of the early color demonstrations, how they were described and understood, and whether or not they were deemed capable of highlighting the features of electronic color imaging. Although there were breaks and gaps in this period of innovation, the scientific, industrial, and cultural position of color television during these early years would help shape the reception of the technology as it began to further penetrate the popular imagination in the 1940s and become a viable and standardized consumer good in the 1950s.

"PAINTING TELEPICTURES": EARLY EXPERIMENTS AND DEMONSTRATIONS

The individual credited with being the first to *display* a successful color system was Baird, who held a demonstration in London on July 3, 1928.[11] His 120-line mechanical system employed a rapidly rotating Nipkow disc with three sets of holes cut into spiral patterns that were covered with red, green, and blue filters. When the disc spun, the images were scanned with alternating lines of the three colors—an interlacing scanning system that helped cut down on flicker (a detectable fading on the screen that occurs between scanning cycles). The receiver then picked up the scanned red, green, and blue images one color at a time and projected them onto a very small screen where the colors were blended. After a demonstration of what was then called daytime television (a monochrome screen that could be viewed not only in a dark room but also in natural or bright light) on the roof of Baird's Long Acre lab, Baird led his guests—mostly reporters and scientists—downstairs, where he had set up a room for the color system. What happened next was meticulously described by the *Manchester Guardian*:

> The receiver in this case gave a somewhat smaller image, about half as large again as an average cigarette card but the detail was perfect. When the sitter opened his mouth his teeth were clearly visible; so were his eyelids and the whites of his eyes and other small details about his face. . . . He picked up a deep red colored cloth and wound it round his head, winked, and put out his tongue. The red of the cloth stood out vividly against the pink of his face, while his tongue showed as a lighter pink. He changed the red cloth for a blue one and then, dropping that, put on a policeman's helmet, the badge in the center standing out clearly against the dark blue background. The color television proved so attractive that the sitter was kept for a long time doing various things at the request of the spectators. A cigarette showed up white with a pink spot on the end when it was lit. The fingernails on a hand held out were just visible and the glitter of a ring showed on one of the fingers.[12]

Baird had begun working on his color television not long after he had successfully developed a black and white system, an experience he touted as "seeing by wireless."[13] He also simultaneously worked on a number of variations and improvements on television between 1926 and 1929, including Phonovision (recorded television signals on a gramophone record), long-distance television, stereoscopic television (an early version of 3D), and "noctovision" (infrared television). Although he would not work to refine color television to any serious degree until the late 1930s and early 1940s, when he combined it with stereoscopic television, Baird's multiple demonstrations of color television in this brief period of his initial interest in color impressed government officials and members of the press. An article published in the *Journal of the Royal Society of Arts* reported on Baird's successful demonstration of color to the British Association meeting in Glasgow in 1928:

> The images transmitted, consisting as they did of only fifteen elemental strips [scanning lines], showed a surprising amount of detail: in the human face, the whites of the eyes, the colour of a protruded tongue, and the teeth were clearly reproduced. Mixtures of strawberries, raspberries and leaves were recognisable: not only the colour

but the tones and shades of irises, poppies and marguerites [daisies] could be seen. The chief difficulty occurs, of course, with whites, in which the relative strengths of red, green and blue have to be carefully balanced: fortunately, the visual accommodation is large, however, and it is remarkable to what extent light may differ from white and yet appear but slightly tinted.[14]

For such a small image with so few scan lines, the amount of detail is certainly notable, as is the reported legibility of the color. Baird was displaying what would be understood as the most "natural" of the vivid colors through flowers, fruits, and faces, and he focused especially on variations of red (one of the most challenging colors to reproduce) through the tongue, red cloth, poppies, strawberries, and raspberries. We will see this develop as a common feature and collection of objects in early color demonstrations.

The following summer (1929), mechanical color was demonstrated in the United States at AT&T Bell Labs with a system that used filters and discs like Baird's but that also contained two distinct features: a bank of photocells at the receiving end that picked up the color signals (and was said to catch the depths and subtleties of the red hues even better than Baird's)[15] as well as a set of mirrors that worked to mix the colors and display the image on the screen (see figures 1.3–1.5). In his description of the "beam scanning" method employed in the Bell color system, Ives, whose research into photoelectronic cells led to his groundbreaking work on the transmission and reception of television signals, linked his research on color television to previous achievements in telephony and in the science of color photography.[16] Since his youth, Ives had been involved in the development of color photography, initially through his father, Frederic E. Ives, who was a pioneer in the field, having developed Kromskop, the first commercially available color photography system in England and the United States, in the late 1880s. In reporting on H. E. Ives's work, *Science* claimed that this "new method of color television is essentially a combination of these two achievements of father and son."[17] The younger Ives had also worked on an early color facsimile prototype, which successfully transmitted a color image using color separations in 1924. While recognizing that "principles used in three-color photography" formed the basis of his understanding of how *additive* color (color created by mixing primary colors of light) functioned and that there had

FIGURE 1.3 Bell Labs color television system, 1929. From "Two-way Television and a Pictorial Account of Its Background," developed by Bell Telephone Laboratories (with AT&T), April 1930, 18.

always been an assumed parallel between color photography and color television, Ives's particular method did not have any "close counterpart" in color photography and could not be replicated in that medium.[18] In other words, color television was conceptually related to—and perhaps indebted to—color photography, but television's need for high-speed colored light sources "capable of following the variation of the television signal current" made its demands and processes unique.

Calling television in color (inaccurately) "an American achievement," the *Western Electric News* described Ives's June 1929 demonstration as:

a score or more of New York newspaper men, gathered recently in the Bell Laboratories, walked past a piece of apparatus enclosed in a heavy curtain and, one by one, peered into an aperture that resem-

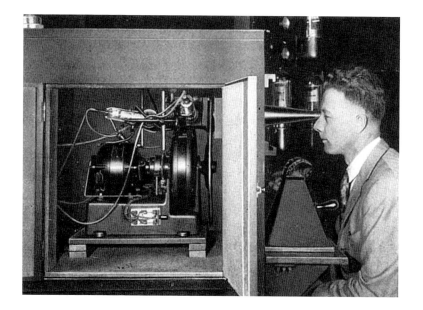

FIGURE 1.4 "Peephole" viewer on the Bell Labs color receiver. From "Two-way Television and a Pictorial Account of Its Background," Bell Labs, 1930.

bled the eyepiece of a telescope. What each of them saw first was an American flag rippling in the breeze, each star outlined against a field of blue; each stripe clearly defined in red or white.[19]

After the flag was waved, a man held up a color photo of Al Jolson in blackface singing "Sonny Boy," which he then put down in order to pick up a series of other objects: children's play balls in orange, green, and red, a slice of watermelon, and a geranium.[20] Then, to show off the qualities of electronic color in movement, "the stage was cleared and a young girl, Miss Charlotte Papillion, mounted a high stool before the dance blue light." As she played with a string of red beads, "her every movement, from a white toothed smile to an alluring wink, was clearly visible."[21]

Ives organized another demonstration close to two weeks later for more journalists, an engineer from the Federal Radio Commission (FRC), and a representative from the radio division of the Bureau of Standards. The press likened the demonstration to an "old fashioned peep show," as

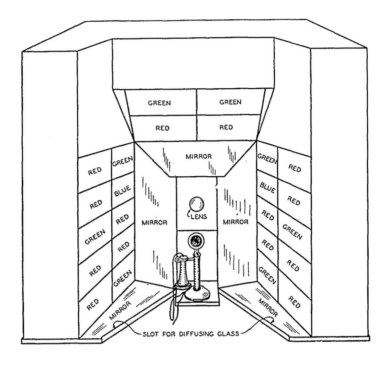

FIGURE 1.5 From Herbert E. Ives and A. L. Johnsrud, "Scanning in Colors from a Beam Scanning Method," *Journal of the Optical Society of America* 20, no. 1 (1930): 20.

the receiver was actually positioned in a booth and the screen itself was extremely small and was located at the end of what was compared to a spyglass. The *Washington Post* said, "It was like looking at a moving picture about as big as a postage stamp, excepting instead of a film you were seeing the real thing and in beautiful colors. . . . It was a marvelous achievement—one of the most highly satisfactory demonstrations we have ever seen."[22]

Demonstrations for the press, government officials, and the public occurred at a stage within the process of technological innovation at which the technology has been successfully and reliably operated in the lab. These demonstrations were intended as grand announcements that would lay claim to a particular innovation. They were public relations moments that combined scholarly scientific address, branding, and a touch of the spectacle of a carnival midway.

Despite the similarities in their demonstrations, Baird and Ives were working out of two distinct models for the funding and development of technological innovations—the independent model and the corporate model—which impacted the ways they arranged and sometimes even performed their demonstrations. Baird was an independent inventor, working virtually alone before he formed his own company, the Baird Development Company, in 1927. Ives, on the other hand, was employed in AT&T's research division, which meant he worked alongside various scientists, engineers, and technicians, and he was overseen by higher-ups in the company's corporate structure who would have had highly specific directives for those working in the lab. The corporate structure impacted not only the lab culture and the process, financing, and ownership of the technologies, but also the context, setting, and framing of the demonstrations. For example, since Baird was independent, he felt compelled to seek out validation from both established institutions and commercial operations, along with alternative sources of financing. In 1925, he accepted payment of twenty-five pounds a week to demonstrate his still rather crude monochrome system three times a day for three weeks at Selfridges, London's largest department store. This was the first public demonstration of television anywhere and was a hit with shoppers, if not an immediate sensation among scientists and business-men. It was also most likely not the way that AT&T would have ever initially presented a new technology. (Although they might have, at a later stage, taken it on a tour through popular spaces in order to expose it to a wide swath of consumers.) However, Baird also needed to present his invention in a more formal way to a community with influence and power. Therefore, a year after his Selfridges display, Baird brought a more refined version of his black and white system to the Royal Insti-tution of Great Britain. Ives, on the other hand, brought in reporters and officials who would be key to the eventual approval of a television system, including members of the FRC and the Bureau of Standards, for his first announced demonstrations.

Demonstrations of monochrome television systems had been per-formed in a very similar way to the color demonstrations, of course, as they came out of the same or similar (corporate and independent) lab environments. However, there were differences, especially when one compares the objects that were placed in front of the camera for black and white demonstrations with the objects in color demonstrations.

FIGURE 1.6 RCA's Felix the Cat doll. Sarnoff Collection, file 1814.
COURTESY OF THE HAGLEY MUSEUM AND LIBRARY.

FIGURE 1.7 John Logie Baird's ventriloquist dummy "Stookie Bill" was often used in his television experiments and demonstrations. USED WITH PERMISSION FROM THE SCIENCE MUSEUM/SCIENCE & SOCIETY PICTURE LIBRARY, U.K.

These distinctions reveal insights into the creators' beliefs about and intentions for these systems.

Many early in-lab tests of black and white television captured still imagery—the most famous being RCA's Felix the Cat, used in the majority of their in-lab experiments from 1928 to 1932 (see figure 1.6). These still objects used in the lab were also often used in formal demonstrations. Examples include Baird's "Stookie Bill" (see figure 1.7) and the dollar sign Farnsworth used in his 1928 transmission in front of the press.

In her dissertation on displays of television at fairs and exhibition sites in the early part of the twentieth century, Weber states that early television demonstrations in these contexts were done in studio-like settings and often involved still images and film strips that were "scanned by a tele-cine apparatus and, transformed by electric information, transmitted to nearby receivers."[23] The still imagery allowed for consistency and predictability in the image, especially as live transmissions by mechanical systems could easily be affected by weather or other forms of interference or disruption. Yet there were also live components to most of these demonstrations. (This combination of the live, still, and filmed would also define color television demonstrations.) In his first demonstration of monochrome mechanical television, Baird used head-and-shoulder views of both Stookie Bill and William, his (human) office boy. William and the other live models Baird would use in subsequent demonstrations (sometimes he brought up the officials and reporters watching the demonstration to serve as subjects, much to their delight) would often be asked to look at the camera and open their mouths wide. Their open mouths would look like large deep black holes in the center of the screen. Baird also sometimes used performers—comedians, actors, and singers—to do short versions of their acts in front of the camera. The demonstrations at AT&T were said to more often than not put live bodies in front of the screen, mostly showing close-ups of faces. In 1927, for instance, Ives's demonstration of "long-distance" television (between Washington, DC, New Jersey, and New York) to scientists, press, and officials involved an on-screen guest appearance by Secretary of Commerce Herbert Hoover and what could be understood as a mini variety show, featuring a vaudeville act, a speech, and a performance of "humorous dialog talk."[24] Due to the low resolution of the experimental systems and the extreme lighting needed to capture the most basic of images, monochromatic objects with high contrast (or performers wearing harsh monochromatic makeup that provided a similar contrast for faces) seemed to be sensible choices.

In order to demonstrate the unique qualities of *color* television, a variety of colored objects and subjects had to be shown live for at least part of the demonstration. They needed to best present the capabilities of the system by showing color as stable, consistent, vibrant, clear, and "natural." These early moments of color display are fascinating in their simultaneous quest for realism in and spectacularization of the image, as well as in their use of particular objects for display that connect not only to other cultural products and ideologies but also to other moments of innovation in media and cultural technologies.

Based on the press reports, the Baird demonstration, as a performance containing some measure of spontaneity, showing the man with the red cloth and other objects, is perhaps more easy to interpret, as it was somewhat similar to many of the earliest silent films—shot to emphasize detail and "natural" movement of the body, as well as hue and contrast. There are similar performances in both Bell Labs demonstrations, with the girl who holds objects, plays with red beads, and flirts with the camera. (Although here, the peep show quality of this system and the gender of the performer distinctly alters the character of the viewing experience.) And yet, close-ups in both black and white and color demonstrations were always noted to be the most interesting and clear images seen on those early tiny screens. The close-ups on objects of nature, such as flowers and types of red fruit (strawberries and watermelons were especially favored), were a common element of all these demonstrations. Certain colors are more difficult to contain or keep fixed—specifically red, as it has a tendency to bleed, especially when it is placed against white. So it was perhaps both the vibrancy and the challenge that red offered that led Baird and Ives to include so many red objects in their demonstrations. Similarly, the American flag also provided an opportunity not only for an expression of nationalism but also for the placement of three challenging colors together—red, white, and blue—without them bleeding into each other.

While these objects may have been selected for what they could reveal about the color system on display, they also carry cultural, historical, and industrial resonances, especially when presented in a particular order. Looking more closely at two of the 1929 Bell Labs demonstrations described in the press, we find an odd addition to the usual collection of colorful fruits and flowers and a person in motion: a color photo of Al Jolson singing "Sonny Boy," which came right after the waving of an American flag and right before a slice of watermelon. In 1929, Jolson was an enormous star, which might serve as reason enough to use him in this moment; yet his image was closely linked to both minstrel performance and another media technology: film sound. He had starred in a Vitaphone short as early as 1926 as part of the Warner Bros. early sound experiments. Of course, he was also in *The Jazz Singer* in 1927, and Jolson's first full talkie, *The Singing Fool*—the film in which "Sonny Boy" was featured and performed in blackface—broke box office records in 1928. This makes the Jolson image a curious and yet not altogether unexpected choice for these demonstrations. Curious in that one would have to ask what a silent, still image of a singing minstrel performer had to do with color television; and not altogether unexpected in that Jolson was already used as a sign or carrier of innovation (sound films) and that racist or stereotyped imagery of African Americans more generally has a historical connection with moments of innovation in and/or dissemination of media technologies. (This includes early race films in the cinema, radio's movement into serial narratives in the late 1920s with *Amos 'n' Andy*, and *Amos 'n' Andy* being used as the feature program of RCA's demonstration of television at the 1939 world's fair.) While certainly watermelons were one of the more vibrant fruits commonly used in such demonstrations in order to show off the red hues and the contrast of the green rind and black seeds, when used in conjunction with the image of Jolson, one cannot help but think of the ways that watermelons have been used in racist imagery in the United States. For example, in the very early period of silent films, at the turn of the nineteenth century, there was a series of shorts of African Americans eating watermelons, most of which could be also categorized as "expression films"—those works meant to highlight the detail and movement of the face and therefore emphasize the unique properties of the technology of the cinema. Examples include *A Watermelon Feast* (American Mutoscope, 1896), *The Watermelon Contest* (Edison, 1900), *Who Said Watermelon?* (Lubin, 1902), *New Watermelon Contest* (Lubin, 1903), and *The Watermelon Patch* (Porter, 1905). In *Lynching and Spectacle: Witnessing Racial Violence in America, 1890–1940*, Amy Louise Wood writes,

> Particularly popular throughout this period . . . were films of African American men devouring watermelons, in which the eaters appear ravenous and animalistic, juice and flesh running down their chins. Though they present simple caricatures, the scenes captured white fears of black sexual bestiality but neutralized those fears by placing them in the comic setting of a plantation feast.[25]

The coupling of these two still images of Jolson and the watermelon, then, speaks to and repeats a larger tradition of relying on specific types of powerful and problematic racial imagery to display or demonstrate technological innovation in both film and television.

We can also note that these early demonstrations of color television systems used both still images, in order to allow the viewer to rest on the more clear, stable, and easy moments of the display of color, and images in motion, to show the potential of the medium to broadcast realistic moving images of living objects. There is both utility and scientific reasoning behind the selection and arrangement of objects placed before the camera, along with deeper cultural connections and symbolic gestures that inform the reception of those objects. In trying to capture the interest of and entertain those present at the demonstrations, while also highlighting particular qualities of the technology, these moments of display exist as complex ruminations on the potential applications, cultural intersections, implications, and meanings of color television.

Soon after the Ives demonstrations were conducted, color television experiments in the United States were shelved in favor of honing less complicated and less expensive black and white systems. (Baird, however, continued his color television work throughout the 1930s.) Color was not picked up again in earnest by the American industry until Peter Goldmark developed a part-electronic, part-mechanical system for CBS much later in the 1930s.

THE EXPERIMENTAL YEARS LEADING
UP TO STANDARDIZATION

After demonstrating a series of television innovations in the late 1920s—long-distance television, two-way television, and color television—AT&T began to lose interest in funding more television research, and by the 1930s, engineers at Bell Labs had turned their sights to other technologies. In contrast, RCA picked up television research at the start of the 1930s under the leadership of Vladimir Zworykin, an engineer who while working at Westinghouse at the start of the decade had obtained a number of television related patents, including patents for the iconoscope camera tube and the kinescope picture tube, which would form the basis of all-electronic television. A year or so before he joined RCA, Zworykin had acquired his first patent for a color television system, and he would work to perfect it while at RCA. David Sarnoff, who had become president of RCA in 1930, was a huge proponent of television and desired, almost more than anything else, for his company to be the first to develop and successfully market an all-electronic system. As Benjamin Gross has discussed in his dissertation on RCA's development of LCD (liquid crystal display), Sarnoff prioritized research and development, establishing laboratories that served as centers for applied research and product development (most notably the RCA laboratories founded in Princeton, New Jersey, in 1942).[26] During World War II, the research turned to wartime communications technologies, such as those relating to radar, but television research continued as well, with color becoming

FIGURE 1.8 A 1940 photo of an image on Baird's 600-line color television.

a focus after the war. As a result of Sarnoff's support of Zworykin's re-search and tenacity in acquiring television related patents, the company did succeed in producing an electronic monochrome television system that was first shown to the public on a large scale at the 1939 world's fair. However, the company would not begin working on *color* television specifically until the 1940s (this will be covered in more detail in chapter 2), around the time that CBS was pushing for FCC approval of their own color system.

Baird continued his experiments with color television in the 1930s, broadcasting color images almost daily from his laboratories in London's Crystal Palace. For a time, he became especially interested in com-bining "stereoscopic television" (a concept based on the same principle as the common stereoscope device used to view photographs in a way that presents solidity and depth—an approximation of 3D) with color in order to create the ultimate immersive and "real" viewing experience.

When that system of color stereoscopic television proved to be cumbersome and unpractical, Baird concentrated on perfecting his mechanical monochrome system (in hopes that it would be permanently adopted by the BBC and eventually become the U.K. standard), as well as devising a part-mechanical, part-electronic color system. Employing a rotating RGB disc in front of a newly RCA-trademarked cathode ray tube, Baird demonstrated that color system in 1939, while also working toward a high-definition color device. Although he once again had in mind 3D television as an ideal (he had displayed a monochrome version in 1928), he managed to give more depth and clarity to his color television image by increasing the resolution to bring it to a level of "high definition." In 1941, he demonstrated a 600-line color system (see figure 1.8) employing a cathode ray tube and scanning three interlaced 200-line frames onto a large screen (twenty-four by twenty-four inches).[27] The resulting images were impressive to those who attended the demonstrations, although, as Baird himself admitted, the biggest challenge was to get the "colors of the human skin" correct.[28] *Wireless World* reported:

> The various tone values were reproduced with a degree of truth comparable with the Technicolor films which we are now used to seeing at the cinema. A notable point in connection with viewing the colour pictures is an apparent stereoscopic effect which makes the picture stand out to a remarkable degree.[29]

While this iteration of Baird's color system was not technically stereoscopic, the reporter was speaking to a sense or experience of being pulled into a highly detailed moving image in color, which adds to the "degree of truth" that a color image can claim about its representation of the natural world. (We will see this claim made about color television's immersive effect throughout the chapters of this book.) A year later, Baird revealed a stereoscopic color system that was more streamlined than his earlier model and that no longer required the viewer to wear special glasses, use a stereoscope, or sit in one precise spot in relation to the screen. The demonstrations of this device were a success and generated much excitement; however, his color and stereoscopic technologies were never made available to the public, as Baird continued to struggle financially during the war years and was in ill health. Moreover, neither his monochrome nor color systems were ultimately accepted into use by the BBC, due to what the broadcasting company considered insurmountable technical problems with Baird's early monochrome cameras and, a decade later, to Baird's extended illness coupled with the postwar dissolution of a governmental plan to institute a new high-definition color television standard. Instead, the BBC adopted a 405-line electronic system by Marconi-EMI, which served as the model for the U.K. standard for decades. However, only a few years before his death in 1946, Baird demonstrated a cathode ray tube in an all-electronic two-color system, employing his newly developed telechrome tubes and boasting the potential for a 1,000-line image. Although none of Baird's television technologies made it to the consumer marketplace, his ideas were influential, and in many ways, his innovations were said to surpass those of his primary competition in the color television field during the 1940s, CBS.

Around the time of Baird's successful demonstrations of his high-definition color system in the early 1940s, Goldmark at CBS had begun to demonstrate his part-electronic field-sequential system, which relied on an image-dissector tube, a three-color rotating disc, and a sped-up version of Baird's original scanning method. Goldmark's first demonstration, on August 28, 1940, was for CBS executives, who felt so positive about the development that they arranged for Goldmark to show it to FCC commissioners—including the chairman, James L. Fly—a month later. The company also initiated a public relations campaign for their new color system, with events and press screenings, in an effort to both boost their corporate image as a technological innovator and hopefully delay the approval of the RCA-backed black and white standard for television, which was already being considered by the NTSC and which CBS considered too technologically limiting. Reports of the quality of the CBS image were generally positive, even though some (especially U.K. reporters) complained that Goldmark had stolen Baird's system. In demonstrations, the images of "flowers, flags, maps, bathing beauties, fabrics, a watermelon and marine views" on the CBS color receiver were, as a *New York Times* reporter put it, "so clear . . . that a bumble-bee alighting on a marigold seemed to be in the room."[30] As part of their series of demonstrations to journalists and appliance retailers, CBS also broadcast shots of paintings from a major art exhibit (see figure 1.9).

Although CBS did not succeed in altering the outcome of the FCC/NTSC approval process for a black and white standard for television, the

Pale delicate colors of bowl of flowers provide an exacting test for the CBS color television system. All colors will be reproduced at receiver by mixture of the primary colors, red, green and blue, which are represented in the filters of the color drum and disc (*below*).

Flowers televised appear with their colors accurately reproduced. Kodachrome reproduction of color television image does not do entire justice to it. In particular, horizontal lines on image picked up by camera at close range are not apparent to the eye at normal viewing distance.

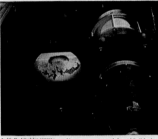

Inside the television camera inverted image appears on ground glass at left. Color drum at right, with red, green and blue filters, spins at 1,200 r. p. m. Filters pick out own colors in subject, transmit them separately to inside of electronic scanning tube to right of drum.

Color disc, held by Inventor Peter C. Goldmark, spins in front of cathode-ray tube. Synchronized with color drum, disc transmits the successive single-color images picked up by camera. Persistence of vision in eyes blends separate color images into integrated full-color picture.

In the television studio, Victor Moore, Vera Zorina and William Gaxton perform for color television camera (*left*). Color television can handle hundreds of thousands of different shades and tones of all colors as against 30 shades of gray for black-and-white television.

Performers televised show program possibilities of color television. Exaggerated in reproduction, loss of image detail is compensated by colors, which convey information lost in black-and-white transmission. Color image resists room illumination much better than black-and-white.

FIGURE 1.9 "Color and Big-Screen Images Open New Horizons," *Life*, September 22, 1941, 53.

company did manage to prove that color was an imminent practical possibility for the industry. The NTSC also agreed to eventually form a panel on the topic of color television, and RCA initiated further research into the technology. Although the war would put the question of commercial television on hold, television research continued in the context of military communication technologies. As a result, once the war ended, CBS would begin to tout their new "high-definition" UHF color system, which will be discussed in detail in the following chapter.

CHAPTER TWO

Natural Vision versus "Tele-Vision"

Defining and Standardizing Color

The movement toward standardization of a color television system in the postwar era was in large part discussed and determined in relation to historical developments in color theory (philosophical, psychological, and physical), colorimetry (the measurement of color), color design and industry, psychophysics, psychology, and, of course, what had already been established for monochrome television. The structures and definitions that formed the basis for color standards in both commercial and artistic use developed out of an array of scholarly and industrial fields during the first part of the twentieth century, all of which were primarily centered on the question of how to understand and quantify the relationship between the observer and the colors that appear to exist in the world. Some early to mid-twentieth-century forms of color management and/or standardization came out of the industrial and design arts—such as textile, paint, printing, and plastics—and were devised specifically with consumers in mind. For example, the Munsell and Ostwald systems, which were both refined and implemented in the first two decades of the century and were roughly based on Newton's color circle, are empirical approaches to identification and quantification of the perception of color values. The CIE (Commission Internationale de l'Eclairage, or International Commission on Illumination) system of color, developed in the 1930s, also worked to standardize the perception and use of color, but was the first to define and express color spaces—mathematical models of the range of colors that can be created out of primary pigments (RGB, for example, uses red, green, and blue to construct a model of all possible colors)—in a more complex way.

FIGURE 2.1 Illustration of the inner workings of an RCA color system from the cover of the October 1949 issue of *Radio Age*.

It was these systems and models that formed the basis for the post-war expansion in the business of the deliberate naming, arranging, selecting, marketing, and branding of color by color experts (who also went by such titles as "color forecasters," "color engineers," and "color stylists").[1] While Regina Blaszczyk marks the 1920s as the initiation of the "color revolution," she also identifies the postwar period as the moment in which that revolution intensified and expanded, arguing that "the color explosion of the postwar years was evidence of the extravagances of a growth economy and the maturation of American consumer society."[2] As Penny Sparke reminds us, color was also a way to distinguish oneself in a time of acute cultural homogenization and mass production. Women in particular responded to the increased use of color in products, furnishings, and appliances as the act of display in the home became "a form of self-identification" for the housewife.[3]

Color television promised to put the color explosion on vivid display, highlighting and selling the products tinted so carefully and consciously by color consultants. Yet while standardization in the language, management, and use of color for design and for consumer products was established by the 1940s, standards for electronic color had only begun to be hashed out among regulators, engineers, and the television industry. The meeting of these areas—the television specific and the color specific—in the processes and systems of standardization is at the heart of this chapter. This history of color measurement, management, and perception informs not only the innovation of color reproductive technologies such as color television, but also the manner in which those technologies are tested, standardized, and manufactured by industry and used and understood by consumers. This chapter will trace the conceptual tools—from the philosophical to the scientific to the commercial—developed to help systematize and stabilize our vexed and complex relationship to color. It will also explore the history of color reproduction and standard setting in a number of industries, including, most relevantly, that of film and television.

SCIENCE, PHILOSOPHY, AND THE SEEING SUBJECT

Even though color has been highly rationalized and standardized, subjectivity and unpredictability are also assumed features of both color television and the human eye. The mechanisms of vision and perception are especially complicated when it comes to the sensory experience of color. As art historian John Gage notes, the differences and possibilities that arise when we consider both the objective aspects of color (the scientifically quantifiable stimuli that produce an experience of color in an observer) and the subjective outcome of the sensory process, raise weighty metaphysical issues.[4] Over the past few centuries, this disjuncture has led to a diversity of theoretical claims and articulations of the meanings and experiences of color—in fields as diverse as art history, psychology, linguistics, philosophy, cognitive science, neuroscience, physics, design, and even marketing and advertising. For example, during the 1950s, the then increasingly popular hypothesis of linguistic relativity (the idea that people who speak different languages might also think differently) centered on studies of color language and color cognition, since it was recognized that reception and classification of color depended on both biology and language and was, to varying degrees, understood to be a subjective process.[5]

The fundamental question that has structured much of the debate around color since the sixteenth century is whether or not color exists as a sui generis property in objects in the physical world, outside of the mind of the perceiver. In his seminal study of color, *Opticks*, published in 1704, Isaac Newton located color in light (he identified seven spectral hues) as it is reflected off objects, thereby disproving the existing theory that pure light was colorless or white. However, he also was clear that color, as we understand it, exists in the mind, "for the rays, to speak properly, are not coloured. In them is nothing else than a certain power and disposition to stir up a sensation of this or that colour."[6] René Descartes and John Locke, however, argued that there were no colors at all in the physical world (not even in light); rather, colors exist only as *sensations* (or sensory ideas) in our visual perception.[7] In his highly influential work, *Zur Farbenlehre* (*Theory of Colors*), Goethe asserted that the origin of color is the interplay between dark and light, and emphasized the role that shadow plays as an element of color.[8] Goethe was presenting a description of his experimentation (at times with the aid of a camera obscura) on the phenomenon of color, and in doing so, he argued that instead of focusing so much on white light as the source of a spectrum of color (as Newton did), one should analyze color's relationship to darkness as well as to light, to perception, and to subjectivity. He even speculated on what would later be called color psychology—the meanings and responses that particular colors generate for people. Yet Wittgenstein said that, rather than a theory, Goethe's work was really a "vague schematic outline" of the properties and interactions of color.[9] Jonathan Crary also notes that while many questioned the validity of Goethe's findings or their relation to scientific "truth," the importance of his work lies in a "key delineation of subjective vision, a post-Kantian notion that is both a product and constituent of modernity." Crary continues,

> What is important about Goethe's account of subjective vision is the inseparability of two models usually presented as distinct and irreconcilable: a physiological observer who will be described in increasing detail by the empirical sciences in the nineteenth century, *and* an observer posited by various "romanticisms" as the active, autonomous producer of his or her own visual experience.[10]

For Goethe, the origination of color was neither only in the mind nor only in the world but a highly involved process of input and information provided by the world coupled with human perception and sensation—the biological response of a standard or healthy eye. Goethe delineated three types of color in relation to their points of origin: (1) physiological colors, which originate in the eye; (2) physical colors, which are "produced by certain material mediums"; and (3) chemical colors, "which we can produce, and more or less fix, in certain bodies."[11] Physiological colors were the most compelling ones for Goethe, as they represented the way that color perception simultaneously obeyed the laws of nature and appeared to maintain a rather radical subjectivity.[12] In *On Vision and Colors*, Arthur Schopenhauer—who engaged directly with Goethe's work, even duplicating some of his experiments—recognized the significance of physiological color but studied the changes that occur specifically in the retina when perceiving color.[13] Schopenhauer's study on color stemmed from his larger theory of perception and cognition that at its core argued for the intellectual nature of perception—meaning that while the senses provide access to the raw data of the world, it is our intellect, our knowledge of such things as "space, time, and causality," that can make sense of what we are seeing/ feeling/hearing/smelling.[14] George Stahl, who notes that Schopenhauer was the first to bring the study of color into the realm of philosophy, explains that "there can be, according to Schopenhauer, no object without subject and no subject without object, since perceptions are defined by both." Stahl continues:

A key element of Schopenhauer's theory of perception is the transformation of subjective *sensations*, emanating from the object world, into objective representations, which comes about, as Schopenhauer shows, by the inference of the understanding. Schopenhauer was the first to make this fundamental separation between sensation and representation and the role the understanding plays in establishing the relation between the two.[15]

Color for Schopenhauer was a physiological process—an effect of the cause of "sensation brought about by an external stimulus" and a part of his theory of intuitive perception.[16]

The phenomenon of afterimages was key to Goethe's and Schopenhauer's ideas about the perception of color. As Crary has noted, afterimages—images that linger in one's vision after the initial stimulus or object is no longer in one's sight—had been identified and described since antiquity and yet, until the early nineteenth century, they were thought of as either spectral deceptions or physical imperfections in the eye.[17] Goethe's and Schopenhauer's work during this period (along with the work of others such as Jan Purkinje and A. S. Davis) treated the afterimage not as a visual or psychic disturbance or aberration but rather as an essential component of the physiological processes of cognition and perception.[18] In the following paragraph, Goethe describes how readers might experiment with their own vision to activate afterimages:

> Those who wish to take the most effectual means for observing the appearance in nature—suppose in a garden—should fix the eyes on the bright flowers selected for the purpose, and, immediately after, look on the gravel path. This will be studded with spots of the opposite color. The experiment is practicable on a cloudy day, and even in the brightest sunshine, for the sun-light, by enhancing the brilliancy of the flower, renders it fit to produce the compensatory color sufficiently distinct to be perceptible even in a bright light. Thus peonies produce beautiful green, marigolds vivid blue spectra.[19]

Both Goethe and Schopenhauer noticed that the afterimage appears as the complementary color of the original object viewed—violet for yellow, green for red, et cetera. Their studies served to normalize afterimages but also forced a reconsideration of the belief that vision was autonomous and mechanical and pushed toward an understanding of it as subjective and corporeal. As Mary Ann Doane has pointed out, this move toward the subjectivization of vision was accompanied by an "inevitable production of anxiety linked with the revelation of a body that cannot even trust its own senses, when vision is uprooted from the world and destabilized."[20] The afterimage, and its accompanying theory of the persistence of vision was, of course, used to explain the ability of pictures in motion—at a specific speed—to "trick" the eye into seeing continuous movement.[21] Afterimages that were studied specifically in relation to color perception were, as Doane notes, often described as being a result of trauma or fatigue in response to the shock of exposure to and then release from an especially vivid or bright color.[22] (The classic example would be the response of the eye to fixating on a vibrant red for a time and then suddenly looking at a white sheet of paper.)

In his book on color in early film, Joshua Yumibe discusses the work of Joseph Plateau, a Belgian physiologist whose research on afterimages in the 1820s and '30s formed the basis for his development of the optical toys the anorthoscope and the phenakistoscope, which were meant to demonstrate the functions of color perception along with the phenomenon of persistence of vision.[23] Yumibe states, "More than just proffering playful experimentation, these toys worked to shape the viewer's subjective perception to an orderly system that rationalized space, time, and color in ways that would bridge one person's individual experience to another's."[24]

When it came to the electronic transmission of color, afterimages were noted and analyzed in both radar imagery and color television in the mid-twentieth century. The perceived coherence of television imagery—whether monochrome or color—is based on models or understandings of vision similar to those that make both film and optical toys function, based on the premise that the eye will fill in the gaps and assume coherence and movement when a series of images are presented at a particular rate. For television, the process of scanning (first with the Nipkow disc, in 1884) in both mechanical and, later, electronic television systems involves the transmission of images one line at a time, at a particular rate, in order to give the effect of motion.[25] Adding color to the scanning process not only made it more complex but also introduced more possibility for errors—some of which were related to the production of color trails, flicker, or afterimages. In two mid-century studies, the cathode ray tube screen was found to produce "Purkinje afterimages" or "Bidwell's ghost" (both terms refer to a very clear type of afterimage that is stimulated in the eye after exposure to a brief flash of light). These early studies were initiated because of complaints made by radar operators in the late 1940s about an "illusory sweep," a second yellow-tinged sweep line seen rotating behind the actual (blue-tinged) sweep line on their cathode ray tube radar screens. This extra rotating sweep line existed as a potentially dangerous distraction or point of confusion for operators, who often took the presence of the illusory sweep as a sign of equipment failure.[26] The researchers found that the illusory sweep line afterimage would not appear if the pulse rate of the light was reduced or the sweep sped up.[27] Later in this chapter, we will see how the specific technical issues in the electronic transmission of color had to be addressed and then incorporated into a standard for the recording, transmission, and perception (by a traditionally constructed "standard observer") of color. However, standardization—or the process of calculating, measuring, and predicting colors and their various permutations and interactions—was of interest to color scholars as early as the 1830s.

As Sean F. Johnston has discussed, there are two areas of research that fed into the development of color measurement systems (such as the science of colorimetry and the systems of color harmony): (1) empirical research into the makeup and interaction of color (which led to empirical explanatory systems and mapping); and (2) research into "the nature of human vision."[28] Moreover, Johnston locates the interest in measuring and classifying color in the mid- to late 1800s as stemming from a few interrelated communities and their attending interests: artists, scientists, and philologists (those who study the history of written language).[29] Artists, of course, were interested in understanding and perhaps even managing the way that color signified and could be created through mixing and materials. Scientists wanted to expand upon Newton's approach and develop detailed systems for recognizing and predicting the color that would result from particular combinations related to hue, brightness, and saturation; and philologists were engaged with the process of and systems related to color naming and language.

Three of the major figures from this period were Thomas Young, James Clark Maxwell, and Hermann von Helmholtz, who developed the three-color theory of combination—the belief that all colors derive from the mixing together of the three primary colors: red, blue, and green. Additionally, Helmholtz—a German physicist, philosopher, and

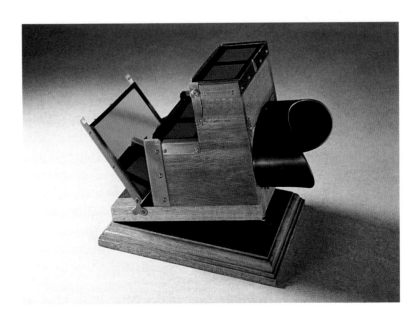

FIGURE 2.2 An Ives Kromskop. PHOTO USED WITH PERMISSION FROM THE SCIENCE
MUSEUM/SCIENCE & SOCIETY PICTURE LIBRARY, U.K.

physician, whose research interests centered on questions of human
perception and who, in partnership with Young, developed the theory
of "trichromatic color vision"—delineated the distinction between *additive* and *subtractive* color mixing in order to explain why the processes
of mixing colors through light and mixing colors through pigments
differ.[30] According to Helmholtz's theory, historian of science Richard
Kremer explains, additive mixing (which is what happens in color television) "occurs when two or more light rays of different wavelengths
illuminate the same spot on the retina, either simultaneously or in rapid
succession. Subtractive mixing results from the physical combination of
different pigments. The former was thus a physiological (or psychological) process . . . ; the latter was a physical process."[31] As discussed briefly
in the previous chapter, Frederic E. Ives, a pioneer in the development
of photography and its techniques, experimented with an additive color
process in the late nineteenth century, which greatly informed the color
television research of his son, Herbert, who developed facsimile and
television technologies at AT&T. Based on Maxwell's theories, the elder

FIGURE 2.3 William Saville Kent, "Butterfly and Flowers" (1898), an Ives Kromogram (as seen through the Kromskop). PRIVATE COLLECTION OF MARK JACOBS. COURTESY OF MARK JACOBS COLLECTION.

Ives developed a system wherein three photos were taken of an object through three separate red, green, and blue filters. The three resulting transparencies were then viewed through a mechanism Ives called a Kromskop, which through the use of screens, reflectors, and red, green, and blue filters, appeared to combine the transparencies into a single complete color image (see figures 2.2 and 2.3).

By the end of the nineteenth century, design, industry, education, and the move toward organization-based management and standard systems for color began to take hold, as color and its deployment became more central to consumerism and mass media. The work of Albert Munsell, an artist and educator, would serve to hasten color's industrialization and subsequent scientific and industrial management.[32] Munsell, according to Blaszczyk, was first interested in color education and the development of a color system that would be used both by artists and by commercial agents, as he believed that there was an array of preferred colors that signified good taste and others (those that he considered "gaudy") that needed to be marginalized in their use. He was a proponent of color education, even developing school supplies such as paints, colored paper, colored spheres, and crayons for teaching his system in the classroom. As Blaszczyk writes, "Munsell believed this great divide in taste, and the general visual chaos of the day, stemmed from a lack of color education and a paucity of good design tools. There was no universal language for describing color, no standard curriculum in color theory, and no mechanism for coordinating colors across merchandise categories."[33] Munsell was engaged in the study of color harmony—a concept that had already been explored in the nineteenth century in the work of Michel Eugéne Chevreul, Ogden Rood, Milton Bradley, and Louis Prang[34]—but he was especially interested in promoting the use of what in his color atlas he called the "middle colors" (neutral shades), which he deemed to be the most pleasing aesthetically.

While colorimetry is an empirical approach to the study and measurement of color perception, color harmony also provides maps and/or wheels of color that encourage "proper" color usage. The use of color harmony systems, which seek to find pleasing interrelationships between colors and to avoid color clashes, was considered educative for artists, industry, and young students. The Munsell color system, developed at the turn of the twentieth century, was based on the research Munsell did with his Lumenometer—an improved daylight photometer used to measure color and light. While Munsell's work was recognized as sound by scientists and deemed intriguing by educators, he did not have much success promoting his system until he began to work with the American textile industry.[35] As Blaszczyk describes, the system's real success began after Munsell's death, when his son took over the Munsell Color Company and established its research laboratory in Baltimore, not far from the Bureau of Standards. It was at this point that the use of Munsell's system shifted, along with much of the rest of color practice, from color education and exploration to color science, management, and standardization.

PROFESSIONALIZATION, COMMERCIALISM, AND THE INSTITUTIONALIZATION OF COLOR STANDARDS

Johnston marks the early twentieth century (between 1900 and World War I) as the institutionalization period of colorimetry, and the Munsell Color Company's growing connection with the Bureau of Standards was a significant contributor to that moment. This time was also the period of what David F. Noble calls the "standardization movement" in science and industry, which was deeply connected to the intensification of mass production.[36] The large national laboratories established during this period, such as the American National Bureau of Standards (NBS), the British National Physical Laboratory, and the German Physikalisch-Technische Reichsanstalt (Imperial Institute for Physics and Technology), were all engaged in research meant to obtain accurate measurements of color in order to define and maintain national standards to be used as reference points by industry and government.[37] As Johnston puts it, "In America the idea of 'standardization' was touted as a means of reducing commercial complexity and improving the country's competitiveness in its products. The regulation of light and color were key components of this scheme."[38] The Munsell Color Company collaborated with the NBS throughout the late 1910s and '20s, funding a number of scientists at the bureau and refining the specifications of its systems based on the resulting reports and recommendations coming out of the laboratory.[39] Some industries established their own standards and labs connected to color measurement, standards, and color vision. (Such labs mentioned by Johnston include the National Electric Lamp Association, the United Gas Improvement Company, the Optical Society of America, and Eastman Kodak.)[40] It is important to note that the work done by the Optical Society of America (OSA) during this period helped promote research done by committees and ensured that the research involved a range of experts in vision from both the academy and business. Its committee on colorimetry also worked to standardize terminology in 1919, which represented another trend in color standardization that would continue through the start of World War II.[41] As Johnston notes, the OSA color committee released a report in 1922 (which became, as color scientist Dorothy Nickerson claims, a "bible" for those working on color[42]) defining color not as a subjective, mental, or psychological process, but, according to Johnston, as a "specific and replicable response to a physical phenomenon" and "implicit in this was the assumption that, neglecting physiological differences between the eyes of individuals, color was an invariant sensation common to all observers."[43] Later in this chapter, we will see how the work of the NTSC in the late 1940s mimics, references, and then also alters some of the organizational structures and systems—particularly those of the OSA—established during this period.[44]

While the organizations and committees mentioned above researched the physical and psychological basis for color perception in vision as they related to standards for colorimetry, other industry bodies were setting color standards in product manufacturing. A similar scientific management of "color chaos" was employed in American textile mills and auto plants as manufacturers sought to harness the commercial appeal of colored goods.[45] Dovetailing with a heightened sense of wartime nationalism, American industry sought to set their own nationally used color production palette with, for example, the Standard Color Card of America (put out by the Textile Color Card Association, known after 1955 as the Color Association of the United States) which was released in 1915 in hopes of coordinating color production across a range of consumer goods industries.[46] This card, which contained samples of one hundred labeled colors, was a deliberate movement away from a reliance on the French color cards that had been used previously in American industry. The Inter-Society Color Council (ISCC), which was made up of delegates from various national societies on color, was formed in 1931 to foster standardization, naming, and specification of color across various industries.[47] Included in the ISCC were the American Ceramic Society, the American Psychological Association, the Society of Motion Picture Engineers (SMPE—later to be known as SMPTE when television was added to the title in 1950), and the Technical Association of the Pulp and Paper Industry. Examples of the council's work in the 1930s and early 1940s (some of which was done with the NBS) include setting colors for the U.S. Textile Color Card Association, used by clothing manufacturers, and deciding upon standards for the coloring of pharmaceuticals across brands, for theatrical light filters, and even for railway signal colors.[48] In an article for the SMPTE journal in 1940, H. P. Gage of Corning Glass described the function of the society:

> It is supposed (1) to secure papers of interest to the Society, to be presented at conventions and published; (2) to secure agreement on technical matters involving many individuals or harmonize diverse interests, particularly when such interests are represented in other societies; (3) to standardize; (4) to collect authoritative information; or (5) to encourage research.[49]

The ISCC represented a move to *standardize the standardization* of color by instituting reference points, research norms, and nomenclature that could be used and referenced across industry, science, psychology, and art. Again, the work of scholars such as Noble reminds us that the scientific management and standardization of innovation and production at all levels was promising more than just efficiency, predictability, and

FIGURE 2.4 An example of color harmony at work in industry.
Saturday Evening Post, July 20, 1929.

profitability. Noble quotes Harlow Person, economist and director of the Taylor Society during the 1920s, as proclaiming:

> Stabilization of material forces is not sufficient; human relations must be stabilized; stabilization of production is not sufficient; merchandising must be stabilized. Stabilization of production and merchandising is not sufficient; general administration must be stabilized. Stabilization of an individual enterprise is not sufficient; all enterprises in the industry must be stabilized. Stabilization of one industry is not sufficient; all industries of a nation must be stabilized. Stabilization of national industry alone is not sufficient; international economics must be stabilized. Achievement of any of these ends is a step toward a more balanced and harmonious industrial and social life; each end is but a means to another greater end.[50]

After World War I, "nearly everyone concerned with moving consumer goods was interested in color," writes Blaszczyk, as advertising agencies were pushing for the heightened use of color in printing, packaging, product design, and advertisements, "color specialists," and those in the business of interior design were encouraging consumers to use more color in the home and training them how to do so with detailed design and color guides.[51] Women, who had been identified as the primary consumers and as expert homemakers, were considered particularly vulnerable to the sway of the look and color of products and goods but also thought to have the most potential as color specialists.[52] Such "colorists," who would commonly wed basic ideas about psychology with marketing and design concepts, were becoming more common by the 1920s.[53] Of course, one of the most famous female color consultants was Natalie Kalmus, the head color consultant for Technicolor from 1933 to 1949, during the company's heyday in Hollywood, who not only advised on technical issues related to color film but also charted and coordinated the use of every color element of the mise-en-scène (wardrobe, set design, etc.) in order to deploy color in such a way as to enhance narrative and stimulate specific emotions in the viewer.[54]

As in the film industry, the broadcast networks would employ color experts and rely on theories of color harmony in calibrating their cameras and plotting out their set and costume design. In a series of color workshops held by NBC in the early 1950s, it was explained that the network was using the Container Corporation of America's *Color Harmony*

Manual to set their color standards. This manual was based on the Ost-wald color system, which, as Gage notes, represents one of three classes of traditional theories of color harmony: (1) those regarding the spectrum of white light as in some sense analogous to the musical scale, so that it could be treated in a musical way (Newtonian); (2) those requiring the presence of all "primary" colors in any harmonious assortment, or in a "complementary" arrangement (as in Goethe's theory); and (3) those regarding the value content of hues as the primary determinant of their harmonious juxtaposition (as expressed in Ostwald's color system).[55] In the 1920s, William Ostwald had worked with the German paint industry to create what he believed to be a highly rationalized system of harmony based on bringing together mathematical calibrations of color with a consideration of psychological sensations produced by color stimuli. He first developed a gray scale and then applied that gray scale to the twenty-four hues of his color circle. In general, Ostwald's theory concludes that equal hues and equal chroma result in color harmony or balance.

Ostwald's work occurred during what has been called the color revolution, a time in which color was appearing in many mediated and non-mediated forms and was understood to have a powerful influence both on mood or emotion and on purchasing decisions.[56] It was also a period in which the scientific management of color—not only through the development of systems but also through the proliferation of professional color forecasters, color stylists, and color engineers—took hold and in which the first four color advertisements were produced (in 1924).[57] Hazel Adler, for example, used and promoted "Taylor's System of Color Harmony," developed by painter Henry Fitch Taylor (profiting from confusion or association with the already well-known and unrelated Taylor system of management), in her work as a color consultant for large manufacturing companies such as Kohler, B. F. Goodrich, and the Ford Motor Company, where she helped select colors for the Model A, as well as working on designing both goods and home decorating guidebooks for Sears.[58]

By the 1930s, "functionalist color," as Blaszczyk describes it, "combined the concerns of the Victorian practical man and the progressive drive for moral uplift in a new approach that put color to work."[59] Color specialists such as Howard Ketcham, Edward Bernays, and Faber Birren (who will be discussed in greater detail in chapter 3) understood color to have deep therapeutic possibilities, with each individual color holding its

Pick a Color from the Rainbow!

DOOR HANDLES *Color-Keyed* TO YOUR KITCHEN!

Exclusive in INTERNATIONAL HARVESTER REFRIGERATORS

Most Exciting Idea in Refrigerators Since the Ice Cube!

Now International Harvester Refrigerators are designed with a *color* flair—as fashionable as they are functional for your new-as-this-minute kitchen! Ten gorgeous colors in sleek door handle plaques to match or contrast with your kitchen color scheme. Easy to switch colors any time you redecorate!

they're *femineered..!*

—and YEARS AHEAD! Scores of chore-saving, women-approved features: Spacious shelves of stainless steel! Pantry-Dor, Butter Keeper, magnetic Bottle Opener! Full-width Freezers, Coldstream Crispers, countless more! Choice of seven models, seven sizes, seven prices. For the name of your nearest dealer, see Classified Telephone Directory.

INTERNATIONAL HARVESTER COMPANY
180 North Michigan Avenue · Chicago 1, Illinois

International Harvester Also Builds Home Freezers . . . McCormick Farm Equipment and Farmall Tractors . . . Motor Trucks . . . Industrial Power

COPYRIGHT, 1951, INTERNATIONAL HARVESTER COMPANY

own psychological implications. This led to a new form of perceived control and careful deployment of color through the 1950s. Color forecasters flourished too during this period by claiming to be able to predict, and possibly inspire, the next color trend in fashion or home design. Color was also an increasingly central part of the postwar landscape, as everything from cars to homes to domestic appliances was becoming available in an entire rainbow of colors from which consumers could choose.

MOVING PICTURE STANDARDS AND COLOR

It wasn't until Hollywood's classical era (1930–1945) that color in film was standardized on a grand scale. However, even though we tend to think of film prior to the advent of Technicolor as predominately black and white, an estimated 80 percent of films were in color by the early 1920s.[60] Color was achieved in cinema's earliest silent years by hand (applied coloring) rather than a technical photographic process (what has been referred to as natural coloring), as early filmmakers borrowed coloring techniques and looks from other forms of visual media of the period, such as photography, the products of chromolithography, and magic lantern slides. Yumibe identifies four types of applied coloring in use at the turn of the twentieth century: tinting, hand coloring, toning, and stenciling.[61] Hand coloring of individual frames of celluloid was an especially laborious and expensive process, the results of which were often temporary, as the heat from the projector could fade or melt away the color. It also could not be standardized (even across multiple prints of the same film) in a meaningful way. Although tinting and dyeing were less time-consuming processes, coloring film became easier and more economical primarily when hand colorists were replaced by machines. Pathé Cinema, for example, a French production house invested in the development and promotion of color stenciling, set up a coloring lab with approximately four hundred workers and eventually employed Jean Méry's mechanical pantograph system for stenciling, which functioned in conjunction with a human tracer, increasing precision, consistency, and the number of color films that could be produced at any given time (see figure 2.6).

The "natural coloring" process was one that utilized many of the concepts and materials of early additive processes in photography, such as

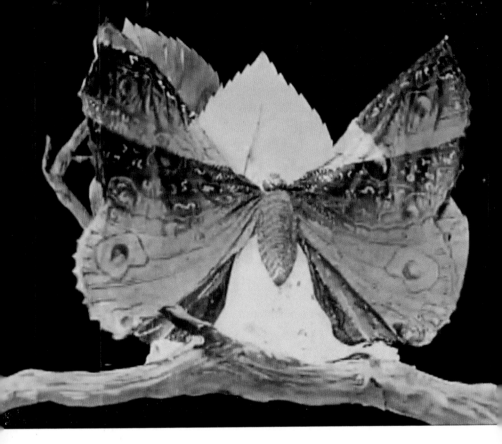

FIGURE 2.6 An example of color stenciling from Pathé Cinema. VIDEO STILL FROM
METAMORPHOSES DU PAPILLON, GASTON VELLE, PATHÉ, 1904.

Kromskop, and did not involve such extensive human labor in the film
lab, as the illusion of a single integrated color image was created on
screen and not imprinted on film. For instance, Gaumont's "chronochrome" film process (first presented to the public in 1912) involved,
on both camera and projector, a triple lens with three filters, one red,
one green, and one blue, the resulting three different colored images
then had to be projected simultaneously to be blended seamlessly on the
screen. While this caused more work at the point of projection (because
the filters had to be adjusted just so in relation to the distance from the
screen, there had to be not only a skilled projectionist at hand but also
often an additional technician) and required supplemental equipment,

the result was a system that was able to capture and then project rich color using standard 35 mm film. And yet the system was ultimately never a commercial success, largely because it did not fit with the established practices and standards of the day, requiring special care and use of its own camera and projector. Kinemacolor, another additive system, did find some success in the commercial marketplace (particularly in the U.K.), even though it didn't provide as complex or rich an image as chronochrome and also required its own specialized equipment.[62] What it did provide to exhibitors was a highly systematic distribution and marketing package based on the branding of color as "equated with quality and prestige."[63] As color film historian Sarah Street describes, Charles Urban, one of Kinemacolor's founders, was not only meticulous in his instructions to U.K. exhibitors in how to best display the color films, but he also gave them notes on musical accompaniment, the creation and use of sound effects, and how to best market the films to "draw in the 'upper strata of local society' to their cinemas, as well as retaining their typical patrons."[64] While the rise of Kinemacolor was short-lived (1910–1914) it did prefigure Technicolor, a color process that would first come on the market in 1916 and then dominate it, both in its technical process and in its systematic and tightly controlled management, from 1922 to 1952 (see figure 2.7).

Color standards and color management were certainly central to the development of color systems for motion pictures during Hollywood's classical era, as studios, working for efficiency and profit along with creativity, had to—as David Bordwell, Kristin Thompson, and Janet Staiger have famously argued—balance standardization and differentiation.[65] Differentiation allowed studios to innovate at the levels of technology, production technique, aesthetics, and narrative in order to mark a film, genre, or theatrical experience as novel or distinct, while standardization allowed for the functions and processes of the system to work smoothly and efficiently. While the addition of color to film offered an opportunity for differentiation, it also caused trouble with the production standards already in place, especially as it was becoming available for use around the same time as Hollywood was slowly transitioning to sound. By 1929, Technicolor had beat out some twenty other companies working on color movie technology and dominated the color film business in Hollywood. While its early two-color printing process did not require any switch

FIGURE 2.7 Ad for Technicolor, 1930.

in the standard dimensions of the film itself, Technicolor did require special cameras and projectors. The two-color printing process proved relatively unstable, so in 1932, the company offered a more predictable three-color subtractive recording and printing process. When the use of Technicolor really began to take off after 1935, the company also began to institute highly coordinated and specific color management techniques across various levels of the production process. Already a carefully managed firm with an in-house research laboratory and a plant that was "a paragon of industrial organization,"[66] Technicolor began to set requirements for a film to be shot using its process: Technicolor cameras were required and could only be rented from Technicolor; a Technicolor cameraman had to be employed to run these cameras; special lighting had to be used; the film magazines had to be inspected daily in Technicolor's lab; the film had to be processed and printed by Technicolor; and finally, studios had to employ and keep on set one of the company's color consultants (Natalie Kalmus being the most famous) to advise on color use throughout the mise-en-scène. In her famous essay, "Color Consciousness," Kalmus describes the role of the on-set color consultant:

> In the preparation of a picture we read the script and prepare a color chart for the entire production, each scene, sequence, set, and character being considered. This chart may be compared to a musical score, and amplifies the picture in a similar manner. The preparation of this chart calls for careful and judicious work. Subtle effects of beauty and feeling are not attained through haphazard methods, but through application of the rules of art and the physical laws of light and color in relation to literary laws and story values. . . . The art director, however, in handling a color picture, must be forever mindful that the human eye is many times more sensitive than the photographic emulsion and many times greater in scope than any process of reproduction. Therefore, he must be able to translate his colors in terms of the process.[67]

Kalmus and Technicolor were simultaneously utilizing the accumulated knowledge around colorimetry, color harmony, perception and cognition, and functional color and connecting it to the specific culture and industry of the classical Hollywood studio system. Their highly involved, mostly efficient, and relatively expensive procedures were used for virtually all color film productions until 1950, when Eastman Kodak began to offer their streamlined and easier to use process, Eastmancolor.

While Technicolor offered a form of commercially standardized packages of services that could be purchased by a studio, there were already institutional models in place for the standardization of a range of aspects of film production that had been established starting in the late 1910s with the formation of SMPE in 1918, the American Society of Cinematographers in 1919, and the Academy of Motion Picture Arts and Sciences' Producers-Technicians Joint Committee in 1927 (renamed the Research Council in 1932). Although these organizations sometimes had shared goals and addressed similar concerns regarding technical developments, needs, and standards, they were also born out of somewhat different ideological and cultural relationships to motion picture technology. As Bordwell, Thompson, and Staiger argue, the formation of SMPE can be understood in relation to the formation of the American Engineering Standards Committee that, beginning in 1918, had worked to coordinate research and other activities across all the various engineering societies. SMPE would mimic that coordination in their work to standardize motion picture technology in the name of efficiency and prosperity, but such standardization would also go a long way to professionalize and raise the status of its members (many of whom were manufacturers). Bordwell, Thompson, and Staiger also note that "the society's conduct was governed by the conception of the engineer as businessman," and that "the society's concern for standardization was thus part of a larger effort to help its companies prosper."[68] Through the organization's journal, meetings, and conferences, SMPE set standards in color (for film, cameras, lighting, laboratory processes and specs, etc.) for the motion picture industry and then did preliminary work leading up to the setting of NTSC standards for color television. SMPE/SMPTE would eventually enter into the discussions on color television standards, recommending and publishing, for example, standards for CBS's high-definition color system in 1942 in the organization's influential journal. It then continued to refine elements of color television production (including developing test patterns and other diagnostic tools) after standards were instituted. However, it ultimately had limited influence, as the processes for and relationships around television standards work quite differently than those for the film industry.

The American Society of Cinematographers maintained a connection to professionalization, standardization, and efficiency too, but adhered to the idea of professionalizing each cinematographer not as a business-man, like SMPE members, but as both "artist and technician."[69] Members shared information, monitored developments in technology, and set standards for what might now be called "best practices." They also consulted with manufacturers as experts, as was the case when Jackson Rose did tests of color rendering for DuPont and Eastman Kodak.[70] The Academy's Research Council was envisioned as a site of contribution by and collaboration with all the studios—a center through which competition between studios could be put aside for the greater good of economy and efficiency for all. This eventually (by 1933) meant that manufacturers and suppliers were also invited into the Academy, which allowed them to consult with engineers and technicians from companies such as Bausch and Lomb and Technicolor (although, since a number of its staff were powerful board members of SMPE, Technicolor worked more closely with that society).

SETTING STANDARDS FOR MONOCHROME TELEVISION

Unlike the voluntary production standards followed by the film industry, standards for the manufacture of television receivers and transmitters—both monochrome and color—were and are ultimately set by governmental regulation, specifically through the FCC.[71] Moreover, in the case of television, standardization had to *precede* commercialization, as receivers produced by various manufacturers had to receive the same number of scanning lines and reassemble them at the same rate. Transmission equipment too had to be designed according to the specific dimensions of the transmission signal, and it was the size of the signal's bandwidth that would ultimately determine the number of channels that could exist on the spectrum.

Although the FCC and other regulatory bodies in the broadcasting industry came to television with the experience of already standardizing and legislating radio broadcasting, television's visual component and its complexity as a consumer technology demanded especially thorough scientific study before the technology entered the commercialization and standard setting stages. Donald G. Fink, an influential member of the Institute of Radio Engineers (IRE), the Advisory Committee on Color Television, and the NTSC, in 1976 acknowledged that there are certain types of electrical engineering technologies—such as the telephone, electrical light, and television—that require "prior standardization of product design" in order to provide a centralized service to the populace. However, he also remarked that standardization brings with it limitations and constraints, as "standards inhibit innovation and prolong obsolescence. . . . In standards-controlled design, the dead hand of the past still lives."[72] He went on to argue, however, that it is television's connection to the eye, "the most sensitive and critical organ evolved by nature," and the precision that television requires at "nearly every feature of the television transmission and reception process" to pull off its illusion of realistic movement and sense of realistic color, that demand a unique and sometimes burdensome level of carefully considered and highly researched system of standards.[73]

The earliest published discussion of standards for television occurred in the pages of *Proceedings of the IRE* in 1929. The authors considered the issues of power, bandwidth, and fidelity in the context of a developing definition of television's potential applications and cultural and economic value. The definition with which they were working was developed by the National Electrical Manufacturers Association and centered mainly on a description of the television viewing process—from optics to operation—and a small note connecting fidelity to content value using language that was likely informed by the public service requirements already built into the Radio Act of 1927, which was the act that constituted and gave regulatory power to the Federal Radio Commission (later the FCC). The definition read,

> Commercial television is the radio transmission and reception of visual images of moving subjects comprising a sufficient proportion of the field of view of the human eye to include large and small objects, persons and groups of persons, the reproduction of which at the receiving point is of such size and fidelity as to possess genuine educational and entertainment value and accomplished so as to give the impression of smooth motion, by an instrument requiring no special skill in operation, having simple means of locating the received image, and automatic means of maintaining its framing.[74]

Attempting to parse out the exact relationship between "genuine educational and entertainment value" and what they later refer to as the "degree of picture detail or number of elements," one of the authors consulted with "various persons engaged in the motion picture and theatrical fields." Their conclusion was that television would need to achieve a "clear reproduction of a semi close-up . . . at least, in the early stages of the art."[75] The authors supported "spectrum economy" in this regard, calling for engineers to develop a service that would meet the basic requirements of clear close-up imagery but would not require too much bandwidth.[76]

The development of standards for monochrome television by committee first began with the Radio Manufacturers Association (RMA), an alliance of radio manufacturers whose leaders (some of whom were RCA employees), after viewing RCA's demonstration of their all-electronic system in 1935, commenced research on a potential timeline for the development of standards for television through its engineering division. Once FCC officials heard that the RMA was initiating standards research, they suggested to the RMA that the organization work with the rest of the television industry to propose collectively agreed upon standards for television and then bring this proposal before the FCC. The RMA organized both a standards committee and a spectrum allocation committee,[77] and in 1938, sent their proposal for a 441-line standard to the FCC, but the FCC did not implement the proposal, even as it announced the following year that it would authorize limited commercial television station operation.[78] It was RCA's move to quickly begin manufacturing sets (based on not yet approved RMA standards) that led the FCC to halt this limited commercial operation and to state that it would only start the operation up again once "the engineering opinion of the industry is prepared to approve any one of the competing systems of broadcasting as the standard system."[79]

As William Boddy has shown, there is ample evidence that RCA and its president, David Sarnoff, were aggressive in their attempts to gain control over the market by moving ahead with the production of RCA sets with the 441-line standard, thereby attempting to establish de facto standards without the consultation and approval of any other organizational or regulatory body.[80] In fact, as Boddy reports, the highly influential Sarnoff threatened to withdraw from the RMA in 1940 if there was not immediate movement on the approval of commercialization and standards.[81] The FCC, noting division and acrimony within the RMA in response to RCA's machinations, supported the development of a new body that would be composed of some members of the RMA but would also include a wider contingent of representatives from the industry.

That body would eventually be the NTSC, and it was understood to be more objective in its assessments. After nine months of research and discussion, there was some debate over the scanning standard (441 lines versus 800); a compromise of 525 lines was agreed upon; and the committee's recommendation was passed on to the FCC, which adopted the recommendations unchanged. Fink argued that this proposal was formulated so quickly because it was "based on technical work done previously under other auspices" (referring primarily to the work of the RMA).[82] Boddy notes that the relatively small number of scanning lines that was approved in 1941 proved to be a limitation for television as the industry grew and the technology improved. Visual quality and frequency bandwidth (set at 6 MHz) would be limited as a result, and consequently, Boddy argues, "U.S. television remain[ed] technologically inferior to other international standards."[83] The decision of the FCC to settle on these standards, and not even to consider the possibility of an all-electronic color system (CBS had provided the FCC with its research and data on its part-electronic color system during the hearings) and the needs it would require, would impact the issues before the second formation of the NTSC (brought together to address color standards specifically) and bring the matter of signal compression even farther to the fore.[84]

COLOR TELEVISION STANDARDS

While Peter Goldmark, chief television engineer at CBS, had demonstrated the CBS field-sequential system to the press in 1940, the first formal demonstration of the system to the FCC occurred in September 1946 as part of the company's petition for ultrahigh frequency (UHF) commercial color adoption. At this point, CBS was engaged in a public relations campaign to bring the public "Quality Television" through high-definition—in both monochrome "fine screen" and in wideband color—through the use of the UHF band. However, since the black and white VHF standards had already been set and manufacturers were eager to continue with the production and distribution of their sets, other factions of the television industry (such as RCA) were demanding "Video Now!" through a countercampaign, insisting on the collective embrace of the FCC approved standard as an act of support of the immediate growth and health of the television industry.[85] Paul Kesten—a CBS vice

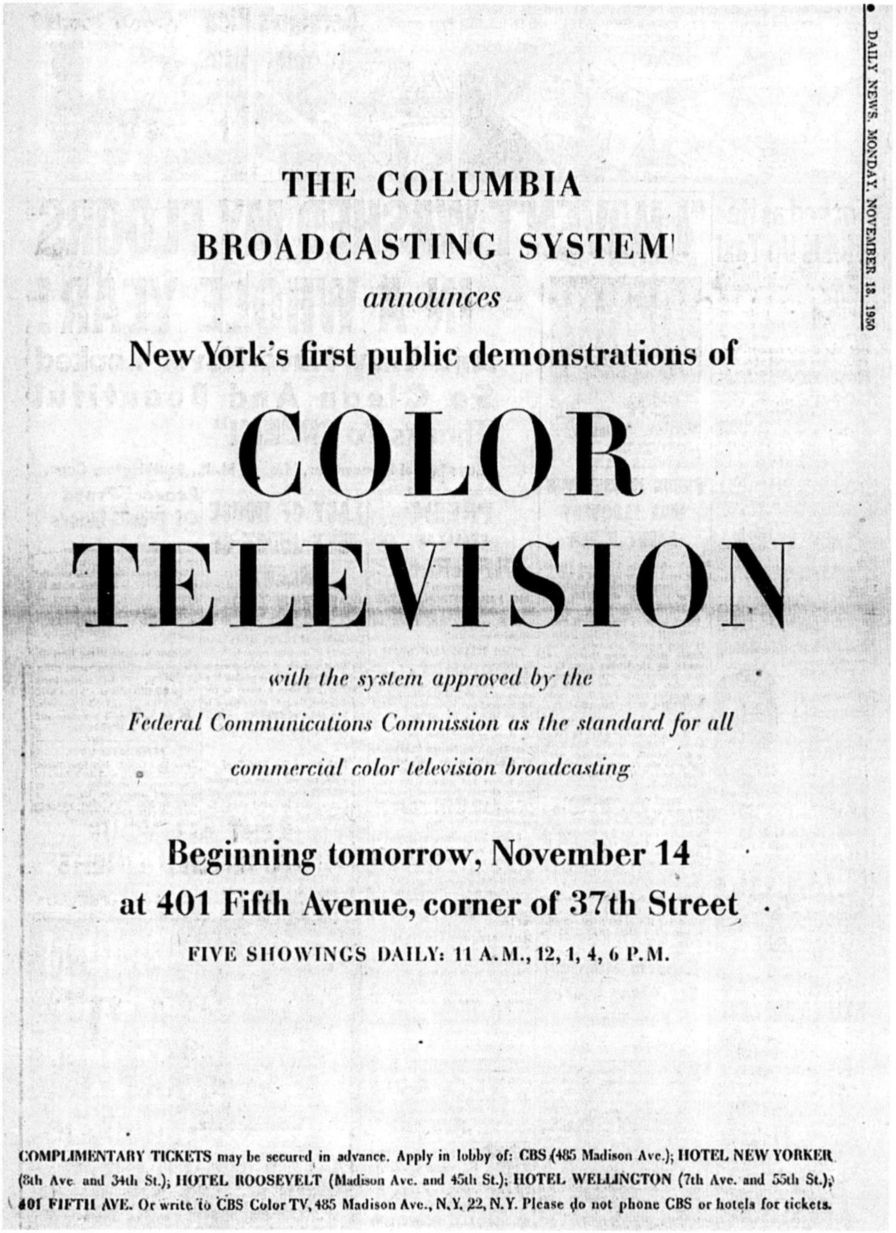
DAILY NEWS, MONDAY, NOVEMBER 13, 1950
THE COLUMBIA BROADCASTING SYSTEM
announces
New York's first public demonstrations of
COLOR TELEVISION
with the system approved by the Federal Communications Commission as the standard for all commercial color television broadcasting
Beginning tomorrow, November 14
at 401 Fifth Avenue, corner of 37th Street
FIVE SHOWINGS DAILY: 11 A.M., 12, 1, 4, 6 P.M.
COMPLIMENTARY TICKETS may be secured in advance. Apply in lobby of: CBS (485 Madison Ave.); HOTEL NEW YORKER (8th Ave. and 34th St.); HOTEL ROOSEVELT (Madison Ave. and 45th St.); HOTEL WELLINGTON (7th Ave. and 55th St.); 401 FIFTH AVE. Or write to CBS Color TV, 485 Madison Ave., N.Y. 22, N.Y. Please do not phone CBS or hotels for tickets.

FIGURE 2.8 An ad in the November 15, 1950, edition of the *Daily News* announcing CBS's first public demonstration of color television.

president, acting as head cheerleader for color both within and without CBS, and a close advisor to network chairman William Paley (who would come to have a complicated and ambivalent relationship to color over the years)—believed that the VHF standard was too restrictive and that this was the perfect moment for the FCC to throw out the lesser standard, as dissemination of sets was still rather limited (an estimated seven thousand of them in 1944), for a standard that promised a better television image, as an investment in the future. Having believed so fully in the idea, CBS purchased a significant number of UHF stations instead of VHF stations, which were readily available at discounted rates, a mistake that would hurt the network financially down the line. CBS was not alone in their mission, as FCC chairman James L. Fly came out in support of the "Quality Television" campaign, as did manufacturers such as Zenith.[86] This occurred at a time when CBS was focused on the development of technology as a prime postwar business strategy, investing in and expanding their research and development department to a staff of 120 working under Goldmark. While not having the manufacturing capability to produce sets on a mass scale, CBS executives (in particular Kesten and Frank Stanton) saw color television as a way to make their mark in the realm of television technology. And due to its complexity, potential for vivid beauty, and high bandwidth needs, color television would be the ideal technology in which to make the argument about the advantages of a "quality" ultrahigh-definition system of television.

The system Goldmark had brought before the FCC in 1946 produced a wideband color signal (12.5 MHz) and had double the line resolution of the 1941 standard. Its receiver also included a colored spinning disc, which harkened back to old mechanical systems of the 1920s but did not make the system antiquated—although it certainly did provide fodder for the competition, who often mocked the color wheel as cumbersome, oversized, and old-fashioned. Prior to showing it formally to the FCC, CBS had held hundreds of demonstrations (often utilizing filmed rather than live footage) for the public, press, affiliates, potential sponsors, and television sales teams across the East Coast. Often monochrome monitors would be placed alongside color ones in an attempt to show the superiority of the color image. Goldmark's team also did daily broadcasts from a CBS studio to department stores, starring the network's "color girl," Patty Painter, who became a regular at almost all of CBS's demonstrations throughout the late 1940s and '50s (see chapter 3 for more on

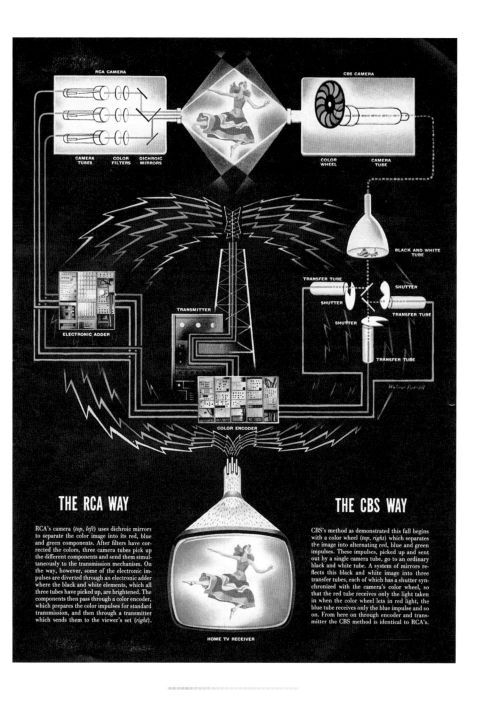

FIGURE 2.9 An illustration of the differences between the RCA and CBS systems from "Upheaval, Markets to Come for a Still-Infant Industry," *Life*, January 4, 1954.

this). Goldmark describes an especially successful live demonstration to the FCC in 1946 by writing, "In an instant starlet Patty Painter, our nineteen-year-old heroine from Beckley, West Virginia, filled the tube. Her skin glowed a natural flesh pink, her long auburn blonde hair glistened and the piquant smile and dancing blue eyes drew appreciative smiles from all of us."[87]

There were three proposals in front of the FCC when the color television hearings got underway in December 1946: CBS's wideband field-sequential system, the television manufacturer DuMont's three-gun picture tube (which was not a fully functional device yet), and RCA's simultaneous system (also wideband but otherwise compatible with the VHF monochrome standards). RCA posed the only significant challenge to CBS's system, even though the CBS system was judged to be superior in side-by-side demonstrations. RCA knew that its system was not ready for approval and made the argument to the FCC that color television in general was not market ready. After the 1946 resignation of Kesten, Frank Stanton, the recently appointed president of CBS (a position formerly held by Paley, who had moved into the chairman of the board role), took on the mantle of color advocacy at the network, arguing for its significance and excellence not only to the FCC but also to Paley, who regularly needed to be convinced of the value of an investment in color. In arguing the case for CBS color, Stanton relied upon his background in market analysis and broadcast audience research, referencing surveys and demonstrations he conducted that seemed to prove the value of the CBS color system in particular to consumers and advertisers.[88] Stanton was also a supporter more generally of CBS's investment in diversification and technological development, having also backed Goldmark in his work on the long-playing (LP) record during the 1940s.[89]

In March 1947, the FCC came out with its ruling—it would deny CBS's petition for color UHF due to what it considered a lack of adequate field testing and the stated belief that the other color systems would "offer the possibility of cheaper receivers and narrower bandwidths that have not yet been fully explored."[90] Most historians agree that it was unlikely that the field testing was the real problem here. Rather, the FCC, reluctant to expand into UHF after having moved the band for FM radio in a somewhat controversial decision in 1945, and wishing for black and white television to take off quickly while also being concerned about the obsolescence of the sets already on the market, chose to buy into

TIME

THE WEEKLY NEWSMAGAZINE

CBS'S FRANK STANTON
He wheeled in color TV.

ARTZYBASHEFF

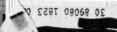

$6.00 A YEAR   (REG. U. S. PAT. OFF.)   VOL. LVI NO. 23

FIGURE 2.10 *Time*, December 4, 1950, features Frank Stanton
and color television on its cover.

the argument that color was simply not ready. Engineers at RCA, who were relieved by the petition denial, returned to the work of perfecting their system, while Paley, deeply disappointed in the decision, took away much of Goldmark's funding for the color project and cut his staff, hoping that he would instead focus on easier and more profitable ventures like the LP. Goldmark's interest in the color project, however, did not wane, and he eventually procured outside funding from pharmaceutical company Smith, Kline and French and cooperation from the University of Pennsylvania Medical School for the modification of his television system as a medical teaching tool. The surgical training demonstration broadcast at the American Medical Association meeting in Atlantic City in 1949 was an enormous hit with attendees and members of the press covering the event. It renewed the excitement about the possibilities of color television more generally and gave more ammunition to Goldmark and Stanton in the fight for continued color research at CBS.

Goldmark's color work once again received support from the network after the FCC formally requested information from the industry on the status of color television in the summer of 1949. Consequently, Goldmark refined his system, both improving its image resolution and also finding a way for it to be transmitted on channels with a 6 MHz (narrowband) bandwidth.[91] It still had a spinning wheel but had been modified in such a way as to no longer affect cabinet size. With its specifications of a 405-line image, 144 fields, and a scan rate of 72 frames per second, it was, however, incompatible with the black and white sets already on the market. The FCC hearings on the fate of color began in the early fall of 1949 and continued for almost a full year. A month into the hearings, RCA and CBS performed separate color demonstrations for the public. While the CBS demonstration went fine, resulting in reporters commenting on the system's "crisp pictures" in their coverage, RCA did not fare nearly as well. In fact, *Variety* famously declared that RCA laid "an off-color egg," as not only did their images lack the "warmth and stability" of CBS's system, but a reporter thought that the RCA reproduction also "did not appear true." The report went on: "Frequently, the images were decidedly off-color, imparting different tones to the subjects. Receivers side-by-side showed different colors from the same transmissions."[92]

There were four main companies competing for their systems to be adopted as the U.S. color standard: RCA, CBS, Color Television Inc. (CTI), and Philco. CBS was pushing for approval of its modified field-sequential system; RCA and Philco had offered dot-sequential systems; and CTI had presented a line-sequential system.[93] Between 1949 and 1953, the central period in which color standards were taken under consideration, three committees were formed to study, test, and report on the state of the various systems: the Joint Technical Advisory Committee, which provided technical advice directly to the FCC; the Senate Advisory Committee on Color Television, commonly referred to as the Condon Committee, as E. U. Condon, the director of the NBS, was its chair; and the NTSC, which was reconstituted in early 1950.[94] The proposed color systems were put through various tests (in the lab, in public settings, and in the home) in order to determine which system would produce the most stable and realistic images in the most cost-effective and least disruptive way. The FCC relied on field testing and the opinions of outside experts because, according to Hugh Slotten, "key commissioners, especially [R. F.] Jones, argued that RCA engineers and their supporters could not be trusted because of the inaccurate and suspiciously self-serving predictions they had made about their [failed] system in 1947."[95] Since all three systems were still only in development at the time of the FCC hearings, engineers—ideally those without vested interests in the outcome of the decision—were thought to be the individuals best suited to weigh the potential that each system had for likely improvements or refinements.

The Condon Committee was the first to complete its study in July 1950, although the group declined to make a clear recommendation for the adoption of a single system "since the committee believes that the decision to adopt a system must include consideration of many social and economic factors not properly the concern of the technical analyst."[96] Nonetheless, they did conclude that RCA was superior in the categories of compatibility, adaptability, flicker and resolution, and effectiveness of channel utilization, while CBS was the best in color fidelity, convertibility, and superposition.[97] CTI was not considered superior in any category, although it was deemed equal to RCA in flicker and resolution. The committee made these judgments based on their own estimation of the demonstrations as well as those of eight independent observers, who viewed the system tests in laboratory settings (rather than doing home tests) and were asked to evaluate their visual experience of each system. For example, observers were asked to rate the amount of flicker they experienced on a scale, using the terms "none," "noticeable," "appreciable," "objectionable," and "painful."[98] Those conducting the tests also used a

"TWIN" VAUGHN MONROES show you how an RCA Victor Big Color TV is like 2 sets in 1. Shown is The *Aldrich* in limed oak grained finish (21CS781). $495.

**NOW YOU CAN ENJOY "LIVING COLOR" PLUS SHARP
BLACK-AND-WHITE IN ONE TV SET FOR $495**

FIGURE 2.11 A 1956 print ad showcases RCA's compatibility
with existing black and white sets.

special colorimeter for measuring the colors produced by each system
and compared them to test charts based on Munsell color scales.

The Condon Committee's report was reviewed by the FCC commissioners and was considered alongside the data originating from the commission's reports on its own color demonstrations and tests. In all, the
color hearings concluded in May 1950 with over ten thousand pages
of transcripts and 265 exhibits, and on September 1, 1950, the FCC released its first "Report on Color Television," which favored CBS's field-sequential system.[99] The commission's opinion on RCA's dot-sequential
system was that there was a lack of fidelity, especially when it came to
"flesh tones"; the texture of the color image produced had a "soft quality"

that was "unsatisfactory"; the system was too vulnerable to interference; the station equipment was too complex; and the receivers were, in the words of the report, "so bulky, so complicated, so difficult to operate, and so expensive that it is inconceivable that the public would purchase them in any quantity."[100] Although it was clear in the report on this first set of hearings and data collection that the FCC considered the CBS system superior, the commission did express concern over the compatibility issue and expressed its hope that CBS would eventually alter its technology enough to overcome the problem. It did not recommend immediate adoption of the CBS system standard; however, in a memo dated September 5, 1950, the FCC stated that they would do just that if the set manufacturers would agree to manufacture receivers capable of receiving both CBS color and black and white signals until the compatibility issue could be resolved.[101] Manufacturers did not comply with this stipulation (some considered it a threat), so, feeling under pressure to institute a standard, on October 11, 1950, the FCC released its "Second Report and Order on Color Television," which formally adopted the CBS system as the U.S. standard for color television. The report claimed the decision was based on color fidelity and "picture texture" and noted that while CBS's system had gone through successful and extensive field testing, RCA's system had not, and that, moreover, CBS color could be transmitted by existing network facilities, but they had no proof that the same could be said for RCA's system.

The 1950 FCC decision was not popular with the television industry at large. Less than a week after CBS's system was approved by the FCC as the color standard, RCA filed suit against the FCC with the Chicago Federal District Court, seeking to halt CBS's entry into the business of color television, arguing that the FCC had overstepped its power, overlooked the public interest, and made a decision that was ultimately "arbitrary and capricious."[102] While the Chicago court and the Supreme Court ultimately upheld the FCC decision, the seven-month-long injunction and the publicity around the court case stalled CBS's advancement. By the time it was all over, the number of black and white sets on the market had increased by 50 percent, RCA had convinced most of the major television manufacturers not to produce CBS color sets, and the Korean War had escalated.

One of the most compelling aspects of RCA's case was that which centered on public interest. The company's lawyers argued that the "large

FIGURE 2.12 CBS color convertor, 1949. AUTHOR'S PRIVATE COLLECTION.

obsolescence loss" resulting from CBS's incompatibility with current sets would greatly inconvenience set owners. CBS had convinced the FCC during the hearings that their already developed adaptors (a device placed on the back of sets that would enable CBS color transmissions to be received in black and white) and convertors (a filter disc device attached to the front of the screen that allowed color viewing on black and white sets) did not place an unreasonable economic burden on the consumer, even though convertors were estimated to cost up to one hundred dollars (see figure 2.12). RCA countered that a "compatible system would save present set owners about a billion dollars and would avoid waste of material and labor, which is vital to conserve in these critical times," in a reference to U.S. wartime conservation.[103] The Supreme Court ultimately found that the FCC had engaged in no wrongdoing during the hearings or in rendering their decision. RCA lost the case, but as many television historians have pointed out, they had succeeded in hobbling the CBS color venture.

FIGURE 2.13 CBS RX-28UHF 1949. USED WITH PERMISSION FROM THE
SCIENCE MUSEUM/SCIENCE & SOCIETY PICTURE LIBRARY, U.K.

CBS aired their first large-scale commercial color program on the
first day that the FCC permitted it: July 25, 1951. Broadcast to an ex-
ceptionally small audience, consisting of those watching the fifty CBS
color receivers located across the country and those industry insiders
attending screenings in a handful of public places across New York City,
Premiere was an hour-long variety special featuring the network's biggest stars. CBS also began regular day and evening colorcasts at that time
(these were sustained by the network, meaning they didn't have sponsors), including a program starring Mel Tormé and another with Mike
Wallace. Despite these broadcasts, CBS's color programming endeavor
was dead on arrival, since "the RCA delaying tactic had already been
successfully fatal to the CBS color system."[104] Making it more difficult
still for CBS was the reluctance of manufacturers to produce sets for
them. The industry was not supportive of CBS color, and the Korean War
was exasperating the problem, as it created uncertainty as to whether
or not the government would place restrictions on the production of

consumer electronics. It was in this context that CBS decided that they had no choice but to manufacture their own sets; they therefore purchased Hytron Electronics, a major producer of radio tubes and a minor producer of television receivers (through its subsidiary, Air King), in April 1951. The deal turned out to be a significant mistake, as there were problems with the Hytron company that became clear after the purchase, including the fact that CBS would have to completely alter its assembly line to make it work for their needs.[105] Some historians now speculate that it was these problems that led CBS to possibly help orchestrate the Office of Defense Mobilization's wartime ban on the production of color televisions in October of that year, even though Stanton vehemently denied the accusation at the time. Nevertheless, whether or not they helped arrange the ban, CBS very quickly complied with it when it was announced, seeing it as a way out of a situation they had come to regret.

NTSC: OPTICS, FIDELITY, AND COMPRESSION

While the NTSC would eventually share its reports and findings with the FCC, it also worked independently of the commission. In fact, it continued its work long after the first approval of a color standard, much to the chagrin of those FCC commissioners who believed the NTSC was undermining their decision. In the end, the NTSC's research would ultimately lead to the new standard that was approved by the FCC in 1953.

The NTSC, disbanded after it had completed its standards work for monochrome television, was reconstituted in January 1950, with its membership expanded and its structure reorganized to fit the particular questions that surrounded the adoption and standardization of a color system. In order to determine the capabilities and potential weaknesses of each system, the NTSC, beginning in the summer of 1951, established various study panels, which:

> conducted fundamental investigations into the nature of human vision, explored the transmissions systems best adapted to such vision, wrote and rewrote signal specifications, conducted field tests of the signals for color reception as well as compatible monochrome reception, studied the special problems of network connections for color, wrote tutorial papers, compiled definitions, and finally arrived at unanimous

agreement on twenty-two signal specifications which now are serving as the basis of color telecasting in the United States.[106]

The members of these panels (predominately engineers) worked with bodies of knowledge on the eye, optics, colorimetry, and the peculiarities of color vision in order to imagine and then create standards around how an average viewer with a "healthy eye" might take in and make sense of electronic color. In this way, an imagined viewer, her perceptual processes and physiology, and the ideal environmental conditions for television viewing were built into the color technology and its accompanying standards.[107] As Sterne and Mulvin remind us, "Color TV is thus a perceptual technology in the deepest sense: a technical formation that requires a set of perceptual operations on the part of its subjects to 'work' at all. The 'colorness' of the color TV picture thus lies somewhere between the inner workings of the camera, the broadcast infrastructure, and the set on one hand, and the inner psychophysical life of viewers on the other."[108] In order to tease out the various "perceptual operations," measure them, and then judge them, the NTSC employed the techniques of psychophysics—the scientific study of the effects of stimulus on the perceptual system. And in doing so, they also took into account the human eye's capacity for failure—in ways that were expected and empirically measured by scientists and engineers—so that allowances for these imperfections were also incorporated into the design of the technology and signal processing and the development of FCC standards. (This was especially true when it came to the study and processes of compression, which would take up a significant amount of time and thought for NTSC's Panel 11, which was tasked with studying "the subjective aspects of color television.") Persistence of vision was often framed as a failure of the eye, as was the inability to discern errors and gaps. Eye fatigue, "color bombardment" (a fatigue effect produced by the 'rapid sequence of primary colors'), and "color flash effects" (a separation in colors that occurs at the edges of the screen image during certain eye movements) were all considered to be related to failed operations of vision and were taken into consideration in the setting of standards and refining of systems. And yet, after all the philosophical and scientific debates about and general acceptance of the subjectivity of color, the process of developing standards for viewing color television relied upon the belief that color vision was measurable, repeatable, predictable, and able to be represented by statistical and scientific models that would serve as the basis for yet more standardization. One such model is based on the "standard observer," which is referenced frequently in the NTSC reports.

All colorimetry for television—which defined systems and standards, and undergirded the work of the NTSC panels—was informed by the recorded optical responses of the standard observer. Established and defined by the CIE in 1931, the standard observer, rather than being a single human observer, is a table of calculations representing the physiological responses of an "average" or "normal" observer.[109] These calculations were the result of laboratory studies of the visual responses of fifty-two volunteers, who were seated in darkened rooms with their chins strapped into position as they looked at a white screen "through an aperture having a 2 degree field of view."[110] These tests measured perceptions of luminosity, the eye's evaluation of chromaticity, color matching, and color mixing. In acknowledging the fact that color television systems are designed with the statistically modeled standard observer in mind, W. T. Wintringham writes in his seminal 1951 article, "Colorimetry for Television," "It is not known how seriously color reproduction is affected by the fact that no observer sees mixtures in the same way as the Standard Observer."[111] Panel 16's report on color performance in broadcasting using the proposed NTSC standard color signal also acknowledged both the subjectivity and the variability in observers and the assessments they make, based on their own physiology, sensitivities, and even taste or ability to analyze or judge images. In the concluding remarks, the panel states: "Regarding color fidelity, the final conclusion is that the appreciation of color is so highly subjective that possibly no setting will prove pleas[ing] to all of a group of critical observers. This need not be too disturbing, for the successes of color motion pictures and color photography show that most people are not critical observers, and that color does in fact add to the pleasantness of a picture."[112] This statement both speaks to the continued belief in the subjectivity of color vision even within the highly regulated and structured world of standard setting for communication technology, and also sets the stage for much of what would be discussed in Panel 11—the concept of the "good enough" image in relation to spectrum economy and signal compression.

While the measurements built into the design of color television systems are based on the standard observer, tests were also administered in the standards process that were psychophysical in nature and that relied on the reporting of observers or test subjects in laboratory settings. In addition, tests were also done both in the home and in more public settings. Field testing is a process that is meant to replicate real-life experience with the technology. Yet many of the demonstrations and tests of the various color systems during the standardization process did anything but replicate real life, as they occurred in darkened labs or hotel conference rooms, in front of large audiences in theaters and studios, and often involved still or filmed images rather than forms of live performance. The test subjects often were not even ordinary viewers themselves, but, as in the case of NTSC's Panel 11, were various types of engineers, panel members, and lab employees who were meant to stand in for the average viewer, but who were not by any means representative. They were mostly white and often male experts with highly specialized technical knowledge.[113] As part of the FCC hearings, both CBS and RCA placed televisions in private homes for a number of months in order to collect data on broadcast signal strength, reception, and image quality. WCBS in New York broadcast for two hours a day in early 1950 to these homes, but the programming, "beyond a single live broadcast with the network's color girl, Patty Painter," consisted mostly of test patterns and photo slides.[114] While demonstrations and tests sometimes had live components to them, they mostly relied on still images and filmed moving images. Genuinely successful live demonstrations were rare in the color standardization period, as liveness created too much potential for disruption, interference, and variation, which is remarkable given that almost all early television programming—both monochrome and eventually color—would be live. Moreover, even filmed moving images were rare; the tests done by the various committees during the color standards period relied mostly on slides of color photographs.

In Panel 11's report on the psychophysical tests performed, the committee noted that instead of live broadcasts, they chose to use only the NTSC mandated test slides and a single reel of 16 mm Eastman Kodak color film, because they wanted to see "substantially identical subject matter" from various labs and from across the systems studies so that they could have clearer guidelines for comparison.[115] In other words, they needed standard images in order to compare image quality, and moreover, the NTSC reasoned that "live-talent performances would in general be too elaborate, costly, and difficult of exact duplication to be suitable for routine laboratory or field tests although live-talent material is of course necessary and desirable as a substantial part of any field-test program."[116] Therefore, all field tests across all panels relied on these same twenty-seven Kodakchrome slides, made especially by Kodak for the NTSC tests, which consisted primarily of medium-, long-, and close-range shots of animals and white people in outdoor settings (what Mulvin and Sterne call "a narrow band of WASP leisure") along with the occasional photo of a fruit bowl, fishing tackle, jewelry, or another such still life.[117] Calling these images early iterations of stock photography, Mulvin and Sterne, who analyzed the use and meaning of these slides in great detail, argue that:

> The images' relatively free-floating status made them ideal test subjects for television: not too heavily invested with a particular set of meanings or interpretive communities, using widely available visual rhetoric, and not depicting anything in particular, as determined by a set of professional cultural intermediaries. They were meant to call attention to color capacities, not to themselves.[118]

Some of the slides appear relatively muted in their color compositions while others would have presented a challenge to the color systems being tested. For example, a slide called "sunflower girl" (see figure 2.14), is a close-up of a young white woman with dark hair, pressing sunflowers up to her face, against the backdrop of a clear blue sky. This image would have required a color system to represent the woman's skin tone in a manner that would be received by viewing subjects as "natural" or "real" while also capturing the vibrancy of the yellow sunflowers and blue sky without allowing for any color bleeding or blurring. The viewing subjects (again, mostly engineers) in the NTSC panels were asked to look at the slides (in a dark room, "sitting as close to the displays as was comfortable") through the various color systems, at varying color bandwidths (12 MHz and 4 MHz, for example), and compare them to the original Kodachrome image. After doing so, they were asked to rate the image quality and identify the tipping point at which an image went from "satisfactory" to "unsatisfactory"—in other words, the moment of "just-noticeable difference."[119] In performing such a test, researchers were attempting to determine how to economize signal size while providing viewers with an acceptable color image.

Two of the most significant and interrelated issues examined by all

FIGURE 2.14 NTSC test slide used by Panel 11. Donald Fink, *Color Television Standards* (New York: McGraw Hill, 1955).

the committees studying color television during the standardization process were compression and fidelity. Due to the fact that color television signals contain more information (broadly, across the categories of brightness, hue, and saturation) than monochrome, color systems as designed would require more bandwidth than the 6 MHz standard. What the FCC preferred, however, was that the color signal be compressed in such a way that it would take out some of the information and detail, thereby making the packet of data smaller and better able to fit onto the already agreed upon "narrowband" standard. Two questions still remained: Which details should be omitted? And what would be a "good enough" color image if compression were prioritized?

As part of his project to reconstruct "a general history of compression," Sterne has developed the term "perceptual technics," which he defines as the "application of perceptual research for the purposes of economizing signals." And as Sterne and Mulvin argue, color television represents "a major node in compression history."[120] Debates and studies in setting standards for both monochrome and color television have been defined in relation to the narrowband versus wideband requirements or capacities of various proposed systems. While wideband systems—of 12 or 16 MHz, for example—would allow for more data and therefore more picture detail, they would also require more space on the spectrum, which would result in a smaller number of television stations. In CBS's UHF proposal, Stanton posited the network as presenting cutting-edge "quality" color technology (in addition to a "fine-screen" monochrome system), based at least partially on an argument that a larger amount of data would provide more visual information to the image and the eye, thus producing a more complex and substantially better visual experience.[121] However, the counterargument to this claim (made by, for example, RCA, in support of its compatible 6 MHz system) was that rather than thinking that compression leads to a reduction in quality, one should acknowledge that there is only so much data or information the eye can take in to reconstruct a realistic and "pleasing" image, which means that some of that data is not necessary but "surplus."[122] Some argued further that, in the words of the Panel 11 report, "most people aren't critical observers" and would therefore not notice or care much about a high-definition image. In the nineteenth century, Hermann von Helmholtz, one of the great and early physiologists of the eye and ear, expressed similar ideas about the insensitivity of the eye, especially when compared to the ear. For a time, Helmholtz believed that the eye's job was largely to synthesize information for coherence, while the ear was the sense organ that could break down and analyze finer details of sensory input.[123] This led him to posit, "The eye has no sense of harmony in the same meaning as the ear. There is no music to the eye." However, Helmholtz would eventually be forced (through evidence gathered from his psychophysical experiments) to confront the fact that there were very real limits and fallibility for the ear, just as there were for the eye, as all sense organs showed themselves (to Thomas Edison and others) to be "flawed instruments."[124] Theoretically, communication devices meant to extend or replicate human perception could have been devised for a set of ideal, rather than flawed, human senses; however, the limits of human perception were instead built into the design of the communication technology. Mara Mills explains that "with perceptual coding irrelevant material is removed before transmission—and never reconstructed."[125] Mills locates the origins of this phenomenon and of media compression more generally in the development and use of artificial voice technologies. She writes:

> Lip-readers, artificial larynx users, and acousticians alike investigated ways to materialize speech, translate it into different media, break it into simple components, or synthesize it from diverse materials. Telephone engineers drew on this research to deduce the absolute minimum parameters through which speech could be transmitted and remade. Today, rather than directly reproduce speech, transmission and recording systems increasingly contain simplified models of speech and hearing; they code and compress speech based on an understanding of the elements that are redundant—those that can be eliminated and later reconstructed—as well as those that are irrelevant to the human ear.[126]

Mills considers this "the politics of modulation," wherein ideas or theories about human perception are "built into transmission systems, the imagined senders and receivers of messages, and the effects of signal-thinking on styles of communication."[127] Sterne has made a similar argument, stating that "in the case of transmission and storage of sound and images perceptual technics use measurements of the limits of human perception to classify signals that move through an infrastructure, thereby transforming the operational character of the infrastructure."[128] In the NTSC recommendations, engineers, advisors, and regulators ultimately sought an approximation of verisimilitude in the image (especially in the case of flesh tones) and yet in the end did not prioritize maximum levels of picture detail, which *might* have constructed a richer and more complex televisual image.[129] In moving in this direction, they considered the limitations of human vision; the limitations of the screen (relatively small at the time); the limitations of the home as viewing space; and the fact that the reception of RGB color signals was "device dependent";[130] along with the many and varied potential problems, bandwidth or spectrum limitations, and other disruptions and interferences that could affect or distort the transmitted electronic image.

It is also important to note that there are specific definitions of fidelity written and referred to by standards organizations in this process. For example, a section of the Panel 11 report reads, "Psychophysical picture fidelity is the degree to which the color of the reproduced scene agrees, element by element, with the color of the corresponding element in the original scene; perceptual picture fidelity is the degree to which the color of objects and lights in the reproduced scene are perceived the same as in the original scene."[131] Psychophysical testing works to compare the physical measurements of a color stimulus with the perception of that color stimulus. The distinction between psychophysical and perceptual fidelity is meant to differentiate between what can be analyzed as a "real," measurable stimulus-response correlation and what is perceived to be an accurate representation or approximation by an observer. This, at least theoretically, allows both the subjectivity of the individual eye and empirical color measurement to be considered.

In an article for a 1951 special issue on color television in the *Proceedings of the IRE*, Fink described the ways that human perception did not exactly line up with what might be considered an accurate representation of a color image: "In color photography it is a truism that an accurate reproduction is usually less satisfactory than a distorted reproduction carefully contrived to impress the viewer as being 'natural,' 'bright,' 'warm,' or 'cold,' depending on the context of the material represented."[132] Fink then used this "truism" as a basis from which to argue that a color television system "should never be called upon to reproduce an image that is more than pleasing" to the human eye, since trying to construct and sustain a perfect color image was costly and, from his point of view, unnecessary.[133] He went on to cite existing "statistical studies of what constitutes a pleasing image," wherein subjects were asked to identify differences in and respond to variables in image quality, such as resolution or flicker, in order to better understand and track what might be "pleasing," "less than pleasing," or "more than pleasing" to viewers.[134] The larger goal, Fink suggested, was for a television system to be calibrated in such a way as to remain steady in the satisfactory range of "pleasing" images.[135] The Condon Committee's 1950 assessment of the quality of televised color images was in line with Fink's, arguing that aesthetic compromises had to be made in light of the expense of a detailed color image and the extra space those images would take up on the spectrum.[136]

While CBS was touting the beauty and detail of its "quality" color images in the late 1940s, others in the industry had their sights set on stabilization, compatibility, and legibility—and an expressed desire for a satisfactory and smooth end to the "color wars." This tension between two often self-serving positions—those seeking the status quo (often, as was the case with set makers, to protect their own economic interests) and those imagining what might be possible for the electronic image *once the technology was perfected*—certainly framed the arguments made before the FCC as well as the type of research taken up by the various advisory groups and committees. In the end, the beliefs held and compromises made by these engineers, regulators, and businessmen in regard to what exactly was necessary and what might be considered surplus remained built into the structures of transmission and reception throughout the rest of the twentieth century and beyond—which, as other scholars have acknowledged, left the American television system with little room for growth or change as color technology developed post standardization.[137]

In 1952, RCA came out with an advancement, a new highly sensitive single-gun color tube that would make both CBS's color wheel and RCA's previous three-gun system obsolete. The tube was demonstrated to the NTSC in the fall of 1952, and by the following January, the NTSC announced that it was recommending RCA's compatible system over the FCC approved CBS system. A few months later, once the Korean War was over and the ban on color receiver manufacturing was lifted, RCA petitioned the FCC for approval of what was being referred to as the NTSC system. RCA and NBC held a series of high-profile public demonstrations in NBC's New York Colonial Theatre,[138] where, as Bradley Chisholm describes, "legislators, journalists, ad agents, even actors and producers, witnessed live broadcasts of musicals and dance performances. The performers strutted in front of color cameras on stage left and could be compared with their full-color video images on a projection-TV monitor on stage right."[139]

Most of the experimental programs aired at this time were variety programs, although bits performed by the cast of *Kukla, Fran and Ollie*, an ad-libbed afternoon puppet program aimed at children but with a substantial adult following, were also part of at least three such broadcasts in 1953. As described in RCA's 1953 petition to the FCC, the field tests (fourteen in total during the first half of 1953) at that stage were mostly to gauge the reception of black and white images via its compatible system. The following is a summary of program content:

A LOOK AT FUTURE OF COLOR RECEPTION

These two television sets are receiving the same picture. Above, a special performance of NBC's *Kukla, Fran & Ollie* is shown on an ordinary black and white set. Below, it is seen on a color set receiving RCA's "compatible" color. Put on for a group of congressmen, this demonstration produced the best TV color to date. RCA's color is compatible because it can be received both in black and white on today's sets and in color on special sets. Recently CBS's color system, which is not compatible but has FCC approval, was shelved by CBS itself. RCA's system does not yet have FCC approval but is so impressive that this seems just a matter of months. When will sets be available? Probably by the end of 1954.

FIGURE 2.15 "A Look at Future of Color Reception," *Life*, May 15, 1953.

TUESDAY, JANUARY 27	A musical revue.
THURSDAY, JANUARY 29	An educational program on the manufacture of stained glass windows.
TUESDAY, FEBRUARY 3	First of two talks by Charles J. Caudle on atomic energy.
THURSDAY, FEBRUARY 5	Dan Blum's collection of dolls and a Siamese dance.
TUESDAY, FEBRUARY 10	Second of two talks by Charles J. Caudle on atomic energy.
THURSDAY, FEBRUARY 12	Excerpts from "Madame Butterfly."
TUESDAY, FEBRUARY 17	Excerpts from "Madame Butterfly."
THURSDAY, FEBRUARY 19	Talk by Ivan Sanderson on caves.
TUESDAY, FEBRUARY 24	Talk by John N. Booth on his experiences in Tibet.
THURSDAY, FEBRUARY 26	A musical revue.
TUESDAY, MARCH 3	Talk by Edward Snow, professional treasure hunter.
THURSDAY, MARCH 5	A musical revue.
THURSDAY, MARCH 12	A musical revue with Jack Lane's birds.
THURSDAY, MARCH 19	*Kukla, Fran and Ollie.*[140]

All of the field tests requested New York viewers to write in to the network, reporting on the quality of the broadcast and with information about their television set (make, model, year, screen size). The fifteen-minute programs were introduced by NBC reporter Ben Grauer:

> The Radio Corporation of America and the National Broadcasting Company present another color television test program. Ladies and gentlemen, greetings to you. This is Ben Grauer speaking to you over Channel 4 of the National Broadcasting Company's experimental station KE2XJV. You are about to view a test of RCA's all-electronic

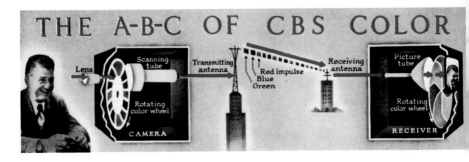

FIGURE 2.16 "The ABC of CBS Color," *Time*, December 4, 1950.

compatible color television system. By "compatible" we mean that it is possible for you to see the color program on your present television sets in black and white. We would like to have you help us with this fifteen-minute test. Please send a card or letter to RCA-NBC Color Television, RCA Building, New York, New York, and let us know how you receive this program. It is important that you include the age and make of your set, size of its screen and anything unusual in your reception. And now on with the show.[141]

RCA did its final official presentation on the NTSC system to the FCC in a rather involved demonstration lasting over two hours and held at the Waldorf Astoria on October 15, 1953. The program included highly choreographed live broadcasts (of action from within the studio and outdoors, and of the NTSC test slides and color test patterns) from CBS, NBC, and DuMont experimental color stations.[142] The response from both the FCC commissioners and the press was reportedly overwhelmingly positive.

While a few companies, such as DuMont, objected to RCA's petition, CBS did not. In fact, Stanton released a public statement in support of the new RCA/NTSC system and soon thereafter announced the development of a device called the Chromacoder, which encoded images from CBS's field-sequential system in the NTSC standard. On December 17, 1953, the FCC announced its approval, but as David Sarnoff's biographer, Eugene Lyons, notes:

Perhaps to cushion the blow to its self-esteem, the Commission extended its endorsement to the NTSC rather than to RCA. Since the two sets of specifications were virtually identical, this made no practical difference. It is a safe guess that the cancellation of their abortive franchise drew sighs of relief from Columbia executives. In a sense it took them off a conspicuous and bruising hook.[143]

Color television had turned out to be a very costly failure for CBS, and while the network continued to develop some technology for the new standard, it was only for a brief time.

CBS would eventually enter into the production of color programming once again, but, besides their work with medical color television, they did abandon their research and development of color technologies. The network's negative experiences—losing money, time, and respect—in the color wars resulted in a long-standing ambivalence about color. There were a few years in the mid- to late 1950s when color programming could be found on the network, but it was pulled completely off the air by the decade's close. It was not until ABC and NBC announced they would convert their full program schedule to color in the mid-1960s that CBS agreed to do the same.

In the following chapter, we will see that CBS was not alone in its post-standards ambivalence toward color, especially during the mid-1950s, when sponsors, critics, and consumers were not altogether ready to embrace the new technology. The NTSC system was also beset by technical issues during its first few years, and RCA struggled to convince consumers and factions of the industry that color was both technically and aesthetically stable and worth the expense.

CHAPTER THREE

Color Adjustments

Experiments, Calibrations, and Color Training, 1950–1955

In June 1951, Goodman Ace addressed the arrival of color television with a good deal of cynicism.[1] Like other critics at the time, he was not convinced of the need for the new technology so early in the medium's development and was instead suspicious of the motives behind the networks' move toward color. In characteristically droll style, Ace wrote, "So color is the transfusion television needs to arouse it from its coma of monotony. Of course it is unfortunate so young a medium needs a shot in the arm so soon, but it's hereditary, following closely the pattern of its parent, the motion-picture industry, developing the same anemic symptoms and doctoring itself with the same miracle-drug, color."[2]

Critics such as Saul Carson, Robert Lewis Shayon, and Jack Gould were also, at various times, of the opinion that color might be a cover for poor programming, motivated by set sales, or the result of particular companies' desires to gain control over aspects of the television industry.[3] Furthermore, coverage of the battle for FCC approval of a color system standard had highlighted the industrial and commercial justifications for color but had not fully addressed the possibilities that color offered for specific narrative and aesthetic developments. This only served to solidify the position taken by some critics that television was first and foremost a commercial (rather than artistic or cultural) object.[4] As Neil Harris has argued, "So suspiciously was television viewed by many critics then, that color sets, the most complex consumer commodity that had ever been mass produced . . . seemed like a wooden victory, a source of shame, a measuring stick to berate all involved with the industry."[5]

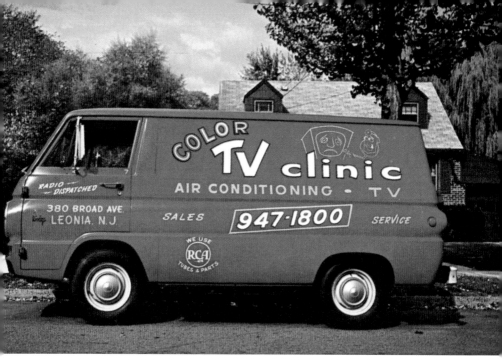

FIGURE 3.1 1965 advertising postcard for color television repair service.

AUTHOR'S PRIVATE COLLECTION.

In the midst of such criticism, RCA/NBC spent the 1950s expanding their investment in and promotion of color while tying their brand closely to it, while CBS (after broadcasting a few color programs, such as *Shower of Stars* and *Ford Star Jubilee,* fairly regularly between 1954 and 1957) abandoned color broadcasting toward the end of the decade, not returning to it until the early 1960s, at which point ABC too began to air color programming.[6] Despite NBC's efforts, *Time* magazine declared color television "the most resounding industrial flop of 1956."[7]

However, at the start of the decade, the process of standardization and the race for FCC approval was still the most visible aspect of the U.S. networks' engagement with color television. Between the time of the initial approval of the CBS system in 1950 and the FCC reversal that set the NTSC standard in 1953, both CBS and NBC aired a number of select programs to a remarkably small number of set owners, most of whom had some sort of relationship with the industry (critics, dealers, sponsors, assorted friends of the networks, etc.). For example, the president of CBS, William Paley, admitted later that, at the time *Premiere* aired in 1951, there were only twenty-five CBS color sets in operation in the New York area.[8] That said, an additional small group of people would have seen NBC's and CBS's public color television demonstrations in the first couple of years of the decade, and there were plans to place color sets in department stores, supermarkets, hotels, and taverns in 1954. "It's possible that most Chicagoans will view their first colorcasts in neighborhood saloons, as they did for black and white," a reporter for the *Chicago Daily News* said, quipping, "It's ironic that many of the first eyes to view colorcasts here will be bloodshot."[9] However, before public sites for color television viewing became a broad experience, the majority of Americans had not yet seen color television, but had heard much about it—especially through the regular press coverage of the "color wars." In terms of envisioning what color television might look like and what it might mean to them, potential consumers/viewers might have seen publicity from the networks, touting the coming of color, but more often, they read descriptions by critics and reporters who painted a mixed picture. Writing about CBS color broadcasts in 1951, for example, John Crosby positions the technology as a glorious distraction:

> You can get drunk as a goat on an hour of CBS color, which I must admit, is a gorgeous thing. After two hours of it, you pass out cold. In this condition of insobriety, folks eagerly attest that they would instantly rush out and buy either a color converter or a whole new set. Then they go home and sleep it off. . . . My chief objection to color at this time is that it may temporarily confuse an already confused industry, which is just five years old, and may retard what some optimists consider its progress.[10]

This chapter focuses on the experimental period of network color in the early 1950s, a time in which there was much anxious rumination on color in all sectors of the television industry, and a good portion of it could be located in the positioning of color, on multiple fronts, as simultaneously trivial and excessive—notions which were intertwined with concerns over the prematurity of color television and its not yet fully standardized processes and functions. Having eventually won the battle for the U.S. color television standard by 1953, RCA/NBC tried to allay some of these concerns with promises and eventual demonstrations

May 14, 1955   **THE**   Price 20 cents

NEW YORKER

FIGURE 3.2 *New Yorker* cover, May 14, 1955.

of careful color management and deployment. The company spent the early part of the 1950s working not only to perfect color technology but also to manage the perception of risk (for sponsors and consumers especially), by simultaneously containing and expanding color use through the introduction of color management techniques. These techniques included employing a system of on-set color harmony, relying on theories of functional color, developing systems of calibration at the points of both production and reception, and implementing widespread color training by color experts and consultants. I argue that these discourses and strategies of management and standardization, taken up primarily by RCA/NBC, had developed both in relationship to the FCC standardization experience and in response to the industrial and cultural anxieties that existed around color's potential for excess, disruption, and triviality. These tactics also influenced the approach to programming during what NBC called its "introductory year," as the network strategized the best genres and programming slots in which to try out color.

As we learned in chapter 2, after a very public battle, the FCC eventually approved the NTSC standard, which was based on RCA's and Philco's separate proposals for a system compatible with existing black and white sets.[11] In the end, the process of standardization—particularly in deciding what exactly was necessary and what might be considered surplus—remained embedded in the very structures of transmission and reception throughout the rest of the twentieth century. It also left Americans with a system of standards that replicated and reinforced assumptions about a television viewer's relationship to the color image and to the viewing process itself; a system that privileged stable, replicable, neither overly rich nor overly defined images that created a *sense* of the natural world but that might not contain all the information available to represent the *closest possible approximation* of the world in full color. A regulatory emphasis on spectrum economy reined in electronic color, limiting it to the minimum amount of color information needed to "trick" the eye into seeing a complete and "good enough" image.

However, even after the standards were formalized, the issue of how to provide a stable and replicable system of color transmission and reception remained. CBS aired color programming while testing and expanding its system during the period right after it was awarded approval but put its system briefly on hold during the Korean War and then ended production of its sets by 1954 and most of its color programming by 1957, by which time NBC was aggressively branding itself in relation to color. However, even though it offered compatibility, which is what eventually won over the FCC on appeal, many noted that the RCA system was not fully developed at the time of its approval, which meant that it would have to be further refined through the mid-1950s. This period then, with a limited color audience and programming schedule, represents an experimental moment in color broadcasting. While RCA's system was serviceable in many ways and even proved to have quite spectacular image quality on occasion, it was also unpredictable, often requiring significant technical management to successfully transmit an image without flicker, bleeds, or degradation. In fact, even after the NTSC system was in full and regular use for many years, it was still considered to be so unreliable that the acronym for the NTSC was often jokingly referred to

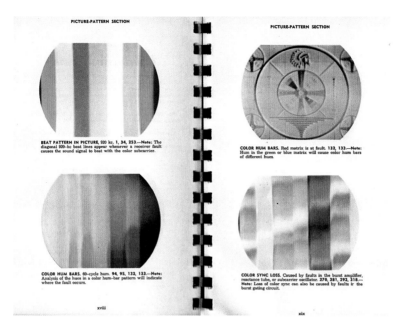

FIGURE 3.3 Identifying problems in color. *Pin-Point Color TV Troubles in 15 Minutes*, ed. Harold Manly, Coyne Electrical School, 1958.

(especially by engineers) as standing for "Never Twice the Same Color," "Never The Same Color," or "No True Skin Color."[12]

The reproduction, transmission, and reception of NTSC color was a complex process involving, in very basic terms, the combination of red, green, and blue (RGB) electrical signals produced from three camera tubes (each capturing the same scene in one of the three primary colors). These signals are then fed to the picture reproducer dot by dot over a video channel and sent to a receiver where the three corresponding primary images are reassembled and superimposed in such a way as to appear as a single cohesive image to the human eye. The NTSC system was designed to divide the color picture signals along the categories of brightness and color information, which is called a luminance-chrominance encoding system. While color receivers would receive and process both sets of signals, monochrome receivers would ignore or filter out the chrominance signal, taking in only the information on the luminance signal.

There was much room for error at all points of the transmission and reception process, leading to distortions and glitches such as no color, no color hold (changing colors or drifting vertical bands of color), incorrect colors, color hum bars, and color snow.[13] The 1950 report from the Condon Committee detailed three general categories of "potential sources of trouble" for reproduction of color in television: improper registration, which arises when the three primary-color images do not precisely line up, leading to blurring at the point of reception; color break-up, which is when the separate primary colors appear at the edges of objects; and color fringing, which describes color trails that can sometimes follow rapidly moving images on the screen.[14] The same report outlined the potential areas of technical failure that could lead to the "unfaithful reproduction of color," which included the incorrect use of filters, interference, and "improper" camera, transmitter, or receiver adjustment.[15] In Panel 11 of the NTSC studies, researchers were testing for what had been understood to be common problems of all color systems on offer, including issues like color bombardment, color flash effects, and the appearance of "residual color" in the scanning process,[16] ultimately concluding that some of these effects had been overstated (such as color bombardment), while others were present and could be mitigated by viewing conditions (for example, by sitting a certain distance from the screen, increasing receiver screen size, or viewing in the dark).

This concern over such effects, however, lingered in press accounts of the technology. In particular, and as discussed in chapter 2, there was talk of eye fatigue and strain (already a concern with black and white sets), as color in motion—especially through a volatile electronic system of transmission and reception—was thought to require possibly too much physiological effort on the part of the viewer and could lead to moments of failure in vision, such as color bleeds in afterimages.[17] Although there was a related concern with early color film systems dating to as early as 1914 with Kinemacolor, the anxieties about vision were intensified for a medium that was in the home, allowed viewers to sit as close to or as far from the set as they pleased, required them to perform their own color adjustments, and maintained a relatively small screen size. In regard to size, many critics noted that monochrome simply worked better with such a small image and that color would only serve to add unnecessary complexity to the screen.[18]

The peculiarities of perception come into play here, as the human eye is more sensitive to some frequencies of light (like green) than others (like red and violet), and color television systems had to account for this unbalanced sensitivity in order to reproduce colors that resonated with viewers' perceptions of the natural world.[19] The idiosyncrasy of human vision was also used as another justification for, and technical answer to, compression.[20] There are variations in color perception across individuals too, as addressed in various sites of expertise, such as in the engineering community by Wintringham, who acknowledged that "no observers sees mixtures [of color] the same way," and more popularly by Gould, who suggested that color tuning does not involve "absolute rights or wrongs . . . since individual tastes do vary and by adjusting the chrome control which regulates color intensity on the screen, one can pick up one's own shadings."[21]

A problem arose, however, from the experimental period, in which some television critics (most of whom were given sets by RCA, for example, or were present at various demonstrations) were fixated on the instability and subjectivity of color television reception and connected that to larger concerns about why the industry was moving into color so soon after black and white sets had begun to be disseminated. Color was often met with ambivalence, as it seemed to many to be simply too much too soon. As a writer for *Life* magazine remarked in January 1954, "With color, the still-intact TV industry undergoes a sudden revolution, which will greatly increase its markets and its scope. Because color will bring confusion, too-quick obsolescence of black and white sets and financial hardships, sections of the TV industry have been reluctant revolutionaries."[22]

As mentioned earlier, some of this concern stemmed from what were perceived to be the questionable motives and political maneuvering of particular networks, set manufacturers, and station operators. There were also many within and outside the television industry who were not completely convinced that the technology was sufficiently developed by 1950 either to set standards (as the technology changed, so might its technical needs) or to become an immediately viable consumer good (because the technology proved to be highly complicated and often temperamental when used in public or press demonstrations and field tests). Color was also excessive in terms of production and studio cost for networks, stations, and sponsors, and thus involved higher ad rates.[23] There were costs for consumers too, as the $1,000–$1,200 price tag for color sets seemed outrageously expensive by the time they eventually entered the market in 1954. Even the very use of color came with repeated warnings from experts to executives and producers that "overuse of color for color's sake must be avoided,"[24] as though color was an excessive addition that threatened to further destabilize an already precarious narrative, commercial, and technical system. As film historians have noted, cinematic color also went through a period in which its excesses were critiqued as decadent or frivolous distractions in the years prior to color's assimilation into the classical Hollywood production system. In 1953, Gould both emphasized the incredible potential color television had for daily life and warned of the problems that color presented (especially in lighting and tuning) that still needed to be solved by networks:

> A new color age soon will be upon us. With the advent of tinted television the country is going to be conscious of color to a degree scarcely imaginable at the moment—in fashions, decorations, art appreciation, entertainment, advertising methods and public tastes. Psychologically, watching color TV in the familiar surroundings of one's own home produces an almost uncanny reaction. Actually turning a knob and seeing the screen light up in different hues amounts in some ways to an almost completely new experience in the meaning of color. . . . But the presence of color TV in the parlor also is a sobering experience in regard to the realities of the tinted medium at the moment. Seeing is still believing and one need not look at color overly long to realize that considerable problems lie ahead, both on the receiving and the transmitting ends.[25]

In Gould's review, we find a framing for color television, repeated during the decades of its development and the early years of its dissemination, that color carried big promises of change and beauty along with a big potential for failure. Color was a risky financial venture that came with a very real possibility of meaningful losses—as both CBS and RCA learned at different points in the 1950s.[26] Moreover, the very public discussions about color's many excesses and volatility only heightened the networks' concerns and acute sense of what was at stake in this new investment. In an industry that promised predictability, reliability, and repetition in programming, form, and service, color was a potentially disruptive force, one that would leave network executives quite literally anxious, but that would also stir up deeper cultural anxieties about the subjectivity and inconstancy of color more generally.

David Batchelor's notion of "chromophobia" is a helpful concept in identifying and parsing the features and origins of this anxiety, as it draws upon one of the more historically significant conceptual frameworks for color. Batchelor explores the West's social and cultural relationship to color through this concept.[27] Arguing that color is often positioned as both dangerous (through associations with notions of "the oriental, the primitive, the vulgar, the queer or the pathological") and trivial (the feminine, the superficial, the cosmetic), Batchelor concludes that "color is routinely excluded from the higher concerns of the mind. It is the Other to the higher values of Western culture. Or perhaps culture is Other to the higher values of color. Or color is the corruption of culture."[28] Batchelor here encapsulates some of the core ideas contained in John Gage's history of the "morality of color," which traces the rather arbitrary and yet historically circumscribed assignment of moral values to colors from the time of the Enlightenment up through the twentieth century.[29] Moreover, the general instability and subjectivity of color perception can trouble the notion of the rational—specifically the scientific quantification and rationalization of color reproduction. Art historian Stephen Melville writes,

> Color can also seem bottomlessly resistant to nomination, attaching itself absolutely to its own specificity and the surfaces on which it has or finds its visibility, even as it also appears subject to endless alteration arising through its juxtaposition with other colors. Subjective and objective, physically fixed and culturally constructed, absolutely proper and endlessly displaced, color can appear as unthinkable scandal.[30]

Chromophobia and related moral associations of color are certainly present in the anxious framing of the reproduction of color during the mid-twentieth century, as color experts worked to contain, manage, label, and harness the power of color, and can be found quite explicitly in both NBC archival documents and in the press accounts from the period that detail the difficulties related to the technical aspects of electronic color transmission and reception and the complications color introduced to the production process. In their own attempts to dispel some of these worries and to contend with the subjectivity and instability of color perception in relation to a color system that was itself sometimes inconsistent or volatile, RCA/NBC employed a variety of approaches and theories (adapted from other industrial and cultural traditions) intended to contain, manage, and stabilize the viewer's experiences of electronic color.

COLOR HARMONY AND MANAGEMENT

The promise of eventual stabilization and standardization of color was central to NBC's campaign to sell the technology not only to consumers but, perhaps more essentially, to sponsors, advertising agencies, producers and affiliates. The commercial nature of television and, more specifically, the fact that, at this point, program producers were often the advertising agencies and sponsors, made this an even more pressing issue, as product sales partially rested on consistency and appeal in product packaging and identification. A 1950 memo to David Sarnoff from Alfred Goldsmith, head of research at RCA and originator of the basic concept of the shadow mask color picture tube (an essential component of RCA's compatible color system) details the ways in which color television would be "considerably more costly" than monochrome as a result of the need to manage its instability and subjectivity:

> Slight deviations in picture brightness or contrast, while undesirable, are not major faults today. In color broadcasting, however, slight errors of this sort would throw the color balance out; would ruin flesh tones; would spoil the realism of the scene; would make the commercially-advertised product look incorrect or unattractive; and would arouse both audience and sponsor protests. In general, it can be assumed that color adjustments must be about ten times as accurate as black-and-white adjustments. This means constant and unremitting care in adjustment—which in turn is translated into higher operating and maintenance costs.[31]

FIGURE 3.4 Undated photo of a color television being calibrated once off the RCA assembly line.
COURTESY OF THE HAGLEY MUSEUM AND LIBRARY.

It was in this context that NBC had to convince both sponsors and audiences that color was worth the added expense and effort. From 1951 to 1954, the network was applying lessons learned from the FCC testing, demonstrations, and standardization process, and from the film industry, most specifically Technicolor. It also looked to the larger industrial design color organizations and processes, since they were also developing their own techniques of color science and management.

Recognizing the significant role of sponsors (and products) in the color project, NBC had included them in the technical standards process at least since the end of 1950. Companies such as Coca Cola and Pet Milk had been included in the audiences of RCA field tests in 1951, along with distributors, dealers, affiliate representatives, and agency personnel.[32] And in autumn 1951, NBC had converted their studio 3H into an "experimental color research studio," in which they also performed field tests and demonstrations to sponsors and others.[33] Even during the final standards test in 1953—the NBC broadcast that was certified by the NTSC as conforming to the new standard specifications—sponsors were present, and part of the demonstration involved the comparison of color televised images of products next to their originals.[34]

In order to convince sponsors and agencies of the advantages of color, while also training their production units in its use and management, throughout 1953 and 1954 NBC deployed its "Color Corps"—a team of color experts consisting of a network art director, an executive producer in charge of color coordination, a technical supervisor, a color director, and a handful of outside color consultants, including Academy Award–winning Hollywood art director Richard Day. The team developed and attended "color clinics" (large demonstrations of products broadcast live in a Rockefeller Center theatre),[35] "color workshops" (training sessions for agency producers), and "color demonstrations" of live entertainment programming and product demonstrations.[36] Targeting both high-profile sponsors (Borden, Bristol Myers, RJ Reynolds) and those with specific color needs (Eastman Kodak, Helena Rubenstein, and various rug manufacturers), the documentation of these events, found in the NBC archives, reveals not only the pitch that the Color Corps made to these advertisers and production people but also the questions raised by attendees, many of which are very revealing of circulating anxieties about the technical and production issues involved in the move to electronic color. Beyond the prevalent questions about costs, most of the concerns regarding color television production had to do with achieving color harmony, expected alterations in production practices, the use of 16 mm color film versus color kinescope, and the establishment of color standards for product and set design. In late 1954, one of NBC's color demonstrations involved a live broadcast of *Macbeth* from their Brooklyn color studio over closed-circuit to twenty-one-inch sets at the American Association of Advertising Agencies annual conference in Manhattan. *Broadcasting-Telecasting* covered the event and described the live broadcast as a "vivid portrayal," while reporting that it was a chance for the network to demonstrate its new twenty-one-inch receivers, educate attendees about color production (including live demonstrations of lighting set-ups and makeup strategies), use product design and color TV (with slides of products such as a Chevrolet and a can of Ajax), and show a color kinescope.[37]

What both sponsors and color experts understood was that if color harmony and calibration were not practiced carefully, colors could appear "off" and thereby threaten to disrupt the selling process. For example, well-known postwar color consultant Howard Ketcham detailed in his 1958 book, *Color Planning for Business and Industry*, the "remarkable things" that the electronic process can do to color.[38] According to Ketcham, red bleeds into other colors—blue is especially vulnerable, with the red bleeds turning blue tones to purple—and this problem is acute in outdoor scenes. He also identified that dark reds do not translate well, yellows appear shades lighter on television, neutral grays are distorted, and pastel colors become brighter or more intense on the screen. The resulting effects on product color could be "appalling" as "preserves turn black; white becomes gray; copperware looks like silver; beer labels show up black; shrimp reproduces so white it looks unreal. Margarine looks like ice cream and rice comes out appearing dirty. Silverware produces a scintillating series of black blurs and necktie colors darken against white shirts."[39]

Representing color accurately in foods is especially important, not only because the wrong color could turn a viewer's stomach (for example, a greenish steak), but also because processed food itself was becoming more and more colorful during this period. Art and design historian Karal Ann Marling describes how making food into bright, sometimes garish, compositions was a postwar fad followed by many home cooks and represented in color magazines and on television. She points to

SEE THE DIFFERENCE COLOR TV MAKES

Food looks so real, you more than see the difference — you almost taste it.

Sports *come alive*. Watch the red-shirted halfback blaze into that big blue line. And look at the heroine in tonight's play. No longer a study in gray, she's a dazzling redhead in a golden dress. And what a difference!

You can now enjoy thrills like this every single day because RCA believed in Color TV from the very first and put its skills and a fortune behind this belief. The result—reasonably priced Color TV that is *performance-proved* — created a new dimension in home entertainment. And it has given you one more good reason to depend on RCA for the first and best in electronics — today, and tomorrow, too.

(RCA) **RADIO CORPORATION OF AMERICA**

FIGURE 3.5 A 1957 RCA ad demonstrates the positive aspects of showing food on TV in color.

Betty Crocker's Picture Cook Book as a prime example of the trend, as the book puts an emphasis on food's "appearance alone—on shape, on surface gloss, on dazzling color."[40] In fact, the book's feature cake of 1951, which Marling says was promoted heavily on TV, was called the Colorvision cake, a vanilla Betty Crocker mix to which cooks would add their favorite color/flavor of gelatin (see figure 3.6).

Color was becoming increasingly important to advertising and branding, and yet television's promise to put those colors on display was complicated by its limited reach and perceived instability.[41] As a writer for *Television Magazine* noted in the April 1954 issue, color introduced new and more highly problematic excesses and complications: "Set designers, artists, industrial designers, and those working with color film already know how to use color. But TV will do more than accentuate the existing color problems; the use of electronically-transmitted color in motion will present entirely new ones."[42] The Judy-Schwerin Research Corporation, which was hired to do a study for NBC on how color would "influence the effectiveness of commercials" concluded that the most important issues to consider in the move to color were these: that packaging would likely have to be redone for color video, specifically hues and the size of lettering; that certain products (like food and furnishings) would benefit more than others; and that demonstrations done in commercials would lose some of their effectiveness as "the color camera may be more concerned with showing objects, scenes and settings than with concentrating for long stretches on the persons appearing in the commercials."[43]

NBC had decided to use the Container Corporation of America's *Color Harmony Manual*, based on the Ostwald color system (discussed in more detail in chapter 2) to set its color standards. NBC created six hundred color-sample chips based on Ostwald's system and used them for testing purposes and in their experimental color broadcasts. Adapting Ostwald's system to the particular needs of color broadcasting allowed NBC to anticipate problematic meetings of different colors as well as to ascertain which colors worked best under particular circumstances. Yet they also had to test how color transmissions would look on black and white monitors, so NBC engineers keyed in the color-testing chips to the Munsell gray scale, which enabled them to take light-reflectant measurements. The translation of the lights and darks on the luminance signal meant that the monochrome image that most early television viewers

FIGURE 3.6 An ad for Betty Crocker's "Colorvision cake," 1951.

would eventually see on their sets was produced primarily for color, with the hope that the shading would translate well into gray scale. However, even with the use of the Munsell gray scale chips, that was not always the case, leading Ketcham to warn that "the demand for compatible color doubles the color problems of TV by compounding those of black-and-white and color."[44] Nevertheless, during a December 1953 color workshop, Norman Grant, NBC's art director, claimed that after the network completed its colorimetry tests they would have all the pigment standards in place, which would allow them to have pigment measurements for each color and where it fit on the gray scale for black and white transmissions; to know what the color would look like on the color television system itself; and to see how the color actually appeared to the naked eye. According to Grant, "In other words, we will have three color chips to represent a single color—allowing us the compatibility information necessary."[45] He also promised that by early 1954, the network would have developed, based on these color chips, standards for inks and dyes, fabrics and costumes, pigments, makeup, and commercial art, as well as film and paint fields. The corporate adoption of harmony expanded to include virtually everything contained within the program's mise-en-scène. As Grant noted:

> Good color balance can be referred to as color harmony. Since harmony equals order, it is necessary for certain standards to be set to retain this order. We try to avoid the sensation of color disharmony in clothing, furnishings, and wherever we have a choice—just as we avoid disharmony of sounds, which we call discord or noise.[46]

Of course, color harmony in mise-en-scène was a lesson NBC was taking from Hollywood's experience with color, and the framing of color television as excessive and trivial resembles the concerns and problems relating to color in film during the 1930s and 1940s. The enforced micromanagement of the Technicolor process in Hollywood studio production was implemented to control the various aesthetic problems and production complications arising out of the peculiarities of its color system. By the time Technicolor came out with its three-strip process and had instituted its on-set management system, it had been criticized for producing candy-coated, often fake-looking color that might lend itself to fantasy, but that held little connection to notions of realism in the minds of many critics and spectators. David Bordwell notes that there was a double bind for color film at that time: if color was artificial or unnatural then audiences would notice and complain; but, the studio heads argued, if color blended in seamlessly then it would not be *sufficiently* noticed and therefore not worth the cost.[47]

As observed by film historian Scott Higgins, in trying to find the right balance with Technicolor in the 1930s, there was a move by studios to employ "the restrained mode" of making color functional without overemphasizing it. In order to achieve such equilibrium, color was managed at every level of the diegesis, limiting color contrasts and balancing hues in order to create "harmonious compositions" of color.[48] After 1935, Technicolor began to institute highly coordinated and specific color management techniques across various levels of the production process. Already a carefully managed firm with an in-house research laboratory and a plant that was "a paragon of industrial organization,"[49] the company began to require the use of Technicolor cameras that were to be run only by Technicolor cameramen and which used only Technicolor film that would be inspected, processed, and printed by the Technicolor laboratories.

According to color film historian Sarah Street, in outlining the components and functions of color consciousness, Technicolor's color consultant Natalie Kalmus stressed that even though color was powerful and meaningful, it "was not supposed to draw attention to itself."[50] Street also notes how Technicolor's use in Britain was often described as being even more restrained than in the United States, and this was ascribed to the former nation's belief in their refined taste and preference for "softer" rather than "strong and vigorous" color.[51]

In both film and television, color harmony and compatibility could also be managed through lighting. Grant underscored the importance of lighting in the workshops, claiming that 60 percent of color design was with light and that *four times* the amount of light would be required for color productions than was used for monochrome. He also discussed the use of gelatins—which could be used to alter set or object colors or to affect hue—as an additional management technique. *Television Magazine* in 1954 noted that color television would demand rigid light control, as light had the potential to alter the look of a product considerably, remarking, "A package that is designed to look fresh under fluorescent lighting in the frozen food section of a supermarket must look the same in the kitchen and on TV."[52] Some of this control could be gained from light correlation charts, which color engineers would use to anticipate the value, hue, pigment, and chroma resulting from specific colored light sources in the studio.[53] Grant emphasized that lighting must be worked into the entire management system of color and that a vigilant on-set color consultant and/or engineer would be needed in order to coordinate all factions of the production process, remarking that "a color TV expert must understand more than lighting. He must have knowledge of the physical and psychological aspects of color as well, and the aesthetic sense to know what colors go well together. He must have the ability to plan color patterns, maintain color control from scene to scene while keeping hot colors down, and to plot out rapidly changing colors."[54]

The Color Corps worked to convince agencies and sponsors that careful scientific management of technology and vision through color harmony and systems of calibration would allow the industry to perfect the deployment of color in ways that would enhance both the televisual aesthetic generally and the look of products specifically, as well as engage the viewer/consumer on a deeper psychological level. In noting the distinct physiological and psychological effects electronic color had on consumers, *Television Magazine* reported that "color in motion delivered in the home will get a different psychological reaction from the color of a magazine ad."[55] Beyond the problems it introduced, color also had positive effects, as moving color images promised to intensify consumer response to programs and products. As a 1951 network pamphlet on color handed out at NBC sponsor demonstrations claimed, "[Color] exerts a powerful influence on human behavior, often dictating the choice of shoes, clothing, automobiles and even food and drink. Color affects our moods, stimulates interest, and adds appreciably to many of our pleasures."[56] In an effort to bolster their arguments about color impact, NBC employed color specialists to conduct studies and present their research on color use and meaning. The resulting studies were then used to sell sponsors the idea of color programming and commercials.

One of NBC's most prominent consultants was Faber Birren, the foremost color practitioner of the day and author of the 1937 book *Functional Color*. Besides NBC and RCA, by the mid-1950s the clients of Birren's consulting company included American Color Trends, DuPont, Condé Nast, Sears, and Walt Disney Studios. He worked with Disney animators in the late 1930s and early 1940s on their use of color in films such as *Fantasia* (Norm Ferguson, Wilfred Jackson, Hamilton Luske, et al., 1940), *Bambi* (David Hand, 1942) and *Pinocchio* (Ben Sharpsteen and

Hamilton Luske, 1940).[57] Birren's "functional color" was a highly practical approach that first became popular during World War II for industrial design, and it was based on the idea that strategic color use could lead to the creation of safer and more pleasant work environments (by reducing fatigue and improving visibility, for example) in everywhere from schools and hospitals to large factories. Birren eventually expanded upon the working assumptions and goals of functional color by considering them in combination with psychological studies and theories of mass marketing. He arrived at an understanding of color as having deep therapeutic possibilities, with each individual color holding its own psychological implications. Birren argued that the "mood-conditioning" functions of color could be brought to bear not only on workplaces and institutions but also on decisions regarding interior design in the home and how companies might select and employ color in relation to their products or brands. In one of the color studies commissioned by NBC and used in their color clinics, Birren claimed that two distinct moods were created by color—the active or the passive—and argued that the television industry needed to be aware of these effects in order to create the desired mood in the viewer/consumer (see below).

THE LIGHT COLORS (ACTIVE)

RED .... exciting, fervid, active

ORANGE .... lively, energetic, forceful

YELLOW .... cheerful, inspiring, vital

THE DARK COLORS (PASSIVE)

GREEN .... peaceful, quieting, refreshing

BLUE .... subduing, sober

PURPLE .... dignified, mournful

WHITE .... pure, clean, youthful

BLACK .... ominous, deadly, depressing

Birren also noted that "pure colors are likely to be severe and that too much harping on any one color is generally distressing" to viewers.[58] These mood effects, it was believed, were powerful messages from sponsors and advertising agencies that would strongly influence consumers' purchasing decisions.

Birren's approach shares some similarities with that of famed psychologist and marketing researcher Ernest Dichter in his "motivational research," which worked to explain the pleasures and attractions of particular consumer goods through the lens of psychology and psychoanalysis. Birren's argument, like Dichter's, hinged on the belief that one could harness the psyche's responses to and associations with an object in the material world, such as lipstick, a type of hat, a model of car, or a product in a specific color. Dichter's Institute for Motivational Research would, in fact, eventually produce a nearly two-hundred-page report a decade later, entitled "Psy-Color-gy," on the impact of color television commercials on viewers, which will be discussed in greater detail in chapter 4. His research team claimed, among other things, that color television was a more effective selling tool than black and white because it was an inherently more emotional, creative, intimate, immediate, and empathetic medium.[59]

The types of studies done by Birren and Dichter, although quite distinct in their approach, codified and packaged not the visual perception of color but the emotional responses color supposedly inspired in its viewers. Although this was just as subjective, variable, and difficult to measure as color perception, the work of color consultants promised once again to be able to predict, control, and standardize color reception. As Blaszczyk has argued, Birren reshaped commercial color practice in the postwar era more generally by convincing big business that he had found a highly effective tool of "social engineering."[60]

LIVING TEST PATTERNS: FLESH AND FIDELITY

In addition to convincing sponsors that color production and reception was a highly regulated and predictable process, networks needed to institute a system of calibration for color cameras that would provide a consistent color image. One strategy used to calibrate and standardize color adjustment was the employment of a regular "color test girl"—a white woman employed as the singular standard of flesh and fidelity—who would stand before cameras in a studio before the broadcast of any color program while technicians and cameramen made color adjustments to better achieve the "true" representation of flesh tones. Beyond on-set harmony and considerations about the colors of products and their packaging, the representation of Caucasian skin was a paramount concern for NBC. For one thing, the FCC was critical of RCA's representation of flesh tones in the 1950 decision, stating that "the inability to accurately reproduce skin tones is a particularly serious handicap. There appears to be no reasonable prospect that these difficulties in the RCA system can be overcome."[61] Critics also pointed to (almost exclusively Caucasian) flesh tones in all color systems as an area in need of improvement, since, for example, the viewer might not be aware of what color suit an actor is wearing in front of the camera, and "if it's a blue suit and comes across on his screen as gray, he has no way of knowing the difference . . . but he does know what color the actor's face should be. . . . If it comes out as lobster red, he knows something is amiss."[62]

Some of these issues would be resolved through standardized makeup palettes, gels, and lighting; yet in a 1954 memo, NBC identified the source of the problem as stemming from, somewhat counterintuitively, the sensitivity and accuracy of the RCA system, stating that, because the RCA compatible system of color picked up the natural red of the skin and lips so accurately, in most instances the flesh tone had to be lightened rather than emphasized to appear natural to the home viewer. The precision camera saw red pigment that was unnoticed by the human eye.[63]

John Crosby noticed this in the NBC color tests and demonstrations too, and remarked that "the trouble isn't that color TV is not true—actually, it's truer than Technicolor—but that it's too true. People's faces, and especially their ears, are a lot redder than we think and the color cameras bring out something we tend not to notice in real life."[64] A 1960 RCA memo on color production recalled, "One of the first discoveries of the [NBC] color coordinators was that the color camera is a more sensitive instrument than the black and white camera and even more discerning than the human eye itself."[65]

FIGURE 3.7 Patty Painter, from "Color on the Air," *Life*, November 20, 1950, 60.

Television Magazine had identified the problems of fidelity and flesh tones as stemming from too little or too great a contrast range, and from the effects of combining multiple colors seen in motion under a variety of lighting conditions at different distances from the camera.[66] The 1950 Condon Committee, though, claimed that it was the delicate nature of color balance that could cause issues in the reproduction of the tones of flesh color, noting that "a slight excess of green, for example, can transform a ruddy glow into a sickly pallor."[67] Color balance required the correct choice of camera color filters to accord with the receiver color primaries and with the lights used in the studio. It also depended upon the correct operation of the transmitter, the correct functioning of the receiver, and the correct adjustment of contrast. CBS lighting designer E. Carlton Winckler stressed the importance of lighting balance in color production, noting that "overlighted skin tones tend to appear light lavender and to bloom, while underlighted skin appears red. It might be pointed out that in monochrome a brightness range of 30 to 1 can be effectively handled, but in color the brightness range is limited to about 15 to 1."[68]

Just as in film and photography, Caucasian skin alone stood as the ultimate test of color fidelity in television, attesting both to the larger institutional structures of racism and to the incorporation of these biases into the very technological standards of visual media. Starting in the mid-1940s with their earliest demonstrations of their color system, CBS used a "five-foot-one-inch, ninety-five pound, ash-blond young woman whose complexion is pure cream and whose lips are a bright ruby red," who was appropriately named Patty Painter.[69] As mentioned in earlier chapters, Painter made appearances at the most important demonstrations, such as the 1946 live broadcast from the CBS experimental studio in Manhattan to the Tappan Zee Inn in Nyack, New York, which was viewed by four members of the FCC. Painter was also featured in CBS's first commercial color broadcast, *Premiere*, and worked as the network's calibration model. CBS also employed Ann Palmer, who in photos appears to be a similarly fair-skinned, young, petite blonde. In choosing such women, the networks asserted that fair skin in particular lent itself to the delicate process of repeated calibration. For instance, a 1953 *New York Times* article profiling Marie McNamara, NBC's primary color girl between 1951 and 1953, who was also in her twenties, with red hair and blue-green eyes (see figure 3.8), claimed:

FIGURE 3.8 Marie McNamara, NBC Colonial Theater, 1954.

What makes Miss McNamara so valuable to the RCA color people is that she has what they call a "natural complexion." In front of the camera she requires no special make-up as do the great majority of people, to combat the vagaries in reproducing color accurately. She also has a "consistent complexion," meaning that her coloring never changes. To keep her job Marie must avoid a sun tan or exposure to bright sunlight.[70]

Joseph Pugliese reminds us that "calibration" is derived from "caliber," which "refers to a degree of social standing or importance, quality, rank; 'stamp,' degree of merit or importance. . . . The term *caliber* underscores questions of power and hierarchy that inflect the physical settings of imaging technologies, as whiteness assumes the gauge of 'merit or importance' that determines who may or may not be visually captured within the calibrated zone of representation."[71] And as work by scholars such as Richard Dyer and Brian Winston has shown, young white women throughout the twentieth century have, problematically, served as the flesh-tone litmus test in color modulation and adjustment in television, film, and photography. For example, stills of white women in colorful dresses, known collectively as "Shirley cards," were used by Kodak in the 1950s and "China Girls" were images of white women placed beside color bars on reel leaders for calibration by lab technicians—a process also eventually standardized by the use of a single Kodak China Girl.[72] The use of white female models as the standard was also a component of the NTSC Panel 11 testing process, which relied primarily on twenty-four Kodachrome images of white people in various settings, a number of which were close-ups of white women with "alabaster" complexions. Consequently, Mulvin and Sterne argue, the "NTSC's test images effectively biased the format toward rendering white people as more lifelike than other races."[73]

Even if live color girls were not used, the substitute systems that were employed also based their calibrations on the assumption of white skin. For example, Dyer discusses the way that in the 1970s, 3M and WGBH Educational Foundation developed a television signal of a "pale orange color"—based on calibrations of the "pleasing" representation of white skin on the screen—that would be recorded on videotape and then used as a point of reference to evaluate the accuracy of subsequent color images.[74] This process was called skinning.

Yet, as Winston has revealed, Technicolor and Kodak researchers found that exact reproduction of color—especially in the case of flesh tones—was perceived by many viewers as less real and/or more distorted than highly modulated or "optimum" representations of color.[75] As a result, heavy lighting and special makeup were used in both film and television to tone down the gaudier coloring that could appear in the representations of white skin on screen. In an RCA memo describing the complexities that arise while trying to "produce a pleasant normal flesh tone" on color television, "reddishness" was identified as the most prevalent problem that could be addressed by makeup. The memo goes on to note that while many different kinds and shades of theatrical makeup had been tried on color television prior to 1954, most turned out to appear too orange or red on screen. NBC eventually turned to Max Factor Pan Stik "street makeup" in olive and medium tones for a few years until

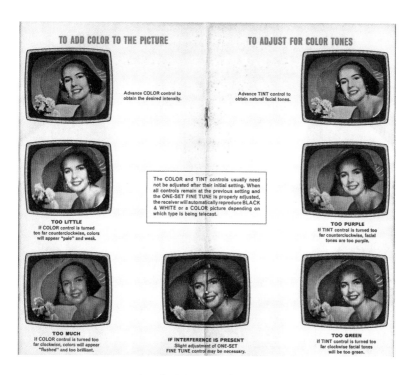

TO ADD COLOR TO THE PICTURE

Advance COLOR control to obtain the desired intensity.

TO ADJUST FOR COLOR TONES

Advance TINT control to obtain natural facial tones.

The COLOR and TINT controls usually need not be adjusted after their initial setting. When all controls remain at the previous setting and the ONE-SET FINE TUNE is properly adjusted, the receiver will automatically reproduce BLACK & WHITE or a COLOR picture depending on which type is being telecast.

TOO LITTLE
If COLOR control is turned too far counterclockwise, colors will appear "pale" and weak.

TOO PURPLE
If TINT control is turned too far counterclockwise, facial tones are too purple.

TOO MUCH
If COLOR control is turned too far clockwise, colors will appear "flushed" and too brilliant.

IF INTERFERENCE IS PRESENT
Slight adjustment of ONE-SET FINE TUNE control may be necessary.

TOO GREEN
If TINT control is turned too far clockwise facial tones will be too green.

FIGURE 3.9 1954 RCA color television manual. AUTHOR'S PRIVATE COLLECTION.

Max Factor worked with the network to "develop a new makeup palette especially for color television."[76]

TINKERING WITH THE SET

It wasn't just at the point of production that color had to be so carefully managed, as systematic approaches to calibration were also important tools that were implemented at the point of reception. Beginning as early as 1953, RCA held color clinics for set manufacturers, distributors, and servicemen that involved a reported twenty-eight hours of instruction on everything from circuitry, components, and color signals to color theory, calibration, and adjustment. When a color set was purchased, a consumer would have to pay an additional installation and one-year service fee ($250 in 1954) on top of the set price.[77] Sets could take up to four hours to install, and "a main difficulty was in making the red, blue, and green images converge properly on the screen. Servicing problems had television store owners at the end of their wits and the bottom of their pocketbooks."[78]

Even with precise adjustments made by trained professionals, outside forces such as interference and consumer tinkering ultimately threatened to upset color fidelity and balance at the reception stage. After installation, for instance, further adjustments could be made by set owners with the help of color cards, which they could hold up to their sets while tuning in the right combination of hue and luminance to avoid bleeds and to provide a more natural-looking image, but this method was hardly a guarantee for the ideal reception of color. RCA's first consumer color television model, CT-100, for example, had over ten knobs dedicated to the adjustment of the color image alone, which made it an incredibly intricate technological object for the average consumer to manipulate and control (see figure 3.10).

In 1953, Richard Salant, executive assistant to Frank Stanton at CBS, was quoted as saying, "There isn't a single color set out there that I could operate at home with any degree of reliability."[79] Crosby agreed: "Much of what finally comes out on the color screen is the result of what the technicians adjusting the set do to it—and ultimately you'll be your own technician and have to fiddle with your own knobs. You can wreak a lot of havoc."[80] Although the networks did not begin to convert fully to color until the 1966–1967 season, by the start of the 1960s, color sets were cheaper in price and equipped with as few as two simple tuning knobs.[81] And as complaints about electronic color's unreliability and its attendant economic risks lessened throughout the decade, more consumers purchased sets and color conversion began to be discussed as an imminent inevitability.[82]

PROGRAM MANAGEMENT:
GENRE AND COLOR'S INTRODUCTORY YEARS

The potential for excess, instability, and triviality assumed in color television also troubled ideas about its relationship to realism in programming. Certainly, color film during the 1940s and '50s was often associated with fantasy and spectacle, while black and white film was assumed to carry with it a documentary-style level of gravitas. Technicolor, which rang false at times to many critics, furthered this connection between

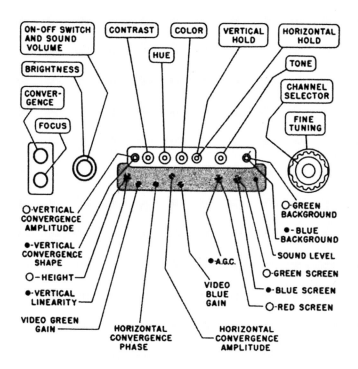

FIGURE 3.10 Controls on the RCA model CT-100. AUTHOR'S PRIVATE COLLECTION.

color and fantasy in moving pictures. Tom Gunning, however, reminds us that color in cinema has historically "played a contradictory role," having both a capacity to represent the indexical and the spectacular and metaphorical,[83] and Steve Neale has argued along similar lines, pointing out the "contradiction between color as an index of realism and color as a mark of fantasy, as an element capable, therefore, of disrupting or detracting from the very realism it is held to inscribe."[84]

As Ed Buscombe asserts in his study of color in film in the 1950s, musical and fantasy films in particular were held to lesser standards of color fidelity and naturalism, as "in these genres, it seems, color may escape the demands of realism. . . . It need no longer be subordinate to plot and the appearance of the real world." Instead, "the audience may give itself up to pleasure."[85] For television, the genre of the live spectacular—tied as it was to excess on multiple levels—became a central site of NBC color experiments in the mid-1950s. However, this was not the only genre to get the color treatment. Due to television's assumed relationship to immediacy, intimacy, and the everyday, along with broadcasting's role as a primary source of information and public service, the addition of color had to maintain at least some connection to the real and/or realistic—especially in its applications outside of entertainment programming. During the first few years of commercial color programming experimentation, NBC was concerned with the question of which genres might best reveal or promote the advantages of color production. For example, certain sports programming provided a very utilitarian argument for color—legibility. It allowed viewers to better locate a ball, identify teams, distinguish where a body ends and the field begins, and so on. Adding color to genres such as variety programs might convey a sense of modernism or freshness, while in others it would add an intensity or emotionality; and some types of programs, it was argued, might do a better job of selling products if they were in color. At a 1953 color clinic, an NBC Color Corps member remarked that "this early in the year nobody can prophesy with certainty just how these shows will respond to color." He continued:

> Each show has its own particular emotional content, so that each will require its own emotional color. [The] RCA color compatible system . . . can handle the lush romanticism of musicals with their emphasis on glamorous backgrounds and the swirling movement of dancing figures, and it can reproduce the utter realism of "life colors"—not merely "life like" colors but the naturalness of color as we see it, for instance, in this very room. It can even, when the subject requires it, go to the equal extremity of black and white.[86]

NBC's plan was to introduce color at all levels of the programming schedule, including sports and daytime programming and a select number of popular prime-time programs, such as *Texaco Star Theatre*. Daytime viewers saw color in *Howdy Doody*, fifteen-minute remote segments of *Home*, and eventually a five-day-a-week daytime drama, *Matinee Theater*, in 1955. The focus on daytime, interestingly enough, was a decision driven by set sales and color demonstrations: this was programming that would be aired during network and station demonstrations and during the business hours of television dealers, department stores, and supermarkets displaying new color sets. This was CBS's priority as well

FIRST WEEK OF REGULAR COLOR TELEVISION AS SEEN ON THE SCREEN

ARTHUR GODFREY PAYS SARDONIC TRIBUTE TO "AIR-CONDITIONED STUDIO"

MARIONETTE SERENADES ED SULLIVAN, INVITES HIM TO BECOME PUPPET TOO

ON NATURE SHOW A BRIGHT-TINTED TANAGER BURSTS INTO A GLEEFUL CHIRP

BEER COMMERCIAL BEGINS WITH SLOGAN SPELLED OUT WITH PLAYING CARDS

FIGURE 3.11 Coverage of cbs's first week on the air in color.
Life, November 22, 1954, 113.

in the early years. In his 1950 testimony before the FCC, Frank Stanton outlined CBS's proposed color plan, which promised "at least 20 hours per week" of color programming over all seven days, with the majority of shows airing before five o'clock.[87] Stanton explained that the daytime audience—primarily made up of women and children—was essential to the early period of dissemination when most viewing of color sets would be public and in which programming would primarily "serve for demonstration purposes in dealer showrooms in the various cities across on the network."[88]

CBS's first color program, and the first commercial colorcast in television history, occurred from 4:30 to 5:30 PM on a Monday in late June 1951. *Premiere* was a variety program starring the network's biggest names—including Arthur Godfrey, Faye Emerson, Ed Sullivan, and Garry Moore, along with the New York City Ballet, the Archie Bleyer Orchestra, and a handful of Broadway musical performers. Patty Painter, referred to on

FIGURE 3.12 Behind the scenes of a one-time color presentation of *Toast of the Town* (CBS), *Life*, November 22, 1954, 113.

the show as both Miss CBS Color and Miss Color Television, also had her own segment, as did William Paley and FCC chairman Wayne Coy. The program had sixteen sponsors and aired through a five-city cable hookup—reaching a minuscule number of viewers in New York, Boston, Philadelphia, Baltimore, and Washington, DC. George Rosen, in *Variety*, felt that *Premiere* lacked "showmanship" and "left much to be desired" in terms of entertainment, and that during parts of the show, "the viewer was conscious of a noticeable lack in contrast between the blue and green colors which predominated: even to the extent that it seems as though the CBS system was limited to a two-color process rather than three."[89] The *Wall Street Journal* reported that many Boston viewers found the broadcast "beautiful" and "beyond expectations," but a Washington observer said that while the image was "pretty," it gave him "a splitting headache." The *Journal* also noted New Yorkers complained that in between each segment the screen went blank while the music continued.[90]

Later that summer, CBS announced that Godfrey, the network's most popular and profitable star at that time, would do an afternoon program in color. However, it never made it to the air, and the last programs to be broadcast through the CBS system of color (before war production shut it down and the NTSC standard was initiated) were relatively unsuccessful broadcasts of football games. For example, the late September colorcast of the California versus Pennsylvania game was considered a great disappointment due to problems with color fringing and imbalance, and the final broadcast of CBS color was the October 20 North Carolina versus Maryland game.[91] The next instance of CBS offering color programs was on the NTSC system in 1953, when the network used one program, *New Revue,* as a space to experiment with color use. Richard Lewine, executive producer of color programs at CBS, explained that their first mistake in that program was using "too much color and too many colors," which, he thought, took too much focus off of the performers. "Economy in the use of color quickly became our rule," he said and noted that they began to develop "color schemes" (the implementation of color harmony) for every show.[92] The network had more success the following year with the regular colorcasts of *Shower of Stars, Arthur Godfrey Talent Scouts,* and *The Perry Como Show.*

Although the vast majority of viewers would continue to see the programming in monochrome, NBC received permission from the FCC in 1953, soon after approval of the NTSC standards, to program a few spe-

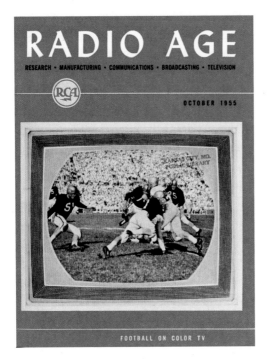

FIGURE 3.13 Sports broadcasting helped sell color in its early years, as it helped viewers distinguish between teams and players and better see the movement of balls and players on the field or court. *Radio Age* cover, October 1955.

cial color events and a handful of episodes of popular programs to be shown to the relatively small number of color television viewers and, more importantly at that time, to critics, station owners, and sponsors. (RCA distributed free color sets to a great number of members of all of those groups.) Interestingly, the first special program was a presentation of a live opera, *Carmen*, in October 1953, which would be followed by another opera, *Hallmark Hall of Fame*'s presentation of *Amahl and the Night Visitors*, a few months later. Independent media technology historian and SMPTE fellow Mark Schubin has argued that opera was a central part of the experimental phase of the most common media technologies, including those involving sound (nineteenth-century stereo sound, telephone, and headphones) and moving images (magic lantern, early silent films, early television demonstrations, early network television broadcasts, and theater television).[93] NBC had in fact aired *Carmen* before, during its first broadcast year in 1939, and had *NBC Opera Theatre* on their schedule for sixteen years, starting in 1948. All networks (including DuMont) featured regular opera series in the late 1940s and early 1950s. While opera might at first seem an unusually highbrow genre for the promotion of the color project, it did suit the needs of the network in terms of the executives' articulated desire to impress critics and sponsors with extravagant, excessive, and spectacular live presentations of productions that had already been widely acknowledged as quality works. And, as Schubin points out, opera's long-standing historical connection to early displays and demonstrations of media technologies likely made it a logical and culturally resonant choice. In 1954, David Sarnoff explained to local station managers that he believed the fastest way to advance color television was for NBC to produce "the famous-star, distinguished-play kind of programs" that would serve as "a conversation piece" and ultimately motivate the purchase of color sets.[94] Richard Pinkham, vice president in charge of NBC programming, made a similar claim in 1956: "The color programs have to create excitement. . . . They've got to be the sort of programs the columnists will write about . . . the kind that will attract unusual public attention and keep color interest spreading on a word-of-mouth basis . . . the kind that will make people feel they're really missing something important if they don't get themselves a color set."[95]

Musical programs also served to introduce audiences and industry insiders to color technology in NBC's early closed-circuit demonstrations in the Colonial Theater throughout the latter half of 1953. Broadway star Nanette Fabray and *Your Hit Parade* dancers performed a series of popular song-and-dance routines in front of an audience made up primarily of critics and sponsors. Before the program began, NBC announcer Ben Grauer informed audiences that they would be displayed on new RCA color receivers as well as standard black and white sets. He instructed, "When the program goes on, glance away occasionally if you can from the color set to the black and white set. You'll see how the program comes in without any loss of picture quality—how it actually provides a better than ever monochrome result without any adjustment to the standard black and white television receiver."[96] By the end of 1953, the network had also aired episodes of *Bob Hope, Colgate Comedy Hour, Hit Parade, Kraft Television, Texaco Star Theatre,* and *Dinah Shore* in color and had plans to greatly expand color programming over the following year.[97]

NBC dubbed 1954 the "Introductory Year" for color television (a seemingly overt dismissal or erasure of the CBS color period) and considered it not just a time in which to test out the technology itself, but also an opportunity to learn what the best uses of color in programming might be. It was also a year of color use that was paid for outright by RCA in order to better support the marketing of color sets. *The Marriage*, the television version of a popular radio program of the same name staring Jessica Tandy and Hume Cronyn, was the first regular series presented in color, even though it only lasted through the summer of 1954. The next regular series was a multicamera family sitcom called *Norby*, which also had only a short life (half a season) on the network. While the sponsor, Eastman Kodak, was considered to be ideal for a color program, the company in the end found the cost of color production too expensive for a program that was not at the top of the ratings.

In what is remembered as one of the most significant moments of NBC's early color period, NBC broadcast the Tournament of Roses Parade on New Year's day 1954, publicizing it as the first West to East Coast color telecast (via mobile unit) in history. Throughout that year, networks continued to air occasional episodes of popular programs in color (NBC's *Your Show of Shows, Colgate Comedy Hour, Camel News Caravan*, for example), and focused on color in sports and in live spectaculars. "Spectacular" was the name NBC president (1953–1955) Sylvester "Pat" Weaver gave to the network's big budget, single-sponsor, prime-time specials that he conceived of as a way to compete against CBS (which was dominating the ratings with programs such as *I Love Lucy, Jack Benny*, and *Arthur Godfrey and Friends*) and to brand NBC programming as distinctive. NBC memos regarding spectaculars stated that color would be built around the "the spectacular plan of 1954," which involved a series of ninety-minute "one-shot" programs (mostly musicals and dramas but also circuses, ice shows, and "aquades") produced by NBC and programmed on a rotating basis (mostly on Saturday, Sunday, and Monday nights) at the rate of four every four weeks.[98] They were aired under different names, including *Color Spread, Hallmark Hall of Fame*, and *Producers Showcase*.[99] These spectaculars are most often discussed by historians in relation to Weaver's desire to highlight liveness in NBC programming. However, it is notable that Weaver was named head of color development for the network in the fall of 1953, when John K. Herbert was brought in as head of sales in an attempt to relieve Weaver's workload and allow him the space to focus on color development. Even though liveness was an essential part of this programming plan, color was his priority. James Baughman has argued that Weaver believed the spectaculars would serve to attract not only the regular or "heavy" viewer

FIGURE 3.14 A 1956 ad promoting both color TV and the
Esther Williams Aqua Spectacle on NBC.

of television, but also the infrequent or "light" viewer.[100] He envisioned these programs as opportunities to lure in the light viewer and sell them on color. In an extended interview with *Broadcasting-Telecasting* in 1955, Weaver claimed to have "never believed, personally, that an extended schedule in color is the thing that will sell color"; instead, he argued that it was the one-off extravagantly produced program that would make viewers realize, "This is a whole different story. This is the big time and that isn't. Then they are going to buy [a color set]."[101] Weaver also saw the model of irregular programming as one that "no one sponsor could underwrite and control," thereby challenging the radio model of financing he disdained.[102] And in fact, NBC color programs were often cosponsored, working on a format of "magazine-style" advertising. However, spectaculars, such as *Satins and Spurs* (1954) and *Alice in Wonderland* (1955), also served the purpose of promoting color in a way that allowed the excesses and potentially unnatural elements of its representation to be more seamlessly incorporated into genres that are intended to be excessive while also providing opportunities for sponsors to try out color without fully committing to it.

By the 1955–1956 season, NBC promised thirty-nine ninety-minute color spectaculars.[103] Calling their programs "extravaganzas" instead of "spectaculars," CBS had a similar focus on live spectacles of color and in 1954, the network announced that they would be airing a color "twin series," sponsored by Chrysler, which would alternate between "once-a-month musical and variety extravaganzas," under the umbrella title of *Shower of Stars*, and dramatic plays and musical comedies broadcast under the title of *Best of Broadway*.[104] CBS also included colorcasts in the monthly program *Ford Star Jubilee*, which was an immediate ratings hit when premiered with a color episode starring Judy Garland in September 1955.

The most notable color spectacular of this period was NBC's live presentation of *Peter Pan* by *Producer's Showcase*, starring the original Tony Award–winning Broadway cast, including headliners Mary Martin as Peter Pan and Cyril Ritchard as Captain Hook. The first broadcast of the production in 1955 was such a success (with an estimated viewing audience of sixty-five million) that it aired twice more with the same cast in 1956 and 1960. Critics loved it, calling it "historic," and "the most polished, finished, and delightful program that has ever been on television."[105] While the vast majority of the audience viewed the two-hour program in black and white, the advertising campaign, of course, pushed color as a major part of its appeal. And, conversely, stills from the live production were used in print campaigns to sell RCA color sets. Most of the reviewers, however, did have the opportunity to see the program in color. John Beaufort, of the *Christian Science Monitor*, wrote that he took up the network's invitation to watch it on a color set in a Radio City viewing room, which also contained black and white sets for comparison. While Beaufort noted that viewers watching it in monochrome still received "many of the production values" of the program, they did miss out on the splendor of the costumes and set design, as well as the vivid shimmer of Tinker Bell's light.[106] The 1956 production of the "Esther Williams Aqua Spectacle" was an enormous undertaking filmed in NBC's Brooklyn studio with an indoor pool used for swimming and waterskiing routines. As they put up $125,000 to make a deal with Williams and finance a national tour for her, NBC clearly expected the special to be an enormous hit and to bring needed attention to the benefits of color production. In the end, however, it was met with tepid reviews, with some critics noting that Williams's acts looked better on film than on television—even if it was in color.[107]

FIGURE 3.15 *Peter Pan* on the cover of *Radio Age*, April 1955.

As for the other two networks, DuMont had only one color program on the air in New York City during the 1954–1955 season, while ABC had none. Frank Marx, ABC's vice president of engineering, told *Billboard*: "ABC has no stake in promoting the sale of color sets and therefore will not produce shows until it is financially profitable to do so," which he predicted would take at least another five years.[108]

During the experimental period explored in this chapter, from the early to the mid-1950s, the use, applications, and meaning of electronic color were still in a state of development and refinement, leading to much discussion and debate about the value of the new technology between industry professionals, among consumers, and in the press. The often unpredictable and volatile color system operating in these early years of color generated a sense of unease among critics, network executives, and audiences that would only be soothed by careful color management and technical refinement. As I have shown, in their attempts to assuage concerns, contend with the vagaries of color television, and manage the perceived risks that went along with the industry's anticipated transition to color, RCA/NBC operationalized color theory and rationalized, in a highly visible way, color production, programming, and reception practices. Color had to be precisely managed and balanced with the following realizations: color itself is highly subjective, as it is a property of light and its modification; color in television was difficult to standardize and stabilize; color was believed to have the power to shift both emotion and vision; commercial imperatives required a rigidity around and control of the technology; color could be seen as either excessive or trivial, or both.

Although working mechanical color television systems had been available since the late 1920s, it took decades to advance the technology to the point that it functioned well enough to satisfy networks, stations, regulators, sponsors, and consumers, and it took many more years to become fully integrated into television's financial, production, aesthetic, and reception processes. Regular color programming began in 1954, with an emphasis on sports and spectaculars, but color television would not be deemed a success until more than a decade later. Even as late as 1959, the press was still predicting both the long anticipated rise of color television and its ultimate demise. Viewers and sponsors remained wary, due to color's various inconsistencies. As a writer for *Popular Electronics* suggested, "Ask the man on the street what he thinks of color TV, and chances are he hasn't even seen it yet. If he has seen it, he will probably say: (1) the quality is poor, (2) it's too expensive, (3) it's too difficult to tune, (4) there aren't enough color programs, and (5) color sets break down too often."[109] Part of solving this poor public perception involved stabilized color television technology, but in the mid- to late 1950s, NBC also sought to convince viewers and advertisers that color was worth the trouble and expense. They did so by taking color on the road, placing it in public places, converting local stations, selling color audiences as a "quality" demographic, and stepping up their campaign to brand color as the future of television and NBC as *the* color network.

CHAPTER FOUR

Colortown, USA

Expansion, Stabilization, and Promotion, 1955–1959

In 1956, NBC and WNBQ—one of NBC's most important owned and operated stations—put on "spectrum spectacular" events, held in conjunction with the National Association of Radio and Television Broadcasters
(NARTB) annual meeting in Chicago in April. These events were created
with the intent to blanket the city, and the conference, in the spectacle
and energy of color. The network spent $165,000 on advertising and
exploitation events for the weeklong celebration of WNBQ's conversion
to "all-color," which *Variety* described as "one of the biggest Windy City
promotion offenses ever mounted."[1] The inauguration event (referred
to as C-Day), broadcast on the *Wide Wide World* and the *Camel News
Caravan,* climaxed with the appearance of Robert Sarnoff, David's son,
who had become first NBC president in 1955 and then chairman of the
board in 1958, taking over leadership from Pat Weaver, who was eventually let go from the network, reportedly due to his clashes with the elder
Sarnoff, who considered Weaver's programming style and choices too
highbrow and needlessly expensive.[2] In Chicago, the younger Robert
Sarnoff pushed a large button on a podium, which switched the color
encoder and marked the very minute in which the station officially made
its transition from monochrome to color. RCA/NBC staff spent the rest of
the week trying to attract the attention not only of Chicago viewers and
advertisers, but most importantly, of NARTB members. While skywriting
planes wrote *Color in the air and color on the air—WNBQ first in color* in
red, green, and blue smoke across the city, on the ground a parade of
trucks carrying one thousand color sets from the manufacturing plant
drove to and parked outside the convention site at the Hilton Hotel. In-

WNBQ, CHICAGO, PAINTS THE TOWN RED!

and blue! and green!

WNBQ LEADS AGAIN, WITH THE WORLD'S FIRST ALL-COLOR STATION!

WNBQ TELEVISION IN CHICAGO

FIGURES 4.1 AND 4.2 An ad for WNBQ, NBC's first all-color station. *Broadcasting-Telecasting,* April–June 1956, 52–54.

side the hotel, "test pattern girls"—models dressed in green, blue, and red, and holding matching color dyed poodles—handed out invitations to an open house at the station for conference attendees. A "color rally," mimicking the form of a traditional political rally, was held in front of the Hilton, with decorations, music, handheld rally signs, and local and national celebrities chanting for color.

The Merchandise Mart, the home of WNBQ, was lit up with red, blue, and green lights during that week. Chicagoans read features on color television in the all of the local papers (see figures 4.1 and 4.2) as well as *Chicago Magazine* and TV *Guide,* while simultaneously being bombarded with multiple television, radio, and print ads featuring "Tommy Tint," a new WNBQ station logo crafted to represent the all-color station. Tommy, a "puckish" animated character with red hair, dressed in a green shirt, blue pants, and socks with "red, green and blue vertical bars,"[3] was usually seen in these campaigns either painting the town ("'gonna paint the town red, 'gonna paint the town green, 'gonna paint it every hue") or preparing to blow it up, pushing the handle of a dynamite plunger ("I'm Tommy Tint, I'm T-N-T, just like color on NBC").[4] A special episode of the locally produced RCA *Color Theatre* held a Tommy Tint contest, boasting prizes that included a color set, two hi-fi radio consoles, and twenty-two portable radios. Tommy's image showed up in the Hilton lobby too, in the form of a "Tommy Tint ice cream party." Fifty red-headed children between the ages of six and nine were the only official invitees, but party favors and red, blue, and green ice cream were handed out to anyone who walked by. At WNBQ's weeklong open house, visiting NARTB convention attendees could tour its four color studios and witness the color equipment in action. They could also go up to the twentieth floor of the Merchandise Mart to walk through the almost completed RCA/NBC exhibition hall and "gallery of color," where color receivers were in continuous operation and an animated exhibit on a wall would trace both the history of television and the specifics of how color television worked. Visitors could also pass through a "viewing corridor," which allowed them to look down onto productions in progress in studios A and B.[5]

While certainly extravagant, the media and promotional and exploitation events produced around the conversion of WNBQ echoed the convergence of familiar interests, strategies, and issues that would define NBC's approach to color during the mid- to late 1950s. Most notably, we find spectacle deployed in such a way as to make people *envision* electronic color through playful references to the RGB model and the writing of color on the cityscape.

At a time when color television had not been seen much by most consumers (as they were still unable or reluctant to purchase their own sets, and color programming was infrequent), it was being marketed and sold on the basis of its vibrancy and verisimilitude—its ability to improve on vision. RCA/NBC took the opportunity of the WNBQ inauguration to make consumers, advertisers, and station managers feel as though they were seeing electronic RGB color everywhere. The WNBQ moment also shows how the network tied a color viewer's sense of place—locally, regionally, nationally—to the commercial aims of the network and national manufacturers. Moreover, these events also demonstrate the importance placed on "local color" at this time, most prominently (and expensively) through the conversion of color stations, but also in the way that audiences were being asked to convert to a new manner of television viewing. Color television was slowly being introduced to communities through the AT&T wires that constituted a television network, but more immediately, it was also being shown to them via touring mobile color units and at the public viewing spaces of department stores, dealer showrooms, taverns, hotels, shopping malls, transportation hubs, and grocery stores that put color receivers and color programming on display. This chapter will explore the manner in which RCA/NBC utilized targeted promotional, advertising, and programming strategies to brand itself as *the* color network. It will also detail the building of a color network through the conversion and building of color stations and studios; the selling of the existing "class" or "quality" color audience to advertisers; and the positioning of color as a tie to and vision for the future. This remains very much RCA/NBC's story, since it was the organization with the most to gain from color television's success, as they would eventually profit not only from programming and advertising, but also from the sale of color receivers. However, CBS's contribution to the form and look of color programming before 1959 (after which they dropped out of color production for a few years) is significant and will also be addressed in this chapter.

THE "CLASS" AUDIENCE

Throughout the 1950s, color sets remained both a novelty and a luxury item, one that was out of reach for the vast majority of Americans.[6] Even though the price of color sets had been halved to about $500 by late 1956 that was still five times the price of the average black and white set. In the context of the majority of household appliances, color television was an anomaly at this time in being unaffordable to the middle class. As discussed in great detail by many historians of mid-century America, the 1950s was a decade of unparalleled prosperity for average white middle-class Americans, who saw their annual income almost triple between the years of 1950 and 1970. During those same years, poverty dropped by around 60 percent, millions moved from urban areas into the suburbs to buy houses and start families, and consumer industries boomed.[7] As a result of such an overall higher standard of living and the economics of mass production, consumer goods that had once been considered inessential were now a part of daily life and, as I discussed briefly in chapter 2, color became an essential component in the economics, design, and planned obsolescence of goods and appliances. As Regina Lee Blaszczyk argues, "The bright postwar landscape, with its color-conditioned schools, its two-tone Chevys and its orange-roofed

Howard Johnson's restaurants, whetted the appetite for more color in the home."[8] As Lynn Spigel and others have shown, black and white television sets (not nearly as good a tool for exhibiting postwar products as color television) were an affordable and essential feature of middle-class suburban homes.[9]

Those who did manage to purchase color sets were what would be called in current parlance "early adopters" and were classified by NBC as being a better class of television viewer—in terms of both status and taste. Taking advantage of the wish for such cachet, products appeared in the marketplace that promised to deliver the color television experience without the high price. For a brief period in the mid- to late 1950s, consumers could purchase (commonly via mail order) inexpensive see-through tinted-plastic overlay sheets that attached to the front of their black and white sets in an effort to enact a low-end do-it-yourself simulation of the color viewing experience (see figure 4.3). These sheets—which came in seven-, ten-, and twelve-inch screen sizes—contained three horizontal bands of color designed like a child's most basic crayon drawing of the fundamentals of landscape and horizon: green on the bottom (grass), light brown or "flesh tone" in the middle (people), and light blue on top (sky). As one viewer recalled, "This was okay if you were watching a show that had a long shot of a city street or Western Prairie, but if it were a close-up of a person, they had green clothes and blue hair."[10]

A slightly more expensive and much more involved at-home solution to color conversion was the mechanical do-it-yourself color converter, of which there were multiple models and kits sold throughout the 1950s. For example, the Col-R-Tel converter, at a price of $150 and modeled after the mechanical elements of the CBS system (see figure 4.3), consisted of a motorized mechanical color wheel, a scanning unit, and a seven-tube convertor, all of which had to be installed by a television repairman or an especially handy set owner. (Another device—the Colordaptor—was similarly constructed.) A more complicated color adaptor, "the color sampler," was described in a 1951 issue of *Popular Mechanics* (see figure 4.4). Readers were instructed on how to build this contraption using a homemade or commercially available color wheel modified by hand to fit the size of a standard television screen, along with a series of pulleys, shafting belts, a constant-speed motor, and some "scrap box findings." The motorized color wheel (complete with brake) would then be placed

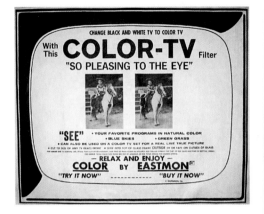

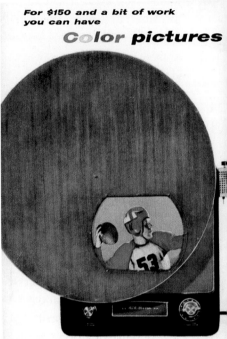

FIGURE 4.3 Ad for Telecolor Filter.

FIGURE 4.4 A Col-R-Tel adaptor. Image from *Popular Mechanics*, October 1955.

in front of the TV screen and the viewer would speed up or slow down the rotation of the wheel so that it would be in sync with the transmission. This would allow some to supposedly "try out" color inexpensively— though the author warns the reader that due to the rough look of the homemade mechanics, "your wife will probably object to having the setup in your living room permanently, but she'll be as delighted as you are with the color pictures."[11] Most owners of the color overlays and those (relatively few) who might have built their own color adapters would have likely eventually recognized what a poor substitute their home-made color experience was for a commercially manufactured color receiver. However, the presence of these devices speaks to the sense that many consumers had of missing out on a color experience while also recognizing just how implausible actually purchasing these new sets seemed to them and their families at the time. They wished to see it, and perhaps even to own it, but not at any cost. Even as late as 1959, out of the estimated forty-five million television sets in use, only 1 percent were estimated to be color.[12]

RCA/NBC was certainly aware that color set ownership was primarily limited to industry insiders and well-off early adopters. While this presented major financial losses for both NBC and its corporate parent as they pushed for color adoption, the network also used the situation to their advantage, selling the class status of color set owners back to sponsors and advertising agencies. Network executives argued, with the help of commissioned ratings and marketing studies, that color set owners were a "quality" audience who were not only wealthy but were also opinion leaders in their communities—actively involved in clubs, hobbies, civic groups, and the arts—and consumers of "other so-called class media" such as the *New Yorker, Fortune, Harper's,* and the *Atlantic.*[13] Additionally, they were more emotionally responsive to commercials and product pitches, retained the names of more brands, and were "more inclined to buy."[14] In 1955, NBC hired famed advertising company BBDO to initiate a long-term study of an unnamed "typical medium-sized" city (later to be revealed as Cincinnati) that researchers called Colortown USA.[15] In BBDO's preliminary report, issued at the end of 1956, the project was described as a "panel-type study based on the probability sample of 4,000," involving 77 color set owners and 144 black and white set owners. The report concluded that color TV owners were wealthy "influential members" of their community and that there were "clear indications of [color television's] effects: increased viewing, more commercial awareness, more product awareness."[16]

In his study of 1960s programming and audience demographics, Mark Alvey used the color studies of the mid-1960s to support his argument that the use of the "quality" audience rhetoric (as opposed to "mass") by network executives started earlier than once thought. However, it is clear from the Colortown study that NBC at least was constructing the notion of a quality audience a decade earlier in order to (as Alvey similarly argues about NBC and its ratings in the mid-60s) shift the interpretation of the small number of color set owners. Lizbeth Cohen locates 1956 as the year that market segmentation was first thought of as a viable alternative to mass marketing. In what was considered a groundbreaking article in the 1956 issue of *Journal of Marketing,* Wendell Smith, a marketing expert who had once worked for RCA, argued for the approach as a solution to the increasing competition in the marketplace, since "attention to smaller or fringe market segments, which may have small potentials individually" could lead to not only

FIGURES 4.5 AND 4.6 Ads that appeal to the "class audience." A 1966 *Playboy* ad claiming a higher color TV ownership among its readers and one in a 1959 series of ads from RCA connecting upper class celebrity, consumerism, and leisure pursuits to color television.

greater profitability but also "a more secure market position."[17] Cohen notes that an article by corporate researcher Pierre Martineau published the same year backed up Smith's overall claim and argued further that the smaller demographic markets—particularly those differentiated by social class—were fundamentally distinct, not only in terms of their access to wealth but also in regard to "mode of thinking," "handling of the world," and the manner in which individuals in the group acquired certain products for "symbolic value."[18] In an article for *Harvard Business Review*, Martineau remarked that one of most significant trends he had identified in the "new customer" was a shift from a "philosophy of saving" to a "more self-indulgent spending, a tendency to equate standard of living with possession of material goods, and great emphasis upon community values."[19] The arguments made by networks about color viewers as a highly desirable market segment echo those made by Martineau and Smith about the "new" consumer. For instance, Sam Tuchman and Thomas Coffin, executives in NBC's research division, voiced a familiar refrain of television marketing in the late 1960s when they said that "one of the most intriguing aspects of color television is that it provides advertisers with the unusual opportunity to reach simultaneously both a 'mass' audience and a 'class' audience."[20] ("Mass" meant most viewers, who could view the program and advertisers' commercials in black and white, while the select "class" audience watched in color.[21]) They added that color viewers were "venturesome" when buying new products; "convenience-orientated," meaning that they would "pay a premium price to save their labor"; and (perhaps most importantly to the industry) "status-minded—consistently moving up-scale in their purchases."[22]

A 1956 issue of *Electrical Merchandising* magazine details a rather fascinating instance of an RCA distributor using color television's status as a luxury item to activate class anxieties and aspirations in potential female buyers. Raymond-Rosen, one of the largest RCA distributors, described this approach as a "highly successful" selling technique centered on the offer of free home demonstrations. After a multimedia ad campaign during National Color Television week announcing the free demonstrations, local salesmen were instructed to "play hard to get" and flagrantly manipulate housewives with ploys to activate their feelings of insecurity and social/class competition. Customers coming into the dealership inquiring after the free home demonstration offer were told that the color set on display was not hooked up (thereby avoiding having to tell her that "there is no program on right now"). It was recommended that at this point salesmen "describe the features to her, let her finger the dials, suggest you might be able to get a set for her to try at home. There is a waiting list but you will see if one is available and telephone her."[23] Salesmen were then expected to use this time before calling the customer to screen her credit and find out her family size, as "prospects should be families with children." (Since, the hope was, the children might lobby "the head of the household" for the purchase of a color set once it was already in the home—much as they would after finding a lost puppy.) After the set was installed in her living room, the housewife would be told to invite her neighbors over to watch it too. "The psychology here is that no woman will part with a color TV once her neighbors have seen it in her living room," remarked the distributor's representative. To close the deal, the salesman was to call the housewife after a few days and tell her that the set would be removed shortly in order to be installed in another woman's home who lived nearby. "When the housewife wants to keep it longer, as she invariably will suggest, you stop around that evening. The family has already been sold in the comfort of their own living room." The distributor boasted that this strategy resulted in 120 home demonstrations in suburban homes in New Jersey during the first week, 64 percent of which reportedly resulted in sales.[24]

While color television ownership was assumed to be both an indicator and a symbol of class and status, there was also an accompanying argument circulating in the industry about the increased emotional, psychological, and visual attention it inspired. The results of studies by rating services and market researchers in the late 1950s and early '60s were similar to the findings contained in the preliminary Colortown report—not only were compatible color programs more highly rated, but color viewers gave greater attention to and maintained better recall of the content of commercials.[25] Some studies posited that this "vigilant attending behavior" was a result of color television's more "realistic presentation" of images and a "greater transfer of information."[26] A 1960 study by Crossley ratings service claimed that the "ratings advantage" of color was so high that when it came to the impact of commercials on viewers "1,000 color homes are equal to 3,589 black and white homes."[27] Perhaps not surprisingly, there is no mention of the possibility that color set owners might have been "heavy viewers" to begin with, which is why they would have invested in the expensive new technology. Instead, there appears to have been an underlying assumption of an inherent quality of the color television image that stimulated an especially engaged and responsive form of attentiveness. While reaching different conclusions from the psychologically based claims Birren and Ketcham were making about functional color, these studies also utilized familiar discourses of fidelity and the heightened level of visual and psychological engagement or intensity assumed to be a part of the perception of moving images in color. As historians of cinematic color have noted, the purported ability of color to affect mood and emotion more generally and to "exceed diegetic meanings" even in the early years of applied color, was very much assumed to be part of its power and potential volatility in film.[28] And yet, while sensuality and the potential for excess and instability were components of the discourse around electronic color, its capacity to elicit and then harness the emotions and attention it inspired were also described in postwar studies as knowable and replicable (and therefore desirable) in television viewership.

In the first few years of the 1960s, the psychological and visual attentiveness of color television viewers was also explored in a study done by researchers at the Institute for Motivational Research (IMR), headed up by the era's best known consumer behavior analyst (referred to by some as the "Sigmund Freud of the supermarket age"), Ernest Dichter.[29] The resulting 157-page report, submitted to the Television Advertising Representatives, served as an argument for advertisers to immediately and enthusiastically turn to color in the production of their commercials. It claimed to have proven that color (when compared to black and white) increased the amount of time audiences watched television; the level of prestige and awareness of sponsors and their products; and "purchase action," the desire and motivation for a viewer to purchase the product advertised.[30] Moreover, the authors of the study asserted:

> In the course of our investigation we have found that audiences respond to the unique, psychological style of color television as if it were a separate medium. . . . These respondents consider color television to be new, progressive, unique, adventuresome, sophisticated, luxurious— they invest in color television the feelings usually reserved for experiences or events which are "first time" and furthermore this is true regardless of length of time of ownership.[31]

In ferreting out the "modalities" (the psychological and sociological advantages of color), the report continued on to make detailed claims about the psychological processes of the meaning and reception of color— both on television and more generally. Like the other studies on color viewing, it asserted the connection between color and increased visual and psychological attentiveness. However, this study took it a step further, claiming that color television inspired in viewers a reduced sense of psychological distance, while also increasing levels of emotional involvement, empathy, creativity, comprehension, sociality, immediacy, a sense of three-dimensionality, and could intensify a sense of realism, while simultaneously simulating "a world of fantasy." Color was also found to be "symbolic of innovation, progress and modernity. . . . Color is symbolic of the better life."[32]

The IMR study used both "depth interviews," which are described in the report as employing "questions designed to encourage spontaneous expression of thoughts, ideas, opinions and feelings—in a free conversational manner"[33] and "projective tests" in the form of surveys, which were given to 379 respondents. Projective techniques in consumer research use stimuli that are constructed in such a way as to access deeper psychological or emotional responses. Questions like those in the IMR survey are therefore purposely ambiguous and unstructured in order to provide interpretative room for a respondent to project her personality, psychology, belief systems, and/or identity onto the question. For instance, a question meant to determine the emotionality of color television, asks "Which one of the following pictures best represents how you feel when watching: a) color television; b) black and white television?"[34] The four possible answers to this question are represented by line drawings of everything from a rectangle to an abstract squiggle (see figure 4.7). These signs and symbols are assumed to represent deeper feelings and associations within the respondent and are interpreted according to an agreed upon meaning by the researchers. Ernest Dichter's star was beginning its decline during the mid-60s, and these types of methods meant to access connections made under the surface of rational or expressed thought would soon go out of style in market research, being replaced by methods considered to be more highly scientific or empirical in nature. However, Dichter's study would still have had great influence on the way networks and advertisers imagined the relationship between viewers and color television and would have supported many of the programming and marketing strategies they had already instituted in the mid- to late 1950s.

COLOR CARAVAN

Attentiveness to commercial imperatives continued to define color programming and production norms at almost every level of the decision making process, both financially and creatively. After the limited success of the "introductory year," RCA began to push NBC to expand color programming in specific directions for the stated purpose of increasing

2. Which one of the following pictures best represents how you feel when watching:

    a)   color television_____

    b)   black and white television_____

W

X

Y

Z

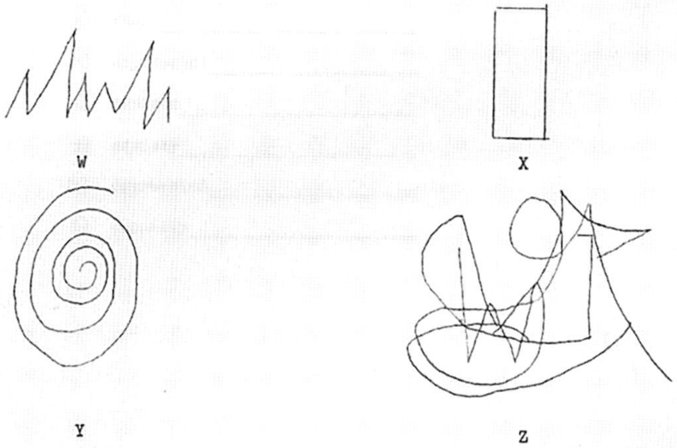

TEST 3.

    Which of these pictures below best represents watching

        Black and White Television _____(A, B or C)

        Color Television_____(A, B or C)

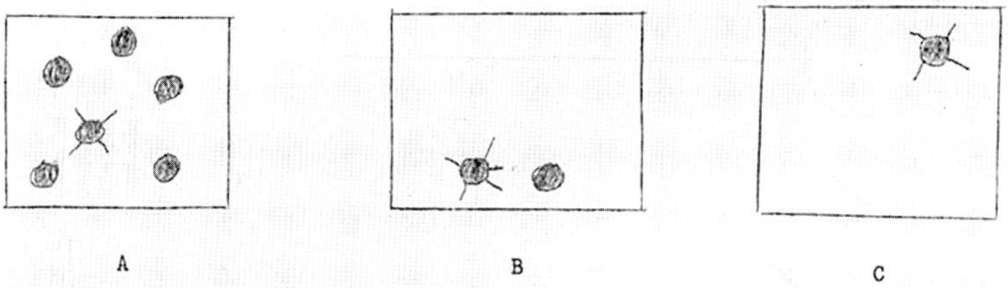

A

B

C

FIGURES 4.7 AND 4.8 Questions from Ernest Dichter's color study. "Psy-color-gy: A Motivational Research Study on Television Commercials in Color," Institute for Motivational Research, 1966.

set sales through linking the network's color programming schedule to dealer needs and showroom hours. RCA had subsidized NBC's introductory year and had also agreed to offset costs of color broadcasts, especially when sponsors seemed unwilling to pay the higher color rates. Instead of targeting and courting sponsors whose products and/or programming would best be served by color, as NBC executives hoped to do, RCA was primarily focused on courting color television set buyers and therefore prioritized the color scheduling around the temporal rhythm of a salesman's workday over other considerations. In one 1955 memo detailing RCA's color programming priorities, an NBC executive opened with the statement, "If our color activities were to be conducted without regard to manufacturing requirements, we would continue to operate under the policies established in 1954, following the introductory year."[35] These earlier color policies centered on the targeting of specific genres, producers, shows, sponsors, and advertisers for color conversion or production, based on their projected color needs and potentialities. While this approach was still certainly at work in color programming and development mid-decade, these policies were also measured against the needs of RCA and its dealers and distributors. With a flurry of press releases, NBC announced its "five-fold expansion"—a color increase of 500 percent over the previous year—for the 1955–1956 season. A good portion of the color would come from the coverage of sports—NCAA football, the World Series, and the Davis Cup. For the daytime schedule, NBC converted *Howdy Doody* and the Sunday afternoon *Hallmark Hall of Fame* series, provided *Wide Wide World, Today,* and *Home* with color mobile unit segments, and premiered *Matinee Theatre,* a four-day-a-week color anthology program offering "live dramas of a nighttime quality . . . presented as national theatre."[36] In the evening schedule, they primarily focused on spectaculars (with Milton Berle being a notable exception)—with the new Sunday night *Color Spread,* along with more color productions included in *Producer's Showcase* and *Max Liebman Presents.*

While RCA was financing a certain number of color programs during these years, NBC also needed regular paying sponsors for their color programs. Most often this meant that once a commitment to a color program was made, a sponsor would be charged at a higher color rate to offset the higher production costs. However, RCA's push for particular program formats at specific times of the day also meant that NBC had to offer certain color shows to advertisers at no extra charge or at reduced rates in order to achieve the right timing for the airing of color programs. While succeeding to attract some color advertisers, this inequity in billing practices also served to eventually frustrate those sponsors footing the full color costs when they agreed upon the standard color rate. The aforementioned memo went on to detail RCA's specific requests, which were that NBC cover as much as possible of the baseball and football schedule in color for bar and club viewing; create regular daytime color for dealer demonstration purposes; and offer a "maximum" lineup of "high appeal" color programs scheduled for "the evenings on which the maximum number of dealers are open for business."[37] RCA singled out *The Milton Berle Show* as the most desirable "high appeal" program, presumably because Berle already had acquired the moniker of "Mr. Television" and was commonly referred to as "the man who had sold a million [black and white] sets" earlier in the decade, and RCA likely imagined he would have the same effect on color sales.

In order to attract more foot traffic in stores selling color televisions, RCA management assisted local dealers in the planning of promotional events and tie-ins. In the summer of 1955, for example, RCA Victor distributors and retailers received promotional kits from RCA containing mailers, photos, display materials (including posters and party streamers), advertising materials, press releases, and an overarching "plan of action" for hosting weekly *Howdy Doody* parties celebrating the start of the program's colorcasts starting in mid-September of that year. It was reported that Polk Bros., one of the largest television dealers in Chicago at the time, successfully hosted five of these Tuesday afternoon parties, wherein children (and their families—most likely their mothers) were invited to watch the first color episodes of the program. Attendees were given refreshments and Howdy Doody–themed gifts for children (such as coloring books, brightly colored balloons, or jigsaw puzzles; see figure 4.9). Children were to be accompanied by adults, as they would "be natural prospects for the purchase of RCA Victor color receivers," and were expected to register themselves in a special Howdy Doody ledger at the front of the door. Adults were also encouraged to enter raffles and contests for prizes related to further involvement in RCA/NBC color events or programming.

RCA encouraged local dealers to hold other "special occasion parties" when NCAA color football broadcasts were on as well as in celebration of holidays such as Thanksgiving and Christmas.[38] One of the longest

FIGURE 4.9 An example of *Howdy Doody* merchandise cross-promoting color television. AUTHOR'S PRIVATE COLLECTION.

running promotional campaigns devised by NBC was National Color TV Week, held every fall at the start of the new broadcast season. It involved a national campaign of local stations, dealers, and distributors that was built around the broadcast of a national spectacular and sometimes local color broadcasts. During the first color week in 1955, there were kickoff parties held in dealer showrooms under banners proclaiming, *Every Night Is Color TV Night,* where prospective buyers could view David Sarnoff declaring to the nation "the fact that color television is HERE," while revisiting the technology's history and the color wars through the lens of RCA/NBC's corporate agenda.[39] RCA was aware that public demonstrations were essential to convincing skeptical consumers that these new sets were stable, pleasurable, easy to use, and a significant and necessary improvement on black and white television. While in-store promotions, exhibitions, and events were intended to bring in female consumers and their children, tavern, lounge, and nightclub color television was believed to be the primary site of male viewership—hence the premium placed on color sports programming.

As Anna McCarthy has detailed in her book *Ambient Television*, bar owners, alcoholic beverage companies and distributors, networks, and set manufacturers, all benefited from the placement of television sets (first black and white and then color) in such masculinized, class-bound social spaces, even though the technology's presence in the bar could also potentially upend established relations between patrons, bars, and the sports industries.[40] While some business owners considered purchasing a color set as an investment in attracting more customers and put sets in their establishments themselves, a number of local RCA distributors rented sets to bars, lounges, clubs, and other well-known public places. RCA had reached out to the National Association of Tavern Owners in order to establish a color television promotion partnership, which included offering, among other things, special pricing deals for taverns, contests for free color set prizes, and advertising in tavern trade magazines. The company predicted in July 1955 that around two thousand bars and taverns would be equipped with color sets within the following two months—in time for colorcasts of several NCAA football games and the World Series that fall.[41] RCA also placed sets in convention centers and waiting rooms in transportation hubs (such as Grand Central station), and offered special pricing to Army, Navy, and Air Force officers' clubs as well as hotels.[42] For instance, they made a deal with New York's Hotel Governor Clinton to install fifty color sets, along with seven hundred black and whites, in their guest rooms. The color sets, of course, would be placed in the more upscale, higher-rate rooms.

RCA also made it a priority to target female consumers where they shopped. This was true both for urban department stores and in the suburban shopping centers and malls that began popping up in the latter half of the decade. In 1955, Brooklyn's Abraham and Straus department store hosted sit-down tea for customers while they watched *Matinee Theatre,* and during the following year, the NBC Color TV Fair went on the road to department stores across the United States, demonstrating color while also bringing in customers with live appearances by television stars such as Diahann Carroll and Peter Boyle, who appeared at Gimbels to kick off the traveling roadshow.

Shopping centers, and eventually enclosed malls, were built with the idea that they would serve as the focal point of community and con-

FIGURE 4.10 "Color TV Makes Homemakers Reach Faster!"
An ad for a local station in Dallas in 1955.

sumer engagement for the growing number of American suburbanites. Entrenched in the values of the new mass consumption society, these sites housed not only national chains and local stores but often also spaces and services intended to create a commercialized public hub of restaurants, playgrounds, movie theaters, laundromats, and chapels. In addition, there were meeting halls and auditoriums used for public education and entertainment that underscored the positioning of the mall at the center of civic life for largely white, middle-class suburbanites. Lizabeth Cohen notes that "well-attended programs and exhibitions" at these sites "taught shoppers about such 'hot' topics of the fifties and sixties as space exploration, color television, modern art, and civics."[43] The demonstrations of color occurring in such malls and department stores were meant to serve as both consumer-citizen education and spectacular enticement. A site of display of new technology in an environment already actively working to stimulate consumer desire that engaged what McCarthy calls "retail spectatorship."[44] McCarthy also notes that such exhibitions in the early years of (black and white) television "were aspirational displays, designed to elevate the store by aligning it with other marketing spectacles of the modern state like world's fairs and expositions."[45] Besides the demonstrations and events held in department stores and malls, color television was also strategically placed in the aisles, on display tables, and near checkout lines of supermarkets and grocery stores. *Tide Magazine* in 1956 reported that RCA's "philosophy" behind the grocery store displays was that "if shoppers see the one hour and forty minutes of color shows each afternoon (*Matinee Theatre, Jinx's Diary, Howdy Doody*), they may hunger for spectaculars and other nighttime and weekend programs in color."[46] The magazine also noted that sponsors likely enjoyed the idea that consumers might see their products in color while at the point of purchase—thereby referencing and supporting a notion of color television as the ultimate inducer of visual desire while also targeting female consumers at what was presumed to be the most vulnerable and emotionally driven moment in her decision making process.

RCA hoped to attract more color television viewers by taking the technology on the road, in much the same way as they did in 1939 after television's introduction at the World's Fair and in 1948, soon after commercial television approval. Traveling across the country to promote and demonstrate color television was the primary job of NBC's Color TV

FIGURE 4.11 RCA's Color TV Caravan. "Color TV Meets the People," *Radio Age*, January 1955, 13.

Caravan, a thirty-two-foot trailer truck containing broadcast equipment, a "complete control room," and eighteen technicians and engineers (see figures 4.11 and 4.12).[47] The caravan provided what RCA referred to as "grassroots" demonstrations of color in cities and small towns across the Midwest and South. One stop was Cleveland's Karamu House—the oldest African American theater in the United States—while another was the Horticultural Yards in Saint Louis. Regional and local fairs were also common sites for the caravan to set up shop—for example, RCA described the eight days spent at the 1954 Mid-South Fair in Memphis as a great success for the caravan. A 150-by-150-foot tent was put up as a "color TV theatre," wherein six fifteen-inch sets presented twenty-minute programs on the hour, seven hours a day (see figure 4.13). In an effort to strengthen ties to and between the community and the affiliate, the programming aired was transmitted by WMCT, which in addition to the transmissions sent to the tent, aired fifteen-minute programs from the caravan at six every evening.[48] The following fall, RCA claimed to have attracted over two million people over sixteen days to a studio constructed in part of the agriculture building at the State Fair of Texas,

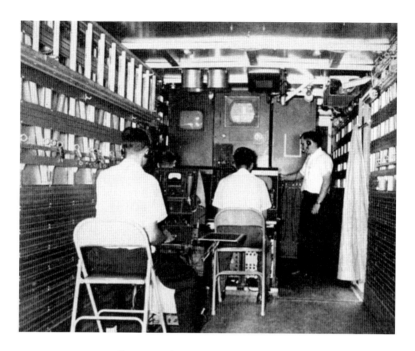

FIGURE 4.12 Inside RCA's Color TV Caravan. "Color TV Meets the People,"
Radio Age, January 1955, 13.

an event that was cosponsored by Dallas Power and Light and two local stations—WFAA and KRLD (see figure 4.14).

Fairgoers watched network and local programs via closed-circuit on a "theater-size screen."[49] Although it gestured strongly toward the modern with its focus on the future of technology and design, RCA's traveling technological roadshow was not unique, either as a form of entertainment or as a business strategy, as it combined the practices and forms of numerous types of touring entertainment, exhibitions, and demonstrations. During the early twentieth century, rural tent shows, medicine shows, vaudeville, itinerant film exhibitions, circuses, and carnivals brought mass amusements and national forms of entertainment to towns and cities across America. Technology was also displayed in roadshow style—some examples include stereoscopy, early film technology, and x-rays—demonstrated in a context that often emphasized the magic of the machine over the content of what it could produce.[50] As Gregory

FIGURES 4.13 AND 4.14 Color TV at the fair in Memphis, Tennessee, and at a fair in Dallas. "Color TV Meets the People," *Radio Age*, January 1955, 13.

Waller has discussed in his history of traveling film exhibitions in the South during the 1930s, film was also used as a tool to sell something else—politicians, health mandates, religion, instructional travelogues, and products such as Studebakers and John Deere farm equipment—to local communities.[51] He also notes that *Billboard*, in their coverage of itinerant film shows during that period, encouraged roadshowmen to make short films of local events and include those reels in the exhibition program as a "surefire way of drumming up business," especially if the exhibitor could "slip in" paid advertising plugs "gently among the other local shots."[52] The Color TV Caravan did this too, focusing on local coverage, advertisers, and, of course, the station itself, but it also made a spectacle out of the technology—the multiple screens, the streamlined modern control room, the presence of technicians and engineers, even emphasizing the presentation of the van itself, which carried "COLOR TELEVISION" in huge rainbow lettering across its side.

After the national tour ended, RCA made the Color TV Caravan available to businesses and organizations for "stockholder or sales meetings, conventions," selling it as an opportunity for a "private wire" (i.e., closed-circuit) way to hold meetings simultaneously in multiple cities, to take groups on virtual tours of their operations, to do product demonstrations or to teach new techniques, and, most importantly for RCA, "to share in and put to work the enormous public interest in color television."[53] AT&T used the caravan for a shareholders' meeting; Electrolux showed a sales demonstration by a Florida salesman to a crowd of 2,500 at the Waldorf; and a close-up surgery, employing the latest surgical techniques, was shown to an audience of veterinarians and other "professional and technical organizations."[54] RCA used the caravan to demonstrate color technology to a range of users, most notably potential set buyers and closed-circuit clients, by highlighting relationships between the local, regional, and national while also promising to collapse the spatial and temporal distance between them. In the state fair tents, locals who were gathered in a familiar community setting were transported elsewhere and at the same time reminded of the connection between their community and the larger network project. Those in industry and business settings were shown not only the way that television could compress time and extend vision but also how color television in particular could allow them to see, work, and learn more effectively. RCA did not increase their sales of sets to consumers in great numbers during this period, but nonetheless they saw the work of the caravan as strengthening ties in the network and to viewers while serving the public interest by spreading the good word of the coming of color. It is likely that most of those families present for the color demonstrations at the Mid-South Fair could not even afford a color set during the 1950s, or even into the 1960s, and yet these decent sized audiences (and RCA) could now say that they had seen color television broadcast by NBC and by their local affiliate. The local affiliate gained publicity through these events through coverage wherein they would appear to have access to and mastery over the most up-to-date technology. RCA and NBC were also hoping that they would eventually cooperate in the color conversion process.

The colorization of local television was a slow and expensive venture for NBC, but one that was necessary for the company to legitimately claim to be a national color network with color programming at all points in the programming schedule. Moreover, because much of the local programming occurred during the day and early evening, peak television dealer hours, RCA and NBC worked together to make local conversion a priority.

COLOR CITY

By the start of 1957, there were 136 NBC stations, 123 CBS stations, and 9 ABC stations *capable* of broadcasting in color, even though few of them actually were doing so.[55] In order to simply broadcast the color programming that would be part of their network package, local stations had to adapt their antenna and transmission system for color. The AT&T network connection lines had to be converted as well; while the 4 MHz black and white radio relay circuits would carry "some sort of color picture," the bandwidth wasn't wide enough to carry all the information, the results being "an inferior color picture, if one is received at all, where the hues may be considerably off from true color."[56] In a 1954 memo to Robert Sarnoff (who was a vice president at that time), NBC's chief engineer, O. B. Hanson, expressed concern that if local stations or manufacturers gave demonstrations using color signals transmitted over AT&T lines at that time, it would be "embarrassing" for the networks, stations, and manufacturer, and would "create poor impressions" in the minds of "important people."[57] However, to move beyond transmission and be able to air locally produced programming and commercials from local sponsors, they would not only have to adapt the relay circuits, but would also have to purchase, at the very least, a color camera, film chain, and likely a videotape machine. Eventually, as color production increased, stations would also need to invest in additional film chains and video recorders, zoom lenses, more lighting, and at least one other studio camera.[58] Of course, all their engineering, creative, and production staff would also have to be fully trained in the technology and in color planning (similar to the work by the Color Corps described in the chapter 3). The majority of stations did not make this full transition until the mid-1960s, but there were a few stations that were fully color converted, capable of not only transmitting network color programming, but also *producing* local color.[59] (NBC reported that they had twenty-six local stations equipped to originate live color by 1961 and CBS and ABC each had seven—although ABC did not have any live color studios producing programming until 1965.)

WLW (NBC) in Cincinnati (NBC's "Colortown") was the first to sign a network contract for color transmission in 1953, and by 1962, it was producing twenty hours a week of local color programming.[60] WKY (CBS) in Oklahoma City and WCCO (CBS) in Minneapolis started live colorcasts, and KTLA (NBC) in Los Angeles broadcast the Tournament of Roses parade via their mobile unit in 1954. NBC's flagship station, WRCA-TV (its call letters were changed to WNBC in 1960) was broadcasting 65 percent of its local live programming in color by the fall of 1956. However, it was NBC's WNBQ, housed in the Merchandise Mart in Chicago, that became the "first all color television station in the world" (even before anything in New York) in 1956, broadcasting all local programs in color at a cost of $1.5 million to the network. "We have chosen this pioneering step," David Sarnoff announced at a press conference, "because Chicago has always been a key city in the operations of the company and the radio and TV industry generally."[61] Chicago had been a major producer of radio programming, maintained one of the largest broadcast audiences in the country, was located near some of the largest television manufacturing plants (new color plants were located in Bloomington and Indianapolis), and was considered by the networks to be *the* connecting node between New York and Los Angeles. It was one of the only locations that, as Christopher Anderson and Michael Curtin have pointed out, could rival New York and Los Angeles "as a center for radio and television production,"[62] thereby also making it an obvious candidate for conversion. In the early 1950s, reviewers began to note a distinct style to Chicago programming, a good portion of which made it onto the network schedule, and began referring to a "Chicago touch" or the "Chicago School" of television.[63] The style, apparent in programs such as those featuring Dave Garroway and Studs Terkel, was described as one that involved a "freshness and informality" and sense of intimacy mixed with a kind of casual sophistication.[64] Producers remarked that the style developed out of necessity, as they lacked the big names and budgets of network production on the coasts. One defining element was that Chicago directors tended to give the camera more room to roam on set, using it "the way an artist uses a brush," as one *Theatre Arts* magazine critic described it in 1951, as the camera "comes alive" and "surveys the goings-on with sly winks, with wide-eyed surprise, and with trembling awareness of the beauty that lurks in the shadows as well as the beauty that dances in the light."[65] The same critic closed her piece by asserting, "If the day ever comes when television establishes a true 'academy,' a place where the young and hopeful may go to learn the art of television programming, Chicago is the only conceivable place for such an institution."[66]

Even though the Chicago school had mostly died out by decade's close, in a very real way WNBQ did become an academy—in a similar manner to the network's use of Studio 3H as a site for learning about the particularities of color—as the station shared the lessons of color production they had acquired during those early years. At the same time that RCA/NBC used WNBQ as a central color network node and key site of color promotion, they also considered it to be an experimental station, often referring to it as a color laboratory for NBC owned and operated stations and affiliates. In the press conference announcing the plan for WNBQ's conversion, David Sarnoff asserted that "all the know-how, all the lessons we learn in this Chicago pilot operation will be made available to other television stations interested in advancing color television as a regular service to the public."[67] Reports coming out of the station, which were shared in trade magazines, were that the station had to modify all of its sets for simplicity, train its personnel in the rules of color harmony, learn how to dolly the heavier color cameras, hire more video engineers (one for each color camera), and alter its lighting practices— but not by much, as they recently learned they could "use less lighting than expected for color."[68] Jules Herbuveaux, NBC vice president and general manager of WNBQ, told *Broadcasting-Telecasting* that color conversion "wasn't as tough as it was cracked up to be," adding, "Color is basic and natural. We live it, wear it, eat it and even ride in it—just look at the nearest parking lot. Now we put an electronic camera on life in all its natural color. . . . Color is natural and that's the way we are treating it."[69] Herbuveaux's statement, even if at least partially true on some level, was also likely an attempt on his part to publicly address and quiet the concerns over "color troubles" that were still very much a part of the discourse that framed the coming of color television. In asserting the naturalness and ease of color in food, clothes, cars, and television, he was also disavowing the established industries and institutions that were continuing to develop, standardize, manage, and market commercial color.

Although wnbq was considered a color success, the station reported that advertisers remained hesitant, mainly due to the low number of sets on the market, even though they were offered color spots at standard rates by the station as part of the "laboratory project." The 10 percent of the station's clients who did advertise in color—such as Sears, Roebuck & Co., DuPont, Canada Dry, Whirlpool, Coca-Cola, Kresge's—were, for the most part, large companies with national profiles.[70] In terms of programming, wnbq was running thirty-three hours a week of local color programs—including *Kukla, Fran and Ollie,* the *Bob and Kay Show,* the variety program *Adults Only,* and the news—along with eight hours a week of network color. Another early color production station in Chicago was wgn-tv, which was owned by the Tribune Company, publisher of the *Chicago Tribune.* Although originally affiliated with both cbs and DuMont (acting as the major production center for the latter), the station became independent after DuMont ceased operations in 1956 and claimed to have produced over one thousand hours of color programming three years later.[71] By the time it had moved into its new all-color television studio in 1961, the station had found its live color niche in sports (covering the White Sox and the Cubs) and children's programming (*Treetop House, Bozo Circus, Bugs Bunny, Garfield Goose,* and *Dick Tracy*).[72]

On May 22, 1958, the dedication of wrc-tv in Washington, DC—the first station designed for color from its inception—was not accompanied by the same level of expansive citywide promotional fanfare that occurred around wnbq's conversion, but the press coverage and recording of the event reveal that it came with its own version of spectacle—one that was political rather than overtly commercial. The old facilities of wrc-tv had been used for closed-circuit demonstrations of color in the 1950s as part of the standards process and were selected for complete reconstruction because of the station's proximity to and relationship with the political scene. The dedication was attended by high-ranking governmental officials, who sat beside the heads of nbc and rca onstage in front of an audience in wrc-tv's studio A. President Dwight D. Eisenhower was the star of the dedication proceedings, first touring

FIGURES 4.15 AND 4.16 On May 22, 1958, Robert Sarnoff, at the dedication of WRC-TV, pushes a button at the podium to signal the transition from black and white to color in one of the oldest color videotape recordings.

the station's technical center (reporting back that the room was "beyond my comprehension but still capable of exciting my wonderment") and then addressed on stage by both Robert Sarnoff (NBC president) and David Sarnoff (RCA chairman of the board) before giving his own brief speech.[73] Eisenhower was positioned in Robert Sarnoff's speech as one in a long line of presidents who contributed to "broadcasting milestones," from Woodrow Wilson, who was the "first to test radio," to Franklin D. Roosevelt, whose "fireside chats" changed the tenor and frequency of presidential address.[74] Eisenhower, who was the first to allow his presidential press conferences to be broadcast, would now, asserted the younger Sarnoff, also be the first president to be broadcast and recorded on color videotape. As he had done in Chicago, Robert Sarnoff once again pushed a button on the podium, a signal to an engineer in the technical center to flip the color burst switch on the encoder, and the television screen filled with color.[75] Sarnoff then announced that the event was being recorded live in color in Burbank, California, which would enable the program to be rebroadcast later on the West Coast "with true fidelity." Robert, like his father, was intent on making the color project a major success for RCA/NBC, and now that he was in charge of policy and financial decision making at the network overall, he would work with newly appointed NBC president, Robert Kinter, to fully convert the network to color.

Of course, it was not just local stations that needed their own color studios to produce programming; networks did too. Starting out by converting small studios in or near their central offices in Manhattan, the networks eventually expanded outside the city to locations that offered more space for color production. CBS was the first to make the move out west. CBS's Television City, located in Fairfax, California, and completed in 1952, did not contain a color soundstage until two years later. The complex was, however, considered a monument to CBS's programming excellence and dominance in the ratings, technical capabilities, engagement with modern art and design, and vision of the future for television production—specifically in its developing relationship with Hollywood studios. As Lynn Spigel has argued, with Television City, CBS "transformed the business of network television from an abstract conglomeration of signals and wires into a physical place of high-tech stages and star-studded glamour that sponsors and audiences recognized as a distinctly new media site."[76] CBS had been first in constructing such a site in Southern California, and yet NBC was the first to build studios there with the *specific needs of color production* in mind. Color City, on land purchased from Warner Brothers and the city of Burbank, was not as distinct in its architectural design or style, but it did allow NBC to once again proclaim a vision of the future based on their history of technical and manufacturing dominance. Color City, as the name implied, was therefore not simply a symbol of the shifting terrain of television financing or the increasing centrality of Hollywood television production, it was also a testament to RCA/NBC's continual and very public assertion that color was the inevitable future of the industry.

While it certainly was the largest and most significant of all the network color studios, Color City was not the first one to be constructed or converted by the networks. CBS had three color studios in New York that were in use at different points in the 1950s: studio 57, located uptown at Fifth Avenue and 109th Street, and used from 1950 to 1951; studios 71 (the first NTSC-equipped CBS studio) and 72, both located in the CBS headquarters on Madison Avenue; and studio 50, located in the theater district, which was renamed the Ed Sullivan Theater in the late '60s.[77] Inside Television City, studio 43C was converted to color in 1954 and two years later, 41C followed suit. Executives at NBC had at times expressed urgency around the conversion or purchase of new color studio space. Besides the experimental color studio 3H, the first NBC studio to be converted, the network also modified another Rockefeller Center studio, 3K, in 1955. Additionally, the network used two Manhattan theaters for live colorcasts: the Colonial Theater on Sixty-second Street, which they first leased in 1953 and then purchased from RKO Pictures three years later, remodeling it to accommodate large-scale productions; and the Ziegfeld Theatre, which they leased from Billy Rose from 1955 until 1963. RCA/NBC also found larger, cheaper spaces outside Manhattan, such as an old Vitagraph studio in Midwood, Brooklyn, purchased in 1952 and then renovated for use in the production of many of the largest color spectaculars, including *Satin and Spurs* (1954) and the *Esther Williams Aqua Spectacle* (1956).

Before committing to the Burbank project, NBC had hired Norman Bel Geddes—one of the period's top industrial designers and the creator of GM's iconic immersive Futurama exhibit at the World's Fair—to consult on the development of studios built specifically for the needs of high output television production. As Joshua Gleich reveals, Bel Geddes designed three extravagant prototypes (named "Atlantis," the "Pilot Studio," and the "Horizontal Studio") for NBC from 1952 to 1956, none of which were selected by the network for a variety of reasons.[78] However, all three design plans incorporated the privileging of live performance, the experience of in-studio audiences, and the efficient use of space to maximize program output. They were also all intended to be located in New York. David Sarnoff had asked Bel Geddes to weigh in on the decision to invest in production in Los Angeles versus New York City, and Bel Geddes came down on the side of New York, based on, Gleich argues, his vision of NBC studios as partly a "theme park" and the fact that the city "remained the country's predominant tourist destination."[79] Colorcasting was a part of Bel Geddes's plans, particularly for the Pilot Studio, which was to be the "showcase theater" in a proposed Color City, to be designed by the architectural firm Harrison & Abramovitz and built on a site directly across from Rockefeller Center on the west side of Sixth Avenue (where the Time & Life Building would eventually be constructed). A November 8, 1954, memo to Pat Weaver and David Sarnoff from John M. Clifford, chairman of the network's plant planning committee, detailed a proposal that had been in the works for over a year at that point.[80] Beyond the "shops, storage area, master control and all necessary technical functions," the plant would include eleven large television studios, including "one large show-case audience studio with a seating capacity of 1,000; four large audience studios each with a seating capacity of 500; [and] six large production studios which can also be used for audiences with temporary seating arrangements."[81] The planning committee estimated that the rent on the midtown Color City would be around $3.5 to $4 million and that the network would have to let their other short-term leases run out and sell both the Hudson theater and the Brooklyn studio in order to cover the cost. They also noted, however, that centralizing operations in one building would cut operating costs considerably.[82]

Ultimately, RCA/NBC made the decision not to invest in a large Manhattan complex, but instead to focus their resources on developing Burbank as their production hub. In his memoir, Pat Weaver claimed that the decision to build in Los Angeles was made not just on the basis of the need for more space, but also on the desire to be near Hollywood talent.[83] Additionally, RCA/NBC executives did not want to be bested by CBS, and the construction of Television City fueled their drive to have a similarly large studio in Southern California. Although Color City's initial phase of construction was completed in 1952 and some black and white programming was produced and aired live there during that time, the 1955 dedication was meant to mark the completion of studio 2—the "first color studio built from the ground up" (see figure 4.17).

Unlike Bel Geddes's elaborate proposed studios or the studios of CBS's Television City, which had been designed in the International Style by the respected local architects William Pereira and Charles Luckman, NBC's Burbank studios were contained in a rather nondescript (but flexible), modernist facility planned and constructed by the Austin Company. It was a highly practical plant built on fifty acres and consisting of 55,000 square feet of built space. Due to the demands of color television production, studio 2, built and equipped at a cost to the network of $3,176,000, contained three times the amount of lighting (at a capacity of 1 million watts) required in studios equipped for black and white and required a high power air-conditioning plant to compensate for the heat generated by such wattage (this amount of lighting was still less than what was initially anticipated for color production).[84] The lights were managed by a Century-Izenour lighting board containing 2,400 controls and allowing for ten light changes within a single scene.[85] Two unique features addressed the problem of how to provide the in-studio audience with a decent view of the production without hemming in the

FIGURE 4.17 Postcard of NBC's Color City in Burbank, California.
AUTHOR'S PRIVATE COLLECTION.

movement and positioning of the cameras (a problem in live television produced in theaters): a fifteen-by-twenty-foot large screen RCA color projector (which also enabled the audience to experience color television on the screen) and a sloping "audience pit," which positioned the audience below floor level only a few feet away from the performers.[86]

NBC marked the studio's dedication with stories planted in various local and national news outlets (including a segment on *Today*), a declaration of "NBC Color TV Week" by California governor Goodwin Knight, and a "big, celebrity packed gathering the night of the dedication" that would lead into the broadcast of *Entertainment 1955*, a high-profile variety show with performances by NBC stars such as Milton Berle, Fred Allen, Dinah Shore, and Dennis Day. In a moment of cross-promotion, well-known television host Ralph Edwards interviewed Adolph Zukor, the founder of Paramount Pictures, about the history and future of film and introduced previews of three upcoming 1955 Paramount films—*The Seven Little Foys*, *Strategic Air Command*, and *You're Never Too Young*. And, in an homage to forms that were considered to be contributing to the development of television as a form, an excerpt of the opera *Tosca* was performed as staged by the NBC Opera Company and there was also a "tribute to nightclubs as a training ground for fresh new talent."[87] Soon after *Entertainment 1955* was broadcast, NBC announced that it would begin construction on another color soundstage—studio 4—that would be completed in time for the 1956 season. It was also during this season that NBC made one of its most significant moves to brand itself as *the* color network.

OF PEACOCKS AND RAINBOWS

In the fall of 1956, NBC commissioned the market research firm Oxtoby-Smith to conduct a study of individual responses to various symbols of color. Logotypes such as colored versions of the NBC chimes as well as a rainbow, a paintbrush, and the proposed NBC peacock were tested in both black and white and in color. The network wanted to find a symbol that brought to mind the vibrancy of color even when viewed in monochrome—and the results were in strong favor of the peacock. Researchers also reported there was no indication of "haughtiness" or "arrogance" associated with the peacock in the minds of the study's subjects. This was a reference to both the perceived regal nature of the bird and a concern that the design itself was too modern or abstract for the average viewer and they might find it alienating. This concern can be read through the lens of a recognized tension between the perception of elitism in modernist art and the clean modernist designs present in mass production and marketing. Spigel notes that television networks (especially CBS) were engaged in producing "everyday modernism," a term that, she argues, encompasses an embrace of modern design at the level of the popular (in contrast to, say, high art) and, on a more abstract level, "signals the general enthusiasm in the postwar period for designs that signified progress, science and forward-looking lifestyles."[88] According to this market study, the abstract design of the peacock succeeded in gesturing both to the familiar or known and to the new or modern.

Before commissioning the peacock study, RCA/NBC executives had made the decision to move away from the three-color xylophone and chimes logo, a symbol first used in 1953, that served as a bridge between NBC's radio past and its future in television (see figure 4.18). The xylophone logo was a visual interpretation of NBC radio's three-note (G-E-C) aural logo that they had been using since 1931. In fact, all of NBC television's network identifications used the G-E-C notes in some way—from

FIGURE 4.18 NBC'S chimes logo.

the NBC microphone symbol to the simple woodblock cutout NBC letters that would light up in sequence as each chime was struck. The chimes were originally devised as a solution to a problem that arose out of network connection—something was needed to ease the transition to the breaks that would occur at the top of the hour in order to allow local outlets their ten seconds of FCC mandated station identification. The sound of the chimes was a cue that the network program had ended and the local station identification could begin. They also worked as a memorable point of brand identification for listeners, and it was the first *sound* logo to receive a trademark, in 1951. NBC hoped that the peacock would serve as a symbol of transition too, both as a marker of the beginning of every NBC colorcast and as a reminder of the network's technological triumph.

The peacock was the creation of in-house art director John J. Graham, who designed the initial iteration of the symbol with eleven crisp feathers of six different colors in a rainbowlike arrangement positioned behind the sleek white modernist abstract representation of the bird's body (see figure 4.19). Beginning in the fall of 1957, the peacock used in the network's broadcast promos was shown first raising its feathers in white outline and then reopening them in color, fanning them out to an orchestral soundtrack that reached a crescendo once the rainbow of feathers was in full bloom. The adoption of this logo was a move to brand NBC color, and the peacock symbol would theoretically be used by all local color stations too, unifying the corporate brand and appearing not only on air, but also on posters, stationery, print advertisements, buildings, displays, billboards, and merchandising and would be distributed to local sales offices through promotional kits. Yet, as Spigel points out, NBC's branding was relatively inconsistent throughout the 1950s, especially when compared to that of CBS.[89] While CBS used variations of its eye logo in all of its branding, NBC continued to use the xylophone chimes at the end of each network program (before the station break) and the peacock at the start, as well as the NBC letters in various fonts (mostly with chimes) and, toward the end of the decade, a design of Graham's that came to be known as the "snake" logo. When used in NBC or RCA print advertisements, the peacock would appear at the bottom, sometimes centered in the middle of a small graphic image of a TV set and other times in a black circle with the word "color" in the middle of the tag "NBC Color Television." RCA would occasionally use versions of the peacock in print ads when it was cross-promoting its sets with NBC programming. At other times, RCA would leave out the peacock, using its own logo and either "The Most Trusted Name in Television" or "Electronics for Living" as a tagline.[90]

While local stations were encouraged to use the peacock in their promotions, sometimes they would use their local logo instead, or, as was the case with WNBQ, their own color character. The rhetoric and hoopla surrounding the opening of local stations WRC-TV and WNBQ described earlier in this chapter demonstrates the importance NBC placed on certain stations within the network. It also reveals how the network wished both to brand stations as unique in relation to local values and styles and to emphasize their status as delivery systems for the programs, practices, ideals, and goals of the national network. Yet there were often conflicts or contradictions between the local practice and the national one that highlighted disconnects. Certainly problematics can arise in the form of content and representation (political, sexual, racial) as one area in which the chain can lose its public sense of cohesiveness, but this can also become apparent in branding, marketing, and advertis-

FIGURE 4.19 NBC's peacock logo.

ing. For example, Spigel has noted that CBS's eye logo, created by CBS's legendary art director, William Golden, "helped create an identity for a CBS corporate culture in which camera operators, set designers, advertisers, secretaries, and virtually all workers were brought together under a single brand."[91] That branding was also supposed to work seamlessly on the national and local level, as CBS sent out promotional kits containing corporate art and instructions for its use in local ad campaigns to all affiliates. And yet the network's modernist aesthetic often clashed with local taste cultures and promotion practices. Golden was, in fact, sent out to CBS sales offices to combat their resistance and train them in the proper use of the promotional kits in an attempt to "redirect the advertising vernacular of local stations toward its more sophisticated New York City tastes."[92]

NBC confronted this problem too in its attempt to brand across stations. The NBC peacock was promoted to stations in a manner similar to what Spigel describes happened at CBS. CBS's eye logo was created not only to distinguish the network from all other networks, but also to distinguish the network's new enterprise—television—from its radio network. NBC used the peacock as a way not only to connote the visual, but also to specifically refer to its investment in and identify moments of color broadcasting, while also using other logos and network IDs in other contexts. And yet it wanted to push for the peacock's use on the local level in order to spread the message about the availability of color on NBC, even in markets where it wasn't yet available. The local stations that were broadcasting in color would obviously have been pleased to link themselves to a nationally recognized logo, as it would connect them to larger claims associated with innovation in color technology. However, there were also many instances when their sales departments would stray from NBC's iconography and even message. Some local stations would choose to use their own IDs along with other symbols of color, such as a painter's palette and paintbrush, in order to invest in their own promotional ideas and campaigns tied to the needs of their community.

In Howard W. Coleman's 1968 anthology on color television, Roy Bacus, general manager of the NBC affiliate WBAP-TV in Dallas/Fort Worth, wrote about his experience with color conversion on the local level, recommending that station managers pay heed to a few points of advice—which combined consistency with the national branding and local flair. In a campaign to "build awareness of color," serving to remind clients, agents, and viewers of a station's conversion, Bacus argued that all on-air IDs should be "as readily recognized as the NBC peacock"; all advertising and printed promotion should preferably be in full-color but at the very least contain one color; the station itself should be decorated in color so that it would look "color-full," but careful "color harmony should prevail"; and finally, even the clothes worn by those working in the station should be color conscious, with "at least one red coat in the house," mostly likely on the station manager, who would be sure to wear it "any time he is making an appearance on behalf of color."[93] While NBC used logos and promotions to brand itself in its headquarters and studios, this "red jacket" approach likely would appear to be too much of a hard sell on the network level. What the network was pushing for was a logo and branding strategy that could position the network in relation to color while also providing a consistent message and image across the lengths and depths of the network—from national to local.

Over time, the peacock, which was altered a number of times over the years, both became a logo for the network on a national and local scale and served its purpose of reminding viewers that NBC was first in color

FIGURE 4.20 CBS's "bloodshot eye" logo.

while also helping black and white set owners identify which programs were being broadcast in color. CBS had also commissioned a logo to signify color, one that was meant both to stay consistent with its black and white eye design and to signify color. The CBS eye was largely considered a modernist masterpiece of design simplicity and recognizability. The manner in which Golden's eye design was initially modified for color, however, was not as clean and brought to mind a bloodshot eye more than it did the idea of color vision (see figure 4.20).

Perhaps because of that negative association, that version of the logo was used infrequently, and in 1965, CBS began to run network identifications for its color programming using the CBS letters followed by a smaller eye. The color identification began with the tonal ID of the network following the movement of each of the three letters (represented first in white) into alignment. Right after an announcer proclaimed, "CBS presents this program in color," a yellow version of the eye logo entered the frame from the left, moving through the letters and transforming them from black and white to color (green, blue, and red). ABC's

FIGURE 4.21 CBS color network ID.   FIGURE 4.22 ABC color network ID.

1960s color ID looked quite similar to CBS's, as it represented its three letters moving from left to right against a black screen as they transformed from a multicolored jumble to the three-color lowercase ABC logo (see figures 4.21 and 4.22).

MODERN DESIGN, VIDEO, AND COLOR PROGRAMMING

Careful design that both relied on and accentuated color occurred not only in marketing, branding, and advertising, of course, but within color programming itself. As we know from chapter 3, NBC employed careful color management and theories of color harmony in their training of production and advertising staff during the first few years of network color. CBS held similar color clinics and programs. Having been trained by color experts, many executives, marketers, and production workers at the networks were cognizant of the ways in which color intersected with the functions of genre, design, marketing, and narrative development. Yet programming often required some trial and error, and the networks received feedback from critics, sponsors, and viewers on what worked and what did not in this regard. Joan Walker of the *Washington Post* detailed what had been, in her opinion, the failures and success of color in relation to genre, arguing that color for outdoor events was unpredictable; panel and talk shows were "the least satisfying as the focus is primarily on faces and they are the most problematic when it comes to color fidelity"; and color served as "more of a distraction than an addition" when it came to drama. She concluded that variety programs were by far the best match for color, remarking, "Color makes a production number look, conservatively, 100 per cent better. The Fred Astaire specials, for instance, got good reviews from the people and critics who saw them in black and white. Everyone who saw them on color sets flipped."[94]

Although some color programming was done by sponsors who had become convinced of the power of color on television (predominately car companies), a significant number of programs, mostly specials or spectaculars, were supported by the networks as showcases for color use and strategy. As such, we can look at the color programming of this period as examples of what the networks and producers prioritized in this context: What staging did they consider to best show off color? How did they use lighting? How was color used to dramatize or emphasize particular narrative or performative moments? Which genres were considered to be a good fit for the spectacularization of color? In addition to the use of color, however, this period of the mid- to late 1950s witnessed the introduction of new video-recording technologies that also had the potential to shift the aesthetics and reception practices of color television: the short-lived lenticular color kinescope, first used in 1956, and color videotape, introduced in 1958. During these years, the coalescing of new recording technologies, new color studios, and modern production techniques, including new forms of lighting and design style, resulted in a distinct look for color on television, one that would be readily recognizable and that would be replicated in a variety of ways across an assortment of genres well into the 1960s.

Up until 1959, CBS was still producing only a handful of regularly scheduled programs in color, such as the *Arthur Godfrey Show*, *Red Skelton*, *The Bob Crosby Show*, *Ford Star Jubilee*, *Climax*, and *Heckle and Jeckle* (an animated program sustained by the network and aired in the afternoon.)[95] Not surprisingly, NBC ran substantially more regular color programs (by 1957 the network's goal was to air two color programs each night), and while some of these programs consisted of the occasional drama, game show, newscast, or sitcom, the vast majority of them were variety shows (like *The Perry Como Show*, *The Jonathan Winters Show*, and *The Dinah Shore Chevy Show*) and anthology programs (like *Studio One*, *Kraft Television Theatre*, and *Lux Video Theatre*). However, even though the network was invested in presenting color on a daily basis, color was most heavily promoted in the context of specials—primarily big-budget musical programs.

Overall, NBC aired fifty-one specials in the 1957–1958 season (the peak year for spectaculars), the majority of them aired in color. Even though Pat Weaver was no longer president as of the close of 1955, these programs represented a continuation of his strategy of connecting color to big singular moments of live spectacle. They were sizable, expensive productions, usually centering on music and dance and often featuring stars from Hollywood or Broadway. For instance, NBC's *Annie Get Your Gun* in 1957 was modeled after the live production of *Peter Pan* and also starred Mary Martin, and it was almost just as much a ratings success, attracting an estimated sixty million viewers. The production took up multiple studios in Color City in an effort to create the impression of an expanse of outdoor space, which then allowed for a scene in which Mary Martin rode a horse at full gallop.[96] *Saturday Color Carnival*, sponsored by RCA and Oldsmobile, was an umbrella title for NBC's ninety-minute Saturday night time slot for color specials, which would often showcase musical, dance, and comedy headliners.[97] In the 1940s and 1950s, Hollywood musicals were a film genre largely associated with the technology of color. As Sarah Street points out, "By 1945 it was practically unthinkable to plan a musical that was not in color."[98] In part, this had to do with the discursive construction of cinematic color (and Technicolor in particular) as having a vexed relationship to notions of realism and a rather consistent association with the spectacular. Due to the musical's generic conventions that required the audience to engage a level of suspension of disbelief in exchange for the pleasures of dance and music, the genre was a forgiving one when it came to color use. In other words, it allowed an easing of the brakes required in restrained mode and allowed for extended moments of color experimentation. This was also largely the case when it came to musical spectaculars in network television.

While CBS aired fewer specials overall (twenty-two in 1957–1958, less than half that of NBC), there were a number of significant color standouts. CBS aired a series (ten in all) of big-budget, sponsored color specials in 1957. *The DuPont Show of the Month*, an umbrella title for the presentation of a range of genres, including drama (*Wuthering Heights*), musicals (*Aladdin*), and variety (*Crescendo*), boasted big names from all areas of entertainment, including Louis Armstrong, Ethel Merman, Rex

FIGURE 4.23 *Cinderella*, 1957. The production of *Cinderella* from the July 1957 issue of *Radio Age*.

FIGURE 4.24 The production of *Cinderella* from the July 1957 issue of *Radio Age*.

Harrison, Shelley Winters, George C. Scott, Elaine Stritch, and Donald O'Connor. However, the special that earned the most attention for the network was a one-off production broadcast on March 31, 1957. Written by Rodgers and Hammerstein expressly for television and starring Julie Andrews, *Cinderella* was viewed by 107 million people, representing 60 percent of the U.S. population at that time. The almost $400,000 production (around the cost of the Academy Awards presentation that year) was described as CBS's answer to NBC's *Peter Pan*. It also was a huge success for its sponsor Pepsi, who had done a major promotional campaign around it, including moments of merchandising and cross-branding, such as their distribution of five million four-page *Cinderella* coloring books in their soda cartons.[99] Because Andrews was still performing in *My Fair Lady* on Broadway, the network kept the production in New York, and therefore was forced to fit six different sets and fifty-six actors into one of their smallest color studios, which was only 4,200 square feet.[100] While the program received somewhat mixed reviews from critics (they almost universally loved the songbook and Andrews's performance, but criticized the production overall), reviewers often commented positively on the color in the set design, while also noting how few people got to see the production that way. "It is heartbreaking to think that the lovely colors Jean and Bill Eckart have used in the sets and costumes can be appreciated only by the comparative few with color sets," wrote a reviewer for the *Chicago Tribune*. "One of the most enchanting shots is the palace staircase at the ball, a cascade of girls in diaphanous gowns of blue, pink, and mauve."[101]

Limited color set ownership was the primary reason why so many people viewed these programs in black and white, but that circumstance was only exacerbated by the fact that the West Coast received only live programs in color during those first few years. Virtually all of the specials on CBS and NBC were broadcast live and were not able to be rebroadcast for time zone delay because the color film used in the color kinescope process available from 1954 to 1955 required more than three hours turnaround time to develop. *Peter Pan*, for example, was aired in color at 4:30 PM in California, much to the upset of sponsors and viewers alike, while other programs, such as *Cinderella*, were rebroadcast only in black and white. *Esther Williams Aqua Spectacle* in 1956 was the first program to be recorded and rebroadcast later with a new type of kinescope system developed by RCA/NBC and Eastman Kodak, which relied on a special black and white 16 mm film stock coated with minuscule lenticular lenses that would produce color images when projected through particular color filters (see figure 4.25). This process meant that the problem of color film's extra processing time was eliminated and programs could be shown in time zone delay; however, the resulting images sometimes suffered from prominent color bleeds and color overlap. The process was used until color videotape became a viable alternative and West Coast viewers watched NBC color programs broadcast using this technology.

Lenticular color kinescopes were a stopgap measure before color video became a feasible and preferable alternative. Ampex first released their two-inch quadruplex black and white videotape in 1956, and it was rather quickly adopted by the networks, although RCA was also working on their own system at that time and hoped to have one that would record color in the near future. By 1958, RCA had added their own color circuits to an Ampex black and white video recorder, thereby arriving at a work-

FIGURE 4.25 *Saturday Night Color Carnival.* Ernie Kovacs's "Silent Show" recorded with the lenticular color kinescope process in 1957.

ing system for recording color programming.[102] Videotape was a vast improvement over the quality of kinescope technology in the recording of live programs, as it resulted in little image deterioration. In fact, the two-inch quadruplex tape had a resolution of four hundred horizontal lines of video resolution, much higher than the less expensive and more practical video systems that would become the standard in the 1980s. Nevertheless, quad video proved incredibly difficult to edit in its early years, as it required hand splicing before an electronic editing machine was introduced in 1963. This meant that most rebroadcast programs that were recorded live on video ended up looking remarkably similar to the initial broadcast. They were reproducible. In general, color video recording was said to present a stable, rich color palette and was thought to do especially well within the confines of network studios.

The first major prime-time program to be recorded on color videotape was *An Evening with Fred Astaire*, which aired on NBC in October 1958 and went on to win nine Emmys, including ones for camerawork and best art direction in a live program. As part of her larger thesis that tele-

Screenshots show two instances of crafting set design through color in *An Evening with Fred Astaire* (NBC, 1958).

vision in the 1950s and '60s was highly influenced by and engaged with forms of modern art, Spigel singled out the Astaire show in her book *TV by Design* as the ultimate example of how "modern design, lighting, and color worked together to create a sense of abstract design and at times even sculptural space" in the color specials of the late 1950s.[103]

The element of the Astaire program that critics and audiences seemed to respond to most, however, was the way that it was able to present the familiar (Astaire himself, dance routines, particular songs, a simple studio stage) in a manner that made it all seem state of the art. As a reviewer for *Billboard* remarked, "Utilizing Jonah Jones' smart jazz backings and David Rose's sweetly swinging arrangements as contrasting musical backdrops, Astaire achieved just the right blend of rich nostalgia and crisp modernity."[104] And it wasn't just the music that blended the traditional and the modern; the stark staging, lighting, and set design were also combined with recognizable formats and performance styles. The "sculptural space" of the sets, designed by Ed Stephenson, relied on color lighting to create a sense of depth and mood out of the studio in NBC's new Color City and did so in a manner that was legible in black and white but became bold and dramatic in color (see figures 4.26 and 4.27). For instance, the show's opening number involved the use of spotlights in a rainbow of colors against a purplish blue floor and yellow horizon reminiscent of a painting by Mark Rothko (see figure 4.28). The circles of colored light acted as marks on which small groupings of male

FIGURE 4.28 Mark Rothko, *No. 61*, 1953, an example of color-field painting.

FIGURE 4.29 Color lighting in *An Evening with Fred Astaire*, which reference forms of modern and pop art.

and female dancers dressed in black and white (with touches of yellow) both were directed by and danced with Astaire, who was often contained in his own separate spotlight (see figure 4.29). In other numbers, more traditional sets—gray city blocks, for example—served as backdrops for the color and movement that came from the dancers' costumes and the lights that subtly shifted hues and shades. Although, as Spigel's work reveals, designers of this period working in black and white were creating highly stylized and often minimalistic sets that referenced the work of abstract modern artists, color brought with it another layer of potential symbolic meaning and additional references to other forms of modern art, such as pop art and color-field painting.

When reviewing such programs, critics commented upon the color use in set design, remarking on the refinement, texture, vibrancy, and stability of color. They also took note of the medium—the unique qualities of color video. In an article on the state of color in 1961, Jack Gould compared the qualities of color on film versus color on videotape, remarking that on film, "the balance between hues seems less delicate than in the case of taped programs," and that there seemed to be an overuse on "a great deal" of color TV of a hard neon blue, which registered well when viewed on black and white sets but was unappealing in color. However, he concluded, "On the production end the use of color is reflecting more imagination. On such shows as *Perry Como's Hour, The Bell Telephone Hour, Dinah Shore*, and *Sing Along with Mitch*, the lighting and interplay of tones can be a feast for the eyes. The ballet sequences on the '*Telephone Hour*' are often especially lovely, soft in texture and of excellent taste." Gould concluded with the familiar refrain, "The best color on TV usually comes when it is employed most sparingly."[105] Four years later, Gould was still arguing that color was most effective in these types of programs: "The most satisfying color usually comes from those shows done in a TV studio . . . and by and large the color is best where costuming, lighting and visual effect are important.[106]

The "less delicate" nature of video color, however, often worked well in the context of live musical and variety stage productions. While the color could appear strong, sometimes even verging on the garish, it matched the overall feeling of excess in these types of programs. Yet, as Gould points out, certain productions of this type managed to harness the stronger edges of video color through such techniques as the use of filters and the mixing in of more neutral or muted tones with those that were more vibrant. Recently, Scott Higgins has remarked on the difference between video recordings of color and color on film in his discussion of the difficulty of analyzing color films of the past that are available only on video. In noting the greater range of color possibilities in film rather than video, he locates the limitations of video color as related to the technology's "trouble rendering very saturated secondary colors like cyan, magenta and especially yellow," even while capable of yielding "highly saturated primaries by activating one set of phosphors."[107]

Over time, a distinctive style developed for a subset of these musical specials. Those that were created with an eye toward capturing the "quality" audience or referred to as "prestige programming" employed a certain level of restraint and engaged the modern sensibility aesthetic through means similar to those used in the production of *An Evening with Fred Astaire*, which, as one reviewer put it, "had c-l-a-s-s written all over its 60 minute format."[108] Using color lighting to create a sense of depth and form, a large expanse of a studio set would be visible to the viewer; and stage design would be uncluttered or even abstract, while costuming would lend itself more to classic lines with touches of not-

FROM NOW ON, YOU CAN ENJO
EVERY PERFORMANCE OF AL
THESE NBC HOUR-LONG NIGHT
TIME DRAMATIC PROGRAMS I
FULL COLOR: THE ALCO
HOUR, GOODYEA
PLAYHOUSE, LUX VIDE
THEATRE, ROBER
MONTGOMERY PRESENT

FIGURE 4.30 *Pontiac Star Parade: Gene Kelly Show*, 1959, NBC.

FIGURE 4.31 A 1956 ad announcing NBC color spectaculars.

too-showy bold colors. This style can be found in episodes of *The Bell Telephone Hour* in the late 1950s, *The Dinah Shore Show, Perry Como, The Steve Allen Plymouth Show* (NBC/ABC), and *The Pontiac Star Parade* (NBC, 1959) and into the 1960s with musical specials such as *Color Me Barbra* (CBS, 1966). A relatively simple iteration of this trend in set design was to strip down the set almost entirely except for the use of color lighting and to often leave elements of the theatrical "behind the scenes" production in the frame, including Fresnel spotlights that faced toward the audience instead of the performers (see figure 4.30). This sort of costume and set design provided a larger visual field, enabling directors to modify form, to highlight objects or people, to set a mood, and to stimulate a viewer's attention.

Color television in the latter half of the 1950s was largely defined through RCA/NBC's push to get color sets into homes, bars, hotels, supermarkets, fairs, and other public spaces. The company took the technology on the road, studied color set owners, and described color viewers in such a way as to better sell color use to sponsors. NBC also began the process of colorizing their network through the conversion of local stations, the building of large color studios, and refining their programming strategies while developing a recognizable aesthetic for color use in live and videotaped productions. In the following chapter, we will see how NBC's strategies finally paid off for the network in the 1960s, the decade of full color conversion. We will also see how, while the color spectacular began to drop off in its use as a format, the discourses that shaped the meaning of color during the next decade began to craft a dual purpose for color: to elicit the fantastical while extending the reach, depth, and detail of vision.

CHAPTER FIVE

The Wonderful World of Color

Network Programming and the Spectacular Real, 1960–1965

Walt Disney playfully calls out to three female lab assistants, the only monochrome figures in the fictional color lab of *Walt Disney's Wonderful World of Color*, "Girls, just a moment. Haven't you got the word? We're in full color!" (see figures 5.1–5.3). The women look at one another and shrug. "Well," Walt continues, "a little bit of color magic will fix it." He claps his hands and points his fingers at them as though casting a spell and shouts, "Bibbidi! Bobbidi! Blue!" in a reference to a scene from the movie *Cinderella* (1950), in which the Fairy Godmother uses her magic to turn Cinderella's ragged clothes into a beautiful ball gown. After Walt works his technological "color magic," each assistant has now turned a single color—red, yellow, or blue. The women look blankly at Walt. "Heh, ha. I must've said the wrong words. Let's see, ah . . . Oh, I know . . ." he says, pointing again at the women, one at a time, at the beat of each word: "*NBC. Color. TV!*" The assistants are now in "full color," complete with subtle shadings in their clothing and hair (blonde, brunette, and redhead) and "natural" seeming complexions. They primp and smile. "Well, that's more like it," says Walt, beaming.

This short scene from the opening segment of the premiere episode of *Walt Disney's Wonderful World of Color* (*WWOC*) on NBC in 1961 encapsulates a number of significant discourses, practices, and concepts related to color production and reception in the early 1960s. The most obvious is, of course, the relationship between NBC and Disney, but the segment also references the color girls and calibration already discussed in chapter 3, the refinement in color use and technologies that occurred during the 1960s, and, most central to this chapter, the generic combination of fantasy and "true life" (stemming from qualities attributed to electronic color such as vibrancy, intensity, and fidelity) that would come to define not only Disney's use of color programming but also some of the most visible forms of color programming on television during this period.

The circumstances leading to the creation of *wwoc* are also indicative of larger trends in color television and representative of Disney and NBC's hopes for the technology. While the Disney studio had previously worked with ABC on the original and highly successful black and white *Disneyland* series, Walt and his brother Roy were always interested in broadcasting their program in color—something that ABC was not fully willing or able to do. (Walt did, however, have the foresight to film new segments of the program in color in anticipation of future reuse.) Eventually, Roy and Walt decided to move their program over to NBC, reportedly due to clashes between ABC executives and Disney.[1] Since it was important to Disney to be associated with technological advancements and because of the company's long held desire to air their television program in color, a partnership with NBC on a show that would be co-sponsored by RCA seemed to be an ideal match. As J. P. Telotte explains, the new title of the program "underscored the new partnership between Disney's fantasy perspective, RCA's color technology, and the natural (or 'wonderful') world, while also suggesting a kind of 'industrialization of vision' at work in the new program, as well as in the larger entertainment industry."[2]

In the opening monologue of the *wwoc* premiere, Walt put his studio at the forefront of the development of sound and color in film, talking first about *Steamboat Willie* (1928) as the first animated *sound* film and then *Flowers and Trees* (1932) as the first animated film to be done in Technicolor. In describing the period after sound but before color, Walt says, "One vital dimension was still missing—color. It was an impractical dream. Something at the end of the rainbow. But in our business, dreams have a way of coming true." This statement, written in the formulaic language of the Hollywood public relations apparatus, obscures a number of historical occurrences and developments in film and electronic color—including a lengthy process of technological innovation and standardization, the extensive history of color research, and the labor and investment that went into developing color for moving images. Yet it also reveals the perceived inevitability of color as part of modern

advancement or progression. Disney and NBC/RCA, companies deeply invested in the idea of their technological and programming dominance, pushed the narrative of color as the inevitable next step in the common discursive framing that implied that the use of color carried with it an element of magic, fantasy, or wish fulfillment—even as the technology was also purportedly presenting the world in all of its "natural" glory.

Other scenes in the premiere episode mixed these contradictory discourses about color's relationship to the fantastical and the indexical. In the episode's first extended segment, Professor Ludwig Von Drake, an uncle of Donald Duck created especially for *wwoc*, explains the basics of color theory and harmony as well as "how color TV works" (see figure 5.4). While there are references and analogies in his "lecture" that are clearly meant for children—for example, when he describes color transmission as volts that fly through the air like "little homing peacocks" (one of many moments of cross-promotion for NBC)—for the most part, it is presented as informational, albeit in a Disneyfied way, of course. However, as this segment moves into the next, the discourse of the wonder of natural beauty presented through the kaleidoscopic view of electronic color, with its synthesis of the real and the magical, reasserts itself. Over documentary footage of scenic American vistas and close-ups on flora and fauna and oceanic life, the program's orchestral theme song swells along with a choir singing such lyrics as "The world is a carousel of color . . . wonderful, wonderful color . . . the blue rolling seas, the red summer rose . . ." (see figure 5.5). It is here that we witness the integration of the visual strategies of documentary with the fantasti-

FIGURES 5.1–5.3 Screenshots from the premiere episode of *Walt Disney's Wonderful World of Color* (NBC), 1961.

cal elements of not only electronic color but also the addition of narrative and aesthetic flourishes associated with fictional programming.

We will find more of this mixed address in the 1960s color programming discussed throughout this chapter, including travel, art appreciation, and nature documentaries, and in some of the fictional programming such as *Bonanza*. Moving from the fantastical to the natural (or at least the spectacle of and immersion in the "natural" color world), the genres of the early to mid-1960s were intended to highlight color technology for the audience, the sponsor, and the network. Critics frequently claimed that color gifted television with a three-dimensional effect. Writing for the *Los Angeles Times* in 1962, Cecil Smith spoke to the "additional dimension" that color provided—one that was an extension of the effects already afforded by television and that was "present whether one is looking at the fabric of a White House chair or a World Series game, the fabulous Lake Tahoe backgrounds of *Bonanza* or the prizes on *The Price Is Right*." He added, "This dimension is not only pictorial. It is emotional," citing the NBC documentary on Van Gogh as one that was so emotional in its color presentation that "it tore at the flesh" as the canvases "boiled and swirled and fumed in angry colors; the Van Gogh sun was so hot it nearly burned you."[3] This visceral effect was also thought to affect the reception of broadcast news reports, bringing viewers closer to the story. Later in the decade, when color reports from the field were more common, newscaster Joel Daly told the *Chicago Tribune* in 1968, "The Vietnam War has been made realistic and vivid—color has had much to do with more accurate TV reporting of the war, and

FIGURE 5.4 A screenshot of Ludwig Von Drake demonstrating color harmony in *wwoc*.

FIGURE 5.5 A screenshot from the "World Is a Carousel of Color" segment of the premier episode of *wwoc*.

the recent reaction to such reports. . . . It has had a great deal to do, for instance, with viewer reaction toward the recent scenes of violence in Chicago. Viewers respond emotionally to color, much more readily than with black and white."[4] Erik Barnouw has also made the claim that the introduction of color film into news reporting helped shift viewers' feelings about the war, adding, "Mud and blood were indistinguishable in black and white; in color, blood was blood. In color, misty Vietnamese landscapes hung with indescribable beauty behind gory actions."[5]

As those scholars studying histories of color film have noted, color technologies have also been thought to provide an extra dimension to the cinematic experience. Yet, in this case of film, the sensual and perceptual experience of color has been discussed as tactile or haptical, borrowing from similar conceptual engagements in art history.[6] Joshua Yumibe provides two films that embody "certain physiological specificity to the aesthetics of color." The haptical color in Alfred Hitchcock's *Vertigo* (1958) contains a "relative flatness" that "invites one to approach its surface and run one's hand—or one's eye acting as a hand—across the textures of the image," while the "projective dimensionality" of Stan Brakhage's hand-colored abstract film *Black Ice* (1994) pitches the images toward the viewer, bringing the "surface toward the viewer in bas- and even high-relief."[7]

Television, however, with its claims of transportation and immediacy, constructs a perceptual embodiment for color television predicated on three-dimensional experientiality. What cinematic and electronic color do share, however, is a complex relationship to realism and sensation. Tom Gunning has discussed how similar paradoxical claims—to the indexical and the purely sensual and/or metaphorical—framed color film during the years when black and white films were the norm.[8] From the beginning of cinema, there was an assumption (similar to the one voiced by Walt Disney above) that the experience of cinema would not be complete, and could not truly represent the human experience of the natural world, without the addition of both sound and color.[9] At the same time, color, in a media world dominated by monochrome, was a marker of difference and therefore, as Gunning argues, could seem as "something superadded to the more dominant form of reproduction." Moreover, Gunning continues, "Color serves as a startling alternative to black and white, evoking a sensual intensity that can overwhelm its realistic and indexical associations even when it appears in color photographic processes."[10] Once color became the norm in film, photography, or in television, however, it lost much of that sensual intensity and metaphorical power. More recently, Richard Misek has discussed the way that color was deemed appropriate for some genres (musicals, fantasies, westerns, histories) and not others (social realism, documentary) from the 1930s until the mid-1950s.[11]

During the period of the early 1960s, color in television was still understood as an innovation, a digression from the black and white standard, and as such there existed the paradox of color as an achievement in both verisimilitude and the sensual fantastical. The genres and programming that I explore in this chapter exist at various points along the spectrum of this paradox, most often containing both claims to varying degrees. I will begin with an overall picture of color television programming and the industrial context in which it was produced during the early 1960s, stopping along the way to reflect briefly on network trends and specific programs. The second half of this chapter will concentrate on the color cultural documentary and its various subgenres in an effort to explore the color paradox as expressed in television in greater detail.

CAROUSEL OF COLOR:
THE STATUS OF COLOR TELEVISION IN THE EARLY 1960S

Network television had a significantly altered financial structure in the 1960s compared to the decade prior. Based largely on the financing and programming model of radio, television in the 1950s had depended primarily on a combination of advertising agencies, independent production companies, and in-house staff to develop, produce, and manage the programming that went on the air. By the start of the '60s, however, programming had shifted to independent production houses (some of them subsidiaries of Hollywood studios) that worked as "essentially production arms" of the network, producing increasingly standardized programs, much more of which was filmed than live. Michele Hilmes has identified the resulting "classic network system" (from roughly 1960 to 1980) as one that was highly centralized at the levels of production, distribution, and exhibition.[12] Critics complained that the shows produced in such a system were too homogeneous, unoriginal, or generic. However, as a result of a combination of cultural and industrial factors (discussed in greater detail later in this chapter), networks also dedicated themselves to presenting more documentary and news programs that were considered a form of public service broadcasting.

While certainly not booming, the business of color television sets was starting to show a profit during this period, as more manufacturers (twelve to be exact) entered the field.[13] Still, while 92 percent of U.S. households owned a television, not quite 10 percent had color television sets at the start of 1965, and that percentage increased only to around 35 to 40 percent by the end of the decade.[14] This slow but steady increase in the dissemination of color sets was likely helped along by the increasing quality and stability of color transmission and reception, and ease in tuning, which was much improved by mid-decade.[15] In addition, the color screen was larger (now available in twenty-three inches) and more nuanced in its presentation of hues. Jack Gould credited the use of new camera equipment from Phillips with improving television's color image, specifically by presenting "soothing pastel shades," a "marked reduction in the artificiality of color images," and the ability to remain stable and avoid loss of texture when switching from one camera to another. Noting that the "tones are beautifully subdued and enjoy a naturalness superior to perhaps anything previously seen on the home screen or in the theater," Gould suggested that this development "might even bring back the costumed dance number to TV," referencing the new ability to show color in detail without blurring and smudging.[16] That said, since CBS was the only network using the new Phillips camera, NBC and ABC appeared to be working with different color calibrations, which meant additional tuning headaches for viewers. "Owners of color television sets these days can hardly be called sedentary spectators," wrote Cynthia Lowry in the *Los Angeles Times*:

> Sometimes, it seems, we spend more time in deep knee bends adjusting the set than sitting back enjoying the show. It is obvious that the three networks have not gotten together to synchronize their palettes. On a Sunday night if one adjusts his set—as directed—to flesh tones on the suntanned face of Efrem Zimbalist Jr. on ABC's *The FBI* and switches over to CBS' *Ed Sullivan*, the latter often looks as if he were suffering from an advanced case of yellow jaundice. That requires some more emergency knob tuning.[17]

NBC remained the network color leader during the 1960s and was rewarded with high ratings and critical praise for its color program-

FIGURE 5.6 An image from *Bonanza* serves as the cover for the color TV special issue of *Radio-Electronics*, January 1966.

FIGURE 5.7 Screenshot of *Bonanza*, season 2, episode 1.

ming.[18] In fact, in the first few years of the decade, it was still the only network doing regular colorcasts. NBC's biggest ratings hit at the time, *Bonanza,* was credited by David Sarnoff and other NBC executives with single-handedly boosting color set sales.[19] Thomas Sarnoff, the youngest son of David and the producer of *Bonanza,* said in an interview, "Where *Matinee Theater* was the spark plug for color television, *Bonanza* really propelled color television forward."[20] NBC placed the Western in an early time slot for family viewing, but also so that it could be on in television showrooms when stores were still open. An article at the close of the decade looking back on the influence the show had on color sales went so far as to claim that, "if you bought a color set in those days it would be installed at 6:30 pm—in order that *Bonanza,* with its technically perfect color, could be used as the test show for proper tuning."[21]

NBC produced the series along with Paramount Studios, while RCA was its sponsor during its first couple of years on the air until Chevrolet took over that role. The family friendly Western dominated the ratings from soon after the show went on the air in 1959 until 1971, when it began to drop in popularity. There were many reasons given for *Bonanza*'s success, including "a star for every age group" and a portrayal of a deep bond between father and sons and of an especially resonant form of masculinity.[22] Yet what was most often repeated in the coverage of the program's success was the crafting of the color film image for television by Paramount studio crews, who brought their experience in working in color films to color television, and the lush outdoor scenes shot not just in backlots but also in a variety of ranch and forest sites throughout California, Nevada, and Arizona. Lake Tahoe, in particular, was singled out in reviews as one of the program's most lush and vivid vistas. A 1963 article in the *Los Angeles Times* profiled *Bonanza*'s on-set color consultant, Edward P. Aneona, as someone who, due to the colorful backdrop of West Coast nature, one might think holds "the easiest job in television," but who instead is shown to be an exacting manager of all elements of the mise-en-scène. Emphasizing the familiar refrain that "a little color goes a long way," Aneona described how, while the outdoor long shots tended to take care of themselves in terms of visual interest, it was the medium and close-up shots "that carry the load," so he and his team added pops of color on costumes and furnishings. "Among us, we come up with a colorful neckerchief for one man, a plaid shirt for another, even such a small thing as some blue Indian beads in the belt of a mountain man. . . . We don't go garish by any means. We must never step across the line of credibility."[23]

ABC, last in the ratings and the very network that lost Disney's anthology to NBC due to issues around color, only began colorcasting in the fall of 1963 with three regularly scheduled color prime-time programs, all animated: *The Jetsons*, *The Flintstones*, and *Beany and Cecil* (along with a few color documentary specials, which will be discussed later in this chapter). Animated color programs had the dual advantage of offering vibrant color while not having to conform to conventions of realism or fidelity. Animated color could be whatever it wanted to be. The vast majority of ABC's prime-time animated series—*Top Cat, Johnny Quest, The Jetsons,* and the highly successful *Flintstones*—were produced by one studio, Hanna-Barbera, which also produced an animated one-hour movie revival of *Alice in Wonderland* for the network in 1966 and a significant

number of Saturday morning cartoons distributed through syndication
to all three networks.

*The New Alice in Wonderland (or What's a Nice Kid Like You Doing in
a Place Like This?)* had an all-star cast, including Sammy Davis Jr. as
the Cheshire Cat and Zsa Zsa Gabor as the Queen of Hearts; a song-
book from the Broadway team Charles Sprouse and Lee Adams; and an
update to the plot and setting (a contemporary Alice falls not through a
mirror, but through the screen of her family's color television); but it was
ultimately a huge critical and ratings flop.

In the mid-1960s, CBS, under the leadership of president James Au-
brey (who helped the network dominate the ratings during the decade,
but whose programming formula of "broads, bosoms and fun" led to
criticisms of program quality) was still being referred to in the press as
a "color laggard."[24] The network continued an ambivalent relationship to
color until they announced that they would fully convert to color during
the 1966–1967 season, following ABC's and NBC's promises to do the

same.[25] However, in the years leading up to their conversion, CBS, at times, would pull almost all their color programs off the air. The season of 1961–1962 was especially notable in this regard, as the network made the inexplicable decision to air its annual broadcast of the Technicolor film *The Wizard of Oz* (MGM, 1939) in black and white instead of the usual color. Cecil Smith explained, "CBS officially gives the same line as ABC has—it will go into color when there are enough color sets to warrant the move. There are industry observers who feel, however, that there's a certain amount of intramural spite in the CBS attitude, that the network feels color gives aid and comfort to its arch enemy, NBC."[26]

When CBS did eventually return to color, network executives were selective in the types of programs that would be presented that way. For example, the bulk of the programs and films added to their color schedule in 1965 were part of the Thursday night lineup of Hollywood movies, were old-style variety shows (hosted by the likes of Red Skelton, Danny Kaye, and Ed Sullivan), or were part of CBS's successful lineup of rural comedies (*Green Acres*, *The Beverly Hillbillies*, *Petticoat Junction*, *Andy Griffith*, *Gomer Pyle*). Shows with a fantastical bent or kid appeal such as *My Favorite Martian* and *Gilligan's Island* were also aired in color for the first time that year.[27]

Fashion and graphic design were increasingly influential in the look of color television programming throughout the decade as mod style, with its strong lines and brilliant—even psychedelic—colors began to infiltrate both popular culture and everyday life. One might think of *Rowan and Martin's Laugh-In*, an NBC show airing in the late 1960s into the early 1970s, as the ultimate example of mod's influence on television, with its neon graphic "joke wall" and groovy psychedelic costumes (see figure 5.9).[28]

It was not just variety programs and the fantastical and animated that were used to push color in programming, however. Documentaries, the television genre most commonly associated with sobriety and public service, were employed in this way as well. For the rest of this chapter, I will examine the 1960s cultural documentary, a genre in which the form and function of color—especially related to the paradox of verisimilitude and the sensual fantastical—is in high relief, referenced endlessly by critics and network executives.

FIGURE 5.9 Screenshot from the 25th anniversary
episode of *Rowan and Martin's Laugh-in.*

COLOR CULTURAL DOCUMENTARIES

A number of scholars have labeled the early 1960s as the Golden Age
of television documentaries, attending to the style and engagement of
political documentaries of this period and how they were considered to
be a corrective to Newton Minow's famous criticism of television as a
"vast wasteland." As Michael Curtin has argued, these programs have to
be understood in relationship to a larger Cold War focus on educational
and cultural reform, global outreach, and interventionist U.S. foreign
policy—in other words, the major tenets of John F. Kennedy's New Frontier programs.[29] Curtin writes that in the early 1960s, "television was the
site where various groups struggled to transform popular images of the
United States and to position it as an active leader of the Free World. . . .
It was hoped that the medium would become an important site for the
production and circulation of images that would win the allegiances of
viewers around the globe to the community of the Free World."[30]

In contrast to these black and white documentaries, the art, nature,
and travel documentaries of the 1960s have received scant attention,
even though they represent a significant portion of the decade's docu-

mentary programming. (According to *Broadcasting* magazine, during the 1965–1966 season alone five hundred hours of travel and adventure documentaries were broadcast.)[31] They too engaged with the world beyond U.S. borders and sought to educate viewers; however, they also trafficked in sensation, pleasure, and the spectacular. Beyond any cultural or political value they might have had, these documentaries on art, nature, and travel, referred to at the time as cultural documentaries, filmed and broadcast in color, were considered to be one of the most successful genres at highlighting the full advantages of electronic color, as they brought together spectacle and vibrancy with a sense of cultural uplift and transportation (see table below). One critic argued in her review of a 1963 art documentary, *Art of Collecting*, that it should have been called the "art of showcasing color TV," and in his glowing review of *Van Gogh: A Self Portrait*, Gould remarked that the program "afforded color television one of its most exciting and lovely moments" and that "even for veteran viewers of color television, the union of the Dutch genius and the electronic age was like opening a new door on tomorrow's possible cultural vistas."[32]

By mid-decade, even local stations equipped for color production were producing color documentaries on local fashion, talent, area histories, and health and civic issues, which were directed to the specific needs and interests of their own communities and advertisers. Impressed by the breadth and volume of such local programming, *Broadcasting* dedicated seven pages of its 1967 special report on color to a story under the headline "Public Served Better through Color TV: Documentaries in Tint Have Broader Appeal Stations Discover."[33]

SELECTED LIST OF COLOR CULTURAL DOCUMENTARIES

1961 .... Japan: East Is West (NBC)

1962 .... Vincent Van Gogh: A Self Portrait (NBC)
The River Nile (NBC)
Shakespeare: Soul of an Age (NBC)
Jacqueline Kennedy's Asian Journey (NBC)

1963 .... The Art of Collecting (NBC)
Elizabeth Taylor in London (CBS)
A Look at Monaco with Princess Grace (CBS)

The Kremlin (NBC)

The Vatican (ABC)

The Saga of Western Man (ABC)

Greece: The Golden Age (NBC)

Wild Kingdom (NBC series)

1964 .... The Louvre, A Golden Prison (NBC)

Sophia Loren in Rome (ABC)

A Tour of Sweden with Inger Stevens (ABC)

Ganges: The Sacred River (NBC)

1965 .... A Visit to Washington with Mr. Lyndon B. Johnson on
Behalf of a More Beautiful America (ABC)

Michelangelo: The Last Giant (NBC)

National Geographic (CBS 1965–1969; series of one-hour
documentaries, starting with Americans on Everest, 1965)

1966 .... Legacy of Rome (ABC), part of The Saga of Western Man

The Royal Palaces of Britain (aired on NBC, produced by BBC)

1967 .... Gauguin in Tahiti (CBS)

I, Leonardo da Vinci (ABC, part of Summer Focus series)

Bravo Picasso! (NBC)

An American Image (NBC)

1969 .... Meet George Washington (NBC)

Many of the cultural documentaries produced at this time were cut from a similar generic and aesthetic cloth, as their creators were interested in crafting saturated landscapes of natural and artistic forms and placing them within educational narratives and historical frameworks. While a few of these productions were part of a series (such as those belonging to *The Saga of Western Man* series on ABC), most of them were one-off specials, moments of high investment public interest programming that would please regulators, bring attention to colorcasting, and allow high-end sponsors to test out their relationship to color. They were also part of television's move toward the global—both in terms of the networks' own desired expansion into foreign markets and in terms of the overall focus on internationalization in U.S. corporate culture. As Curtin has argued, "Prime-time documentary became an important television genre at the very moment that major US corporations were rapidly expanding their operations overseas. . . . Documentary not only pleased government regulators and public officials, but it also helped to make the case of US action to defend these expanding operations."[34] The rise of color programming corresponded with the expansion of global television and, in the case of the cultural documentaries, color expanded the U.S. audiences' horizons culturally and perceptually.

TRAVEL: THE ENDLESS HORIZON

Those cultural documentaries involving travel to or tourism within developed nations—as opposed to those based in the developing world, which tended to be categorized under "nature" or "adventure"—were intended to educate their audiences on the history and culture of countries interesting to Americans either due to their involvement in the discourse of current events or because of their presumed cultural heritage and/or status as centers of taste and tradition. Curtin has asserted that the (mostly black and white) political and social issue documentaries existed in stark contrast to the period's prime-time network entertainment programming, with sitcoms, variety shows, quiz shows, dramas, and the like. Arguing that these documentaries were pitched more toward critics, regulators, and highbrow elites and therefore did not contain the elements of viewer participation, identification, and pleasures of the popular (engagements with celebrity culture, consumerism, etc.), Curtin states that the network documentary "was the antithesis of popular entertainment, stripping away fantasy and facade in order to interrogate problems of the public sphere."[35] While this might have been the case for documentaries such as *Harvest of Shame* (CBS, 1960) or *Red China* (NBC, 1962), such a striking bifurcation did not exist in the color cultural documentaries of the 1960s. These works tended to contain an authoritative and instructional tone that hailed viewers as American citizens invested in their country's heritage, culture, and ideology as well as its position in a global context, while simultaneously offering them the pleasures of visual exploration, storytelling, and celebrity and consumer culture. They were aspirational documentaries that contained highbrow and educational markers and were also, more often than not, serving the purpose of selling and marketing everything from television sets to movie and television stars, the fashion industry, the international and domestic travel and tourism industries, and nations themselves.

FIGURE 5.10 Elizabeth Taylor on the set of *Elizabeth Taylor in London*.
AUTHOR'S PRIVATE COLLECTION.

FIGURE 5.11 Production still from *Sophia Loren in Rome*.
AUTHOR'S PRIVATE COLLECTION.

While the majority of these documentaries did not engage overtly with international politics, a handful of them lingered on the political or made ideological arguments (mostly those set in Eastern Bloc or Communist countries). The Emmy-winning documentary *The Kremlin* (NBC, 1963) is a great example of the latter; as cameras toured the Kremlin, the site was described as the "heart of a great atheistic power" and was used as a pivot point to discuss its political power and symbolism and to enter into subjective treatments of Soviet history, ideology, and culture. While Cold War politics obviously informed both the production and reception of the program, the focus on cultural heritage presumably provided audiences with the opportunity to act as virtual tourists, taking pleasure in the beautiful objects and images while learning more about the culture of a country that was shaping the global landscape and about America's relationship to it.

Another subset of these programs used celebrities as guides to the foreign countries in which they were born. Two documentaries made by the same production team (led by Phillip D'Antoni and Norman Baer) with soundtracks by the famous film composer John Barry, *Elizabeth Taylor in London* (CBS, 1963) and *Sophia Loren in Rome* (ABC, 1964), serve as examples of how consumer culture and educational rhetoric come together in these works as they promise to transport viewers to the glamorous world of international tourism and celebrity while providing lessons in history and cross-cultural exchange. Taylor was paid a record setting $500,000 to film for five weeks in London, and the resulting program, accompanied by much publicity, aired coast to coast on CBS. Yet, much to the chagrin of a number of critics, the program's producers seemed to envision the role of the star as a stylistic and emotional interpreter of London rather than a more traditional historical guide. Taylor was most often filmed walking or looking out upon various sites, dressed in clothing by high-end designers such as Yves Saint Laurent and with hair dressed by the famous stylist Alexandre de Paris as she recites the words of some of the city's most beloved poets, authors, and leaders. In one scene, she morosely reads the lines of Wordsworth's "Upon Westminster Bridge" over a montage of romantic shots of sunsets and cityscapes and the sound of Barry's sweeping soundtrack. Toward the end of her recitation, we find ourselves watching a glamorously coifed and made-up Taylor in close-up emoting as she looks over the city from what we eventually see is an exquisitely decorated terrace in the Dorchester Hotel penthouse suite. A reviewer for *Variety* remarked that "a pompous and so very very cultured" Taylor "got in the way of the cameras," seemingly in competition for attention with London.[36] Yet in the documentary, we see how it worked to engage the sensual perhaps more than the intellectual and how color enhanced the viewers' experience of the look and feel of the objects of luxury—including one of the period's most glamorous movie stars—before the camera (see figure 5.10).

While the Taylor documentary garnered mixed reviews, a similar formula featuring Sophia Loren was considered much more successful in balancing star power with the sights and sounds of a historic European city. Donned in "four different couture outfits from Marc Bohan's autumn Dior collection" over the course of the hour-long broadcast, Loren speaks directly into the camera, smoothly mixing her own biographical details in with the history of the city and Italian politics and culture (see figure 5.11). Gould praised the Loren documentary, claiming, "Rarely have glamour and reporting been so felicitously blended, although the show really had to be seen in color to be fully appreciated."[37]

The accentuating of fashion and celebrity was also very much a part of the anticipated appeal of the documentary *Jacqueline Kennedy's Journey to Asia* (NBC, 1962) on the first lady's inaugural trip to India—a seemingly ideal choice of a documentary locale if one were interested in displaying vibrant hues. However, a number of critics found it flat, dull, and visually stimulating only if a "viewer was lucky enough to have a color TV."[38] A color documentary featuring another first lady, Lady Bird Johnson, not only sought to tour Washington but was also made to promote her campaign to beautify America through gardens, parks, landscaping, and the preservation, renovation, and upkeep of public places in order to raise the psychological, spiritual, and even economic health of the country. *A Visit to Washington with Mrs. Lyndon B. Johnson on Behalf of a More Beautiful America* (ABC, 1965) proved to be a success at least in terms of the visual pleasure it provided viewers, and it was eventually rebroadcast on Easter day. "An enchanting interlude of serenity that healed and refreshed the spirit," proclaimed Gould in his review for the *New York Times*.[39]

The use of documentary to sell the idea of television and its capabilities along with specific notions of cultural heritage, knowledge, and experience was certainly not an altogether new idea in the 1960s. Black and white documentary series of the 1950s, such as *Wide Wide World* (NBC) and *Wisdom* (also NBC), while not maintaining as much of a global focus, promised to bring the world into the home of Americans and to educate them as citizens of culture, history, and art. Although sometimes showing segments filmed abroad, *Wide Wide World* most often focused on American locales and institutions, broadcasting live from a number of different locations at once, as in the case of "Portrait of an American Winter," an episode aired in January 1956, which included a collection of idyllic scenes from Niagara Falls; Burlington, Vermont; Palm Beach; and Milwaukee. The series also brought viewers inside various museums and cultural institutions and sites. Lisa Parks has pointed out that this combination of "travel with a focus on art and culture" answered the call of both the network's public interest mandate and Pat Weaver's desire to combine visual spectacle with intellectually challenging programming. Parks writes, "As a medium of immediacy and mobility (not just physical but cultural), television trespasses into the domains of high culture, granting furtive glimpses into events and practices that are otherwise inaccessible to most."[40]

Further evidence of an early interest in marshaling the documentary form for the project of meeting public interest mandates *and* for the selling of color can be found in a 1954 proposal that Davison Taylor and NBC producer Robert Graff put together for a half-hour documentary anthology series, tentatively titled *Kaleidoscope*, wherein color was "the vital factor, so that if you don't see the show in color, you feel cheated."[41] The proposed episodes would center on everything from movement and exploration ("Airport Control Tower" would use a "camera acting as a passenger" through the entire process of entering the airport through taking off on the runway, and "Underwater Rainbow" would take a color camera underwater in an aquarium filled with colorful fish) to coverage of the work of particular artists (such as Salvador Dali and fashion designers like Christian Dior) and trips to various museums of natural history and art. It also promised to include an episode on "experimental short color films," including abstract, avant-garde, and representational works, and to "tell the story of the birth of Jesus through paintings at the National Gallery" in its premiere episode, airing right before Christmas. While this program never made it on the air in this form, the proposal reads like a series made up of all the various subgenres of color cultural documentaries that the networks would produce during the early 1960s.

In using these documentaries to highlight color technology, the networks were selling an idea about color vision and its connection to expanding cultural, visual, and political horizons, while also emphasizing the sensual pleasures of travel, design, and consumption. And it is here—in the appeal to the sensual and educational—that we may find a connection to early cinema, wherein travelogues, or "scenics," as they were referred to in the press, were used to present content meant to please middle-class sensibilities while also evoking an experiential, exploratory, or contemplative experience for the viewer. As Jennifer Lynn Petersen argues, as a subgenre of the actuality, travelogues of the early twentieth century appeared to be "almost as fascinated with the technology of motion pictures as the places they documented,"[42] following a "logic of collection [of images or isolated scenes] rather than that of narrative progression"[43] and capturing views of the world unique to the moving image, thereby, Petersen asserts, creating a "dream world of cinematic geography."[44] Of course, the color travel films of 1960s television were not as non-narrative as the silent film travelogues Petersen describes, and they were very much a product of the Jet Age; however, both the silent travelogues and the color travel documentaries occur at a point in which the interaction with and display of a new media technology is a component both of the content and of the viewer's experience and expectation. It is also the case that the camera in the color travel documentaries of the 1960s would linger on the scenic more than other televisual forms did. In fact, a *Variety* reviewer criticized *Ganges: The Sacred River* (NBC, 1964) for avoiding politics and culture and instead focusing too much on the crafting of "pretty pictures," even going as far as to claim, "This documentary had the reminiscent quality of a pre–World War II travelogue in its pursuit of the picturesque—the repeated shots of the bathers, the funeral pyres for the dead along the Ganges shores, the Buddhist icons, the long shot of the Taj Mahal, etc."[45] However, presenting "pretty pictures" is precisely what networks and the shows' creators were hoping to do with these color documentaries. They had selected topics that encouraged attentive engagement with the image on the screen, thereby potentially fostering an appreciation for how color alters the experience of viewing and offering new avenues of knowledge.

ART: THE LEARNED EYE

During the years of actively promoting color television, RCA/NBC executives carefully considered which types of programming would stress the usefulness, effectiveness, or pleasure of color for viewers/consumers. Earlier in the 1950s, colorcasts of various sporting events were thought to be a productive and marketable use of the technology because under ideal conditions color would help viewers more readily differentiate between team uniforms, see important marks on the field, and effectively track the movement of the ball or players (and thereby demonstrate a *need* for color). Similarly, color television was widely perceived as a boon to medical education because it provided students with close-up views of live surgeries and other medical procedures, while also representing the colors on and in the body that are essential to the proper identification of healthy organs and to differentiate them from those that might be diseased or malfunctioning. And consumer research studies claimed that color viewing entailed particular modalities that engaged specific components of an audience's emotions, psyche, vision, pleasure, and desire, making them more attentive, engaged, creative, focused, and open consumers/viewers. The use and promotion of many of the cultural documentaries reveal comparable claims regarding electronic color's ability to intensify the pleasure already offered by monochrome television; expand the visual and experiential horizons of viewers through explorations of the natural world; and extend and refine television's technological vision, thereby bringing previously under- or unexplored subjects, objects, and knowledge into clear relief. Color art documentaries in particular were thought to bring these abilities to the fore for audiences, positioning color as a necessity, and were therefore utilized in the years immediately preceding full conversion.

It is important to note that NBC's earliest *nationwide* colorcast was, in fact, an art documentary. *A Visit to the Metropolitan Museum of Art* (1954) was a virtual tour hosted by the museum's director, Francis Henry Taylor.[46] In reviews of the live broadcast from the Met, critics remarked that art was one of the few subjects on television that not only benefited from color but *required* it. Calling it a historic broadcast, the reviewer for *Variety* concluded that "McCarthy vs. the Army won't look any better in spectrum, but Van Gogh's landscapes and a Cezanne still life are something else again."[47] Lynn Spigel, whose research has revealed a long-standing relationship between the leadership of CBS and NBC and New York art culture, also notes that Alfred Barr, the founding director of MoMA, appeared on a color segment of *Home* the following year discussing artists such as Kandinsky and Chagall and their use of color.[48] And in 1967, NBC presented *An American Image*, an hour-long documentary linking American history and landscape to the opening exhibition of the Whitney Museum's new building, "Art of the United States, 1670–1966."[49] Speaking directly to the relationship between the museum and his network's color objectives, Robert Sarnoff, in a 1965 speech to the Friends of the Whitney that was held in the NBC color studio in Rockefeller Center, was said to have predicted, "The museum of the near future is the museum without walls, an open house of treasure that will be brought into millions of homes by color television. . . . Color television is enjoying a fantastic boom. So is art. Both are interrelated."

Sarnoff added that this relationship would be "some small answer to a growing and soon desperate need for our society—the creative use of leisure by a free and educated people."[50] Thirty-five years earlier, his father, David, in an article in the *New York Times*, had suggested the possibility that the growth in art appreciation could connect to the future spread of color television, proclaiming that color broadcasting could eventually make every home an art gallery, extending the "cultural influence" of institutions such as the Louvre and the Metropolitan to millions. In a 1934 address before the college of fine arts at New York University, he reasserted this idea: "If we let our imaginations plunge ahead, we may also dream of television in faithful colors. I believe that dream will come true one day. . . . We may then be shown reproductions of art treasures . . . and have them interpreted to us as we sit by our firesides and see the through the air. A new art appreciation will thus be awakened."[51] These statements by the elder Sarnoff can certainly be understood as an attempt to position broadcasting alongside more high culture pursuits and interests, thereby hopefully quieting criticisms and concerns regarding a network's public interest responsibilities. However, it is also interesting to recognize how monochrome television is skipped over in these moments, as though it is assumed that art can only be represented and appreciated in color. Rarely were such statements made about the absolute centrality of color to the legibility of other forms of televised art, such as theater and musical performances. From the earliest moments of color television's conceptualization, one of its unique strengths was the representation of visual art forms such as painting, sculpture, and design.

Critic Walt Dutton of the *Los Angeles Times* wrote in a 1967 review, "Color television has traveled an astonishing distance—qualitatively as well as geographically—since the early 1950s when people were green and it was difficult to tell where the grass stopped and the sky began. *Bravo Picasso*, Sunday night on NBC, attested to the media's advancement. . . . The telecast was a marvel, flawless save for a momentary loss of color phase whenever cutting to or from the satellite feed."[52] The vast majority of the reviews of color art documentaries emphasized the central role that color played not only in presenting a beautiful image but also in assisting such an image to be completely legible (when compared to monochrome) to the viewer interested in learning more about the craft, meaning, and history of art. In other words, the most common address of these programs was one that was educational and informational, specifically encouraging the development of a tasteful and learned eye in the viewer interested in acquiring the skill of art appreciation. Gould's review of NBC's *Meet George Washington* (1969) encapsulated just this argument: "Color was the searching device that brought out the details of Washington's face and of the scenes of war and politics in which he was the dominant figure. Mr. Hyatt was able to extract from the pictures the kind of vigor, motion, and emotion that painters had tried to put in those pictures. A black and white representation could not have revealed all that the color camera saw."[53] And Barbara Delatiner, critic for *Newsday,* wrote about *The Art of Collecting* (NBC, 1964), "The documentary seen in black and white was like walking through a museum with blinders and sunglasses, but once the tints were tuned in, it was a stunning, beautiful hour."[54]

Even while the use of color in these documentaries was intensifying and clarifying the experience of viewing art on television, the creators could sometimes (perhaps predictably) dip into some heavy-handed visual and oral rhetoric, hanging an artist's works onto grand narratives of American progress and the "great men" of history. The voiceover is the most obvious tool for the creation of these narratives, but the camerawork and editing also worked to train the viewer to see the pieces as part of a tradition or expression of an individual psyche or set of social conditions. The director of *Michelangelo: The Last Giant* (NBC, 1967), likely in an attempt to make a documentary consisting primarily of images of still paintings and sculptures more interesting, crafted a sense of movement through camerawork and editing, which to some critics read as further evidence of an artistic cultural production, while others complained that it obstructed their view of the works and didn't allow them to linger long enough on each image. Delatiner, for example, beseeched, "Really, did the camera have to waver and tilt to prove that the Bacchus is a young man satiate with drink? A few seconds of focusing on the statue's face would have sufficed. . . . Time after time, the documentarian's excesses, their refusal to leave anything to a viewer's imagination, interfered, jarring us and making us want to cry: 'Stop the fooling around and just show the sculpture.'"[55] William Wilson, writing for the *Los Angeles Times,* put it more gently: "Priestly's quick-shift angles and high contrast lighting are undoubtedly good cinema but never was a lily less in need of gilding."[56] Many critics praised the program though, specifically the skill and artistry of producer and writer Lou Ha-zam, who also directed NBC's *Vincent Van Gogh: A Self Portrait* (1962), *Shakespeare: Soul of an Age* (1962), and *The Golden Age of Greece* (1963). Lawrence Laurent of the *Washington Post* wrote, "*Michelangelo: The Last Giant* just might very well be the finest cultural documentary program ever presented on television. Most of the viewers, however, won't be truly aware of its great merit until they see this program in color."[57] Along the same lines, the *Boston Globe*'s critic suggested, "It is quite safe to say that there has seldom, if ever, been such a feast for the eye on television."[58]

Lucy Jarvis, producer of *The Kremlin*, received permission from the French ministry of culture and the department of French national museum to "turn the Louvre into one vast TV studio" for the filming of *The Golden Prison: The Louvre* (NBC, 1964).[59] Because the film was intended to engage not only with the artwork but also with the Louvre as an architectural space (numerous shots were done with dollies, which were moved through the various halls while pointed at the art on the walls) and as a cultural institution (with shots and stills of important moments in the history, upkeep, and management of the museum), the program was criticized by some for not lingering on the paintings long enough, for packing in too much historical detail, and/or for being too short overall.[60] The critical reception of these documentaries reveals, among other things, that their creators were expected to reconstruct an idyllic contemplative experience of an individual's encounter with art in a museum setting while also providing the information viewers needed to fully understand the works' creation, context, and meaning. Unlike museum guides or docents, who would be able to alter the rhythm and pace of when and how they delivered this information to a museumgoer, the camerawork and editing in these productions steered the attention of viewers, requiring them to keep up with the pacing demanded by the generic conventions of the television documentary. The networks' promotion of color television emphasized the technology's ability to bring viewers the experience of immersing themselves in a vibrant world, and while cultural documentaries were a good form in which to display those capabilities, the programs' own artistic and educational objectives were sometimes also considered to be impediments to a viewer's full immersion.

In terms of the art contained in color specials, the vast majority of works presented were in the form of paintings, sculptures, and architecture. Perhaps unsurprisingly, photography was not a central component of these productions. There are a number of explanations for this. For one, very few mainstream museums in the 1950s and '60s had fine art photography on display in general (MoMA being an obvious exception).[61] Color photography, which would have been a fitting subject for these art documentaries, was even more rare, as fine art photography had a highly vexed relationship with the use of color film.

While color in painting was, of course, assumed to play a major role in the collection of any one museum, it was particularly emphasized as a strong formal element in the contemporary movements of pop art (with works by Roy Lichtenstein and Andy Warhol, for example) and abstract expressionism, most significantly in the work of the color-field artists (such as Frank Stella, Mark Rothko, and Gene Davis), which often presented brash, undiluted forms of color in large swaths that confronted the viewer in new ways. These specific movements—especially pop art—also influenced and were influenced by mass media, product design, and consumer culture, which resonated with the palette and uses of color that most Americans would already have been surrounded by in daily life. Americans at this time would have also had regular encounters with color photography, of course, in print magazines, ads, billboards, and the like. However, the use of color in *fine art* photography was another matter.

While the Lumière brothers brought the first commercially available color photo process (Autochrome) to the market in 1907, Kodachrome and Kodak Ektachrome, developed in the 1940s, made color photography less cumbersome; and by 1955, when Kodak was forced to uncouple their (rather inflated) color processing charges from the purchasing of film, color photography became cheaper and therefore more accessible and prevalent. However, ideas about the troublesome nature of color and its purported excessive and vulgar tendencies shaped the status of color art photography well into the 1970s, with many artists and critics claiming that color belonged to the world of advertising and amateur photography, while black and white was considered less literal, more high minded and serious, and offering more artistic control.

FIGURE 5.12 Roman Vishniac, "Estrogen," 1950–1970.
© MARA VISHNIAC KOHN, COURTESY INTERNATIONAL CENTER OF PHOTOGRAPHY.

FIGURE 5.13 William A. Garnett, "Sandbars, Cape Cod, Massachusetts," Cibachrome print, 1966. J. PAUL GETTY MUSEUM, LOS ANGELES. ESTATE OF WILLIAM A. GARNETT.

FIGURE 5.14 "New York," Helen Levitt, 1959. MOMA COLLECTION,
WITH PERMISSION FROM THE FAMILY OF HELEN LEVITT.

The turning point is generally thought to be Stephen Shore's color prints, which were the focus of his solo show for the Met in 1971, and the work of William Eggleston, often credited with bringing an increased level of visibility and prestige to color art photography, who was the first to have a solo exhibit of color prints at MoMA in 1976. Yet photographers such as Paul Outerbridge (who worked both in art and in advertising and commercial photography), Ernst Haas (who brought together photojournalism and art), and Eliot Porter (a prominent nature photographer) produced quality color work that had been recognized by the art community and presented in museum and gallery settings prior to that of Eggleston.

Almost forty years before Eggleston's solo show, MoMA displayed color work in group photography exhibitions such as the one in the spring of 1937, with over eight hundred items, which took up four floors of the museum and included examples of color art photography and a section devoted to the medium's history. In March 1963, the museum hosted Three Photographers in Color, which consisted of slides and talks by three significant color photographers: William Garnett, Helen Levitt, and Roman Vishniac. These particular photographers represented familiar genres of color photography during this period, including nature, street photography, and abstraction. Their work also shared qualities and forms of address with the color television documentaries of the 1960s. Beyond the connection in subject matter—documenting the city, nature, medicine, and the body—the MoMA color photography show and color television relied on similar tropes and beliefs about color, technology, representation, and vision. In Levitt's images, we find color acting as a point of contrast and direction, used with restraint as a way to enliven certain areas or objects within the image, to direct the eye while not detracting from the work's realism. It was a technique of guiding attention that was present in color television in multiple forms but was also an essential part of the color documentary of the 1960s. Levitt was the street photographer whose black and white images of poor and working class neighborhoods in New York City garnered her so much acclaim that in 1959 she was awarded a Guggenheim fellowship, which she used to try her hand at color. The resulting photos were consistent with her already established style but now showed pops of color against gray concrete—for example, bold colors found in graffiti, a lime colored car, fire engine red gumball machines in front of concrete, or a girl's bright pink plastic jump rope.

The photos that Vishniac had on display were of a very different scale from Levitt's images, as they were from his experiments in microphotography. Most well known at the time for his photos of Jewish ghettos during Hitler's rise and reign, Vishniac's interests turned to the "sub-visible" and the merging of art and science, and he began to use color photomicroscopy to capture images of life that exists beyond the capabilities of human vision. These microscopic investigations resulted in images of things such as skin, riboflavin, estrogen, and pancreatic hormones, which resembled lush and layered color landscapes. While Vishniac's work did not make it onto television in the 1960s, the short films he made under the microscope were distributed in educational movies throughout the 1950s and '60s. And even more relevant to the history of color television, his still and moving images serve as an example of the way that color technologies promised a new form of advanced vision that was both praised for its ability to transport viewers to and enmesh them in another natural world or experience while also embodying some of the questions about color's ability to effectively convey realism, rationality, or sobriety. The work of nature photographers of the period such as Garrett and Porter also attests to the often contradictory assumptions about the capabilities of color technology and its relation to the art world. While Vishniac's goal was to reveal the small and unseen, Garrett's aerial camera was focused on the view that could be seen by the human eye but that rarely was. Although originally working in black and white, his photos in Kodachrome revealed patterns and shapes that brought to mind the paintings of abstract expressionists and could often look similar to Vishniac's microscopic landscapes. Porter, working primarily on the ground, was one of the most famous nature and landscape photographers of the twentieth century. Not only was his work hung on museum walls but it also appeared in magazines and books—the most influential being his first, *In Wildness Is the Preservation of the World*, published by Sierra Club Books in 1962, in which each of Porter's images was accompanied by a short piece of writing by Henry David Thoreau. This book, which sold over a million copies, popularized color landscape photography and inspired the Sierra Club to launch a series of nature photography books with a preservationist bent. Porter's imagery resonated with the color nature photography that had entered into the popular imagination through the *National Geographic* magazine, which in the mid-1960s worked with CBS to bring its style and imagery to moving images, with a color television series for families that would be only one of a number of nature documentary programs in color during this period.

NATURE: THE HIDDEN WORLD

Color nature or wildlife series, such as Mutual of Omaha's *Wild Kingdom* (NBC, 1963–1971), *National Geographic* specials (CBS, 1965–1969), *The World of Jacques Cousteau* (CBS, 1966–1968), and later, *The Undersea World of Jacques Cousteau* (ABC, 1968–1975), were in many ways extensions of popular nature photography and arguably connected to the work of color art photographers of the period like Garrett and Vishniac. The programs were also yet another iteration of the promise of color television to extend the eye through technology to places around the globe, under water, into bodies, through a microscope, and eventually into space, reveling in views that had been previously hidden or out of reach.

1965–1966 SEASON

"Americans on Everest" 9/10/1965
"Miss Goodall and the Wild Chimpanzees" 12/22/1965
"Voyage of the Brigantine Yankee" 2/11/1966
"The World of Jacques-Yves Cousteau" 4/28/1966

1966–1967 SEASON

"Dr. Leakey and the Dawn of Man" 11/05/1966
"The Hidden World of Insects" 12/13/1966
"Alaska!" 2/07/1967
"Yankee Sails across Europe" 4/08/1967

1967–1968 SEASON

"Grizzly!" 11/01/1967
"Winged World" 12/11/1967
"Amazon" 2/20/1968
"The Lonely Dorymen" 4/16/1968

1968–1969 SEASON

"America's Wonderlands: The National Parks" 10/23/1968
"Reptiles and Amphibians" 12/03/1968
"Australia: The Timeless Land" 2/18/1969
"Polynesian Adventure" 4/15/1969

1969–1970 SEASON

"The Mystery of Animal Behavior" 10/14/1969
"Siberia: The Endless Horizon" 12/02/1969
"Wild River" 2/10/1970
"Holland Against the Sea" 4/14/1970

In looking at the list of *National Geographic* specials from 1965 to 1970, a number of things stand out: an emphasis on a mix of science and adventure; the assumed American perspective on the world; a clear notion of empire; domination of natural resources; a fascination with sparsely populated, geographically unique, far-flung locales (Australia, Siberia, Alaska, Everest, the Amazon); and a repeated articulation of access to broadly defined, seemingly unified natural domains (the sea, rivers, and mountains; the life systems and social worlds of insects, mammals, reptiles, and birds; etc.). While these themes certainly resonate with the other visual materials produced by the National Geographic Society, they also stress the "endless horizon" that color television technology was thought to afford. Critics were most impressed by both the expansiveness and the detail captured by color cameras on such expeditions, along with the technological finesse and equipment modifications that enabled the crew to capture moving images of hippos traveling underwater on riverbeds, humans scaling Everest, and close-ups of birds flying midair. (This process is similar to the way that contemporary IMAX films also construct an immersive experience through nature films.)

Technological finesse was part of the expertise on display in nature documentaries and accentuated the idea that these programs, when coupled with the new technology of color television, were advancing and augmenting vision in ways that were distinct from monochrome television. Wildlife filmmakers were often put in the position of coming up with their own work-arounds to the challenges of filming in extreme micro and macro scale. One such filmmaker, Gerald Thompson—a British nature documentarian whose films were distributed in the United States by National Geographic—found that, for example, capturing insects on color film presented two major logistical issues: (1) in magnifying the picture, you would also magnify vibrations; and (2) the amount of light required by color film could generate so much heat as to either injure or change the behavior of the insects being filmed. Thompson recalls that the production team on Disney's 1951 True-Life Adventures film *Nature's Half Acres* had chosen relatively large insects—caterpillars and praying mantises—that were more easily captured on screen without special equipment; however, they did not consistently control for the heat from the lights, and therefore, Thompson claims, the caterpillars

FIGURES 5.15 AND 5.16 Screenshots from National Geographic's "Miss Goodall and the Wild Chimpanzees" (CBS, 1965).

on screen were seen "writhing in their death throes because they were being cooked by the lights."[62]

Instead of the predominately first world places and objects explored in the travel and art documentaries discussed earlier in this chapter, these nature programs would center on the flora, fauna, people, and nations deemed "exotic" to the vast majority of American viewers, which meant, more often than not, the landscapes and inhabitants of the developing world. As Cynthia Chris and others have pointed out, many of the nature documentaries of this period (National Geographic's in particular) were, to varying degrees, "sites in which ideologies of post-colonial dependence, race, gender, nature, and science are represented and reinforced."[63] They were also opportunities for program producers to represent and encourage visual and scientific exploration in the television audience. The National Geographic specials were packaged as middlebrow armchair explorations of the beautiful yet "untamed' and "uncivilized" natural world through the eyes of explorers, expeditionists, anthropologists, archeologists, geographers, entomologists, zoologists, and oceanographers. National Geographic's move to television was due in large part to the organization's own investment in and branding around color photography. As a writer for *Broadcasting* explained, "Color is the catalyst that moved the National Geographic Society into television, putting its reputation on the line and proving that patience and perfection in production detail need not equal dullness in a documentary type series. Audiences have agreed. Color may be nature's medium. But it's the salesman's too, whether he be educator, publisher, insurance man, or candlestick maker."[64]

National Geographic magazine, originally established in 1888 as a journal of amateur science, expanded its reach and circulation as its editorial focus shifted into an accessible blend of science and popular entertainment directed at the culturally aspirational middle-class magazine reader of the early twentieth century.[65] The increased space given to photography in the magazine was key to developing its reach and popularity. Its regular use of color photographs, almost exclusively taken with Kodachrome film until 2009, began in the late 1930s and served to both solidify its reliance on the visual and result in a branding of the publication in relationship to a specific type of photo-essay—one that had some similarities to those that might be found in other photo-heavy magazines, such as *Life* and *Look*, but that also maintained its own unique and consistent form, content, and address. Catherine A. Lutz and Jane L. Collins contend that the use of color altered the nature of the magazine's approach to the acquisition and presentation of images, as its photographers began to select subjects on the basis of how vibrant they were, even altering the dress of indigenous people in order to get a more striking color shot.[66] This practice of *National Geographic*'s photographers—which came to be referred to as "the red shirt school of photography," since red was the favorite color for clothes on subjects, as it came out the best on Kodachrome—only added to the reputation of color photography as frivolous, especially when it was contrasted to photojournalism, a field in which color photography did not gain wide acceptance for editorial purposes until the mid-1960s.[67] Lutz and Collins argue that, in addition to the cultural and historical connections to the expos, midways, and world's fairs of the late nineteenth and early twentieth centuries that led *National Geographic* to be "a key actor in presenting 'primitive' people for Western perusal,"[68] the "use of color photography also highlighted the magazine's similarity to museum exhibits—with their highly framed, aestheticized tidbits of traditional culture—rather than to starker news reportage or scientific documentation."[69]

While the televised images produced by National Geographic would not be limited to the "highly framed" aestheticization that defined the photography of the magazine, the society intended the color specials to be moving-image versions of their magazine. And yet the specials also maintained a relationship to another National Geographic product: the films the society produced for classroom and library use. Only a few years before the first National Geographic television special, the society had formed an educational film division, which produced and distributed 16 mm films primarily on scientific and social-scientific topics, as well as some in the humanities. The look and content of these films certainly influenced the form and subject matter of the television specials, even though the specials relied more heavily on spectacle and pleasure. The repurposing of films broadcast on television for classroom use was a practice that had been borrowed from educational film (starting in the 1930s) and was employed by such companies as Disney, who repackaged portions of their True-Life Adventures films into educational shorts, and AT&T, which produced Bell Laboratory Science Series (1956–1964), a collection of hour-long color science films presented as specials first on CBS and then on NBC that were later made available to rent for classroom use. Due in large part to the relationship the two companies had developed through their educational film divisions, one of the major sponsors of the National Geographic series was Encyclopedia Britannica, a company that had by the mid-1940s established a successful educational film arm, producing hundreds of black and white and color educational films (including some now famous ones by Vishniac). Encyclopedia Britannica's owner, William Benton, had grown interested in distributing off-network documentaries (not just those on nature, but also color documentaries such as *The Kremlin*), and they had already sponsored a color children's series, NBC's *Exploring*, on Saturday mornings in 1963, the same year that one of their competitors, World Book (of the *Encyclopedia*), had also begun sponsoring a color nature show directed at family audiences—*Wild Kingdom*.

There were a number of syndicated local, and network nature and animal programs aired in the 1950s in black and white. Some of these programs were nature expedition programs, and others focused solely on animals in what Chris describes as a "show-and-tell format."[70] An example of the latter is *The Zoo Parade* (NBC, 1950–1957), which started as a local show on WNBQ, and was hosted by Marlin Perkins, a conservationist, zoologist, and director of the Lincoln Park Zoo and, later, the Saint Louis Zoological Park. The show also aired in color on the network soon after WNBQ's conversion. Perkins would go on to host *Wild Kingdom*, a half-hour Sunday night family program that combined studio based show-and-tell segments with location footage of the natural habitats of the animals being featured (see figures 5.17 and 5.18). In her history of wildlife documentaries of this period, Chris acknowledges that, while early animal and pet programs, like *The Zoo Parade*, focused on close-up inspections of animals on tabletops in studios and zoos, the wildlife documentaries of the early 1960s utilized many of the filmmaking techniques seen in the theatrical expedition films of the 1920s. While National Geographic programs were hour-long occasional specials, *Wild Kingdom* was a weekly half-hour series. However, as Chris argues, the "organizing principle" for both programs was "a quest—for a particular animal, and for observations about it from which knowledge could be produced—undertaken by an intrepid naturalist-host, like Cousteau or Perkins."[71] Chris doesn't address, however, how crucial color film and television technology were to that aesthetic transition or how showing off color was often one of the primary stated reasons behind such a program's conception and support.

Color film equipment and other forms of technological innovation arguably played the biggest role (or at least received the most press attention) in the Jacques Cousteau documentaries, which were also sponsored by National Geographic and Encyclopedia Britannica. David C. Wolper, producer of Cousteau's ABC series specials along with National Geographic's "The Hidden World" episode (CBS, 1965)—a presentation of the microcosmic world of insects—recalls that it was the way the

FIGURES 5.17 AND 5.18 Screenshots from *Wild Kingdom*,
with Marlin Perkins as host.

Cousteau National Geographic specials looked that initially drew him in. Wolper recalled having said to his wife while watching one of the programs for the first time, "On the TV set, the fish look like they're in a fishbowl. . . . This is beautiful." He called Cousteau shortly thereafter to see if they could work together.[72]

While starting out as special presentations of *National Geographic* (CBS), the adventures of Cousteau and his crew would eventually spin off into a separate series: *The Undersea World of Jacques Cousteau* (ABC, 1968–1975). *Undersea World* was produced jointly by Cousteau's own production company and Wolper. Cousteau had become a well-known figure through his best-selling book, *A Silent World,* and Academy Award–winning 1953 documentary of the same name (directed with Louis Malle), which had for the first time brought color film cameras to the depths of the ocean. He was also known as a technological innovator, having invented the Aqua-Lung, a diving saucer, and a vehicle that could travel 350 meters underwater, and designed cameras and modified film for underwater expeditions. Cousteau put a portion of the $3.5 million given to him and his team by ABC and Wolper for a minimum of twelve one-hour programs toward the creation of one-man jet-propelled subs outfitted with hydraulic claws, sounding gear, and radio equipment. Two remote-controlled color cameras and a set of floodlights were also mounted on each sub and multiple 16 mm cameras, packed into specially made torpedo shaped cases, were held by divers and added to "sleds called troikas which can film as much as 15,000 feet down."[73]

All of this technology enabled the team to, as the show put it, "explore man's last frontier," and to follow Cousteau's oft-quoted motto, *"Il faut aller voir"* (roughly, "We have no choice but to go and see"), capturing images of sweeping sea horizons as well as extreme close-up examinations of sea life. In the opening of most episodes of the series, the audience is introduced to a phenomenon (often a rare one) for the team to investigate, such as the mass mating and procreative cycle of squid off the California coast. Much of the narration (both by Cousteau and by the off-screen voice of Rod Serling, in the series, or Orson Welles, in the specials) position the team's work as scientific observation and documentation and yet, as Alexander Wilson argues, "Cousteau spends a large part of the edited programs on what can loosely be called sightseeing: boating, diving, and underwater photography," in a format of "travelogue cum scientific documentary."[74] At the time of the program's airing, a number of reviewers remarked on the way it immersed viewers in two hidden worlds—life under the sea and daily life on the boat as part of a French crew of divers, oceanographers, technicians, cinematographers, and seaman. Yet the crew was positioned not only as experts and adventurers but also occasionally as naive subjects, as witnessed in Cousteau's description of entering the "coral jungle": "Our first dive in a world so physically striking overwhelms our senses. We are no more explorers than children in a store filled with surprises."[75]

In these underwater documentaries, once again color television alternately overwhelms the senses and enhances and refines vision, bestowing upon viewers the feeling that they too have traveled to a world previously hidden to them, to become adventurers and to see for themselves a world beyond their reach. This sense is enhanced by Serling's narration, as his voice had become synonymous with introductions to the fictional sci-fi worlds of *The Twilight Zone*. In the rhetoric around *Undersea World* and the actions and interests of Cousteau, we can also find an analogous relationship to adventures in another "hidden world" that color television would eventually document and that was very much in the headlines during this period—space exploration. This might be most clearly seen in the 1966 National Geographic CBS special produced by Wolper and narrated by Orson Welles, "The World of Jacques-Yves Cousteau," which followed Cousteau and his "oceanauts" in their deep-sea adventures in underwater living on the *Conshelf III* (continental shelf station), a module he helped design that enabled divers to stay at depths of up to thirty meters for weeks at a time. The special was accompanied by a cover story and multi-page spread in the *National Geographic* magazine in which Cousteau describes the technology and planning behind the *Conshelf* adventure (see figure 5.19). In the relatively mixed reviews of the special, critics found the focus on the lab setting fairly dull compared to Cousteau's previous underwater documentaries, but they remarked on the technical difficulty of filming underwater at such depths and praised the color images that resulted. "Viewers of the forthcoming video special called 'The World of Jacques-Yves Cousteau' will see what is probably the toughest set a cameraman ever tried to light," wrote Jack Gaver for the *Washington Post*. "There were no guidebooks for film at such depths. No one had done it before." Philippe Cousteau, Jacques's son, went on to detail for Gaver the factors that made filming so challenging: no light at the depths of three hundred feet below sea level; a storm at sea level that

FIGURE 5.19 From "Working for Weeks on the Sea Floor," *National Geographic* magazine, April 1966, which served to advertise an upcoming special.

had muddied the waters; the dampness, which would clog the camera; and that the "extra-high-powered lights needed to film indoors made the house unbearably hot within a few minutes."[76]

At the time, Cousteau claimed that the experiment in underwater living that the *Conshelf* expeditions represented were only the beginning and that he believed there was a real future for humanity under the sea. As the *Washington Post* reported, "Since the beginning, [Cousteau] has envisioned fish ranches and under ocean food farms. Now he is thinking about underwater communities, floating artificial islands, and airports. He talks of underwater parking lots and even highways."[77] The training involved and the tracking of the divers' biological processes while under such conditions provided potential models for NASA astronaut training, but the program itself fascinated an audience that was already caught up in the extraordinary and practical meanings of that decade's space race. The modifications to lighting and camera technology that were a part of the televisual presentation of the underwater work also bore striking similarities to the NASA research and experimentation that would occur only a couple of years later.

Cousteau's programs brought color television viewers deep underwater to explore a world unknown to them in a more extreme way than most other cultural documentaries of the time. However, the majority of the programs in this genre, whether centering on travel, art, or nature, were also engaged, at some level, in extending and expanding vision and experience through color. They blended markers of realism with the spectacular, allowing the technology of color television to be read as more immersive, experiential, and even emotional than its monochrome counterpart. In the next chapter, we will see the way this extended, immersive vision expanded even further into a global context with live satellite television, and also through color television's use in the later *Apollo* missions, as that vision accessed the earth's natural satellite—the moon. Chapter 6 will also track how the discourses constructing electronic color's extended immersive view intersected with larger Cold War strategies and ideologies having to do with surveillance, truth-telling, and scientific and technological competition between the United States and the Soviet Union.

CHAPTER SIX

At the End of the Rainbow

Global Expansion, the Space Race, and the Cold War

Surrounded by reporters in the middle of RCA's color television exhibit at the American National Exhibition in Moscow in July 1959, Vice President Richard Nixon is chastised by Nikita Khrushchev for "troubling the waters" by supporting the passing of Captive Nations Week, a soon to be yearly proclamation condemning the Soviet Union for depriving nations of "their national independence and their individual liberties," which had only been signed into law by Eisenhower a few days earlier. Nixon responds to the Soviet leader by declining to comment on the various subjects that he raised at this moment, except to say this: "This, Mr. Khrushchev, is one of the most advanced developments in communication, at least in our country." Nixon points to the color video camera before them. "It is color television, of course. It is, as you will see in a few minutes—when we will see the very picture of your speech and my comments that has been transmitted—it is one of the best means of communication developed. . . . There are some instances where you may be ahead of us, for example, in the development of the thrusts of your rockets for the investigation of outer space. There may be some instances, for example, color television, where we're ahead of you."[1] Khrushchev interrupts Nixon at this point, gesticulating excitedly while laughing and saying, "Wrong! Wrong! We are ahead of you in rockets as well as this technique!" Khrushchev is then interrupted by an RCA representative who interjects and addresses Khrushchev directly in an attempt to get the conversation back to his company's product: "I think it would be interesting for you to know that this program is recording on

FIGURE 6.1 Screenshot of Richard Nixon pointing out the RCA color TV camera recording them to Nikita Khrushchev in the RCA color television exhibit at the American National Exhibition in Moscow in 1959.

AMPEX color tape and it can be played back immediately and you can't tell that it isn't a live program."[2]

Nixon, sounding at times more like an electronics floor salesman than a political leader, dodged Khrushchev's attempts at political and rhetorical engagement and instead repeatedly returned to the topic of color television and videotape as examples of technologies that could increase communication between the two countries. Nixon asserted that the Soviets could learn more about the United States through viewing color television and that Americans could benefit from hearing and seeing the Soviet leader on their screens. Khrushchev countered with accusations of propaganda and raised the possibility of bias in American media and technology, saying at one point, "The apparatus is yours, and you speak English, while I speak Russian. Your words are taped and will be shown and heard. What I say to you about science won't be translated, and so your people won't hear it. These aren't equal conditions."[3]

Unbeknownst to both men was the fact that AMPEX was founded by a Russian who had emigrated to the United States. As Eduard Ivanyan, a Soviet cultural ministry official who was present at the debate, pointed out decades later, "'AMPEX' stood for 'Alexander Matveyevich Ponyatov Excellence.' Ponyatov invented those television cameras. If Nixon or Khrushchev had known that, the debate would have taken on an absolutely different tone. There's no doubt Khrushchev would have won."[4] Ponyatov was also chairman of the board at AMPEX at the time of the exchange.

This infamous meeting between the two world leaders has become known as "the kitchen debate" because, after leaving the RCA exhibit, Khrushchev and Nixon moved on to view a model house and picked up their verbal sparring in its kitchen as they discussed capitalism and Communism in relation to the right to housing, planned obsolescence, and consumer comfort and choice. Consequently, the centrality of the color television technologies and the RCA exhibit has been obscured in the retelling of the event, as the encounter has most commonly been used as an entry point to discuss the intersection of postwar domesticity and consumerism with the Cold War. What is lost in the typical description of the meeting of the two leaders is not only the specific references to color television as an advanced technology (comparable in its significance, according to Nixon, to space rockets), but also the rhetorical framing of color video technologies as central tools for global knowledge, diplomacy, and expansion.

That said, Nixon was not the first to insert color television into the Cold War imaginary. David Sarnoff, for one, had long been tying the development of color to nationalistic pursuits. For example, during the dedication of NBC's Washington station, WRC-TV, in 1958 (discussed in detail in chapter 4), the elder Sarnoff gave a speech in which he inferred that the Soviets had shied away from color technology because of its presumed inherent relationship to veracity. Sarnoff, looking directly at Eisenhower at that event, proclaimed:

> Perhaps there are some persons in the world who may not be very keen about being seen in their true and natural colors. . . . Some of their pronouncements may on occasion bring a blush to their own cheeks. . . . And this camera, I assure you, sir, is relentless in its revelations. Happily, however, this is not so in America; here, we fear

no revelations. We have nothing to hide. On the contrary, we want everyone in the world to see America in its true and natural colors. We want people everywhere to see Americans at work and at play; to see our institutions in action, reflecting their ideals and the ideals of our nation, as well as our and their human imperfections. Here, we do not seek to be anything other than what we are. And what we are is not hidden by curtains and what we say not hidden by censorship.[5]

In this rather bombastic speech, Sarnoff placed electronic color at the center of a Cold War visual regime and culture of surveillance, aligning it with the camera's "relentless" ability to reveal truth and shine a light on those who might wish to hide in the dark or behind an iron curtain. (Nixon too referred—although in a less ominous tone—to color television's potential to reveal Khrushchev's intentions and the truths of Soviet life.) In a manner similar to way it was discussed in the selling and critical reception of the cultural documentaries of the 1960s, electronic color was assumed to have a unique ability to expose the "real" or "natural" as it extended human sight. Moreover, Sarnoff's speech used one of the technical idiosyncrasies of color television (such as its tendency to pick up colors like red in human flesh that may not be seen as easily by the human eye) to claim that the electronic color camera had the capacity to locate "human imperfections" and naturalness as it scrutinized its subject and offered verisimilitude to its viewers. Therefore, its gaze, Sarnoff's logic went, could not be tolerated by the secretive, deceitful, oppressive, and perpetually lurking Communists. It could, however, be embraced by the naturally vibrant capitalist America, rich in values, goods, and democratic ideals, and having "nothing to hide." This rhetoric once again sublimated the subjectivity of color television and instead refigured its promises and capabilities to better fit within the common Cold War ideology and imagery that rested upon the continual monitoring and containment of self and other. Here, color television was not just a tool for selling products or a heightened viewing experience; it was also an idealized and efficient technology for the production of knowledge, truth, detection, and revelation. This rhetoric also referenced the centrality of communications technologies and their advancement during times of war—most essentially, of course, World War II. The advancements in technologies that were operating as organizational and detection devices, such as radar and sonar (particularly the alterations in signal wavelengths that allowed for more precise echoes), were central to both the war effort and the progress and standardization of commercial television. Of course, Sarnoff had his own direct and storied relationship with the military and with the anti-Communist effort. He worked directly under Eisenhower, as a general on his communications staff, overseeing the construction and growth of powerful radio stations that would allow transmissions to all of the Allied forces across Europe, and eventually participating in the establishment of the Voice of America network. He was a vocal opponent of Communism, aligning himself at one point with blacklisting and Senator Joseph McCarthy, and he believed in the power of communications as a tool of political persuasion.[6]

It is also significant that this assertion of color television as evidence of American technological prowess occurred only a couple of years after what came to be known as the Sputnik crisis—a period of cultural reflection and anxiety over the ability of the United States to best the Soviet Union in scientific and technological innovation and in education. After the Soviets' surprise launch of the first satellite, *Sputnik 1*, in October 1957, there was much discussion and grave concern among critics and cultural commentators that by being first to achieve such a successful launch, the Soviet Union was proving itself to be ahead of the United States not only in this area, but also in technology and science more generally. Government officials and citizens alike feared the implications for the advancement of the Soviet military and for U.S. national security. As a consequence, the federal government invested in the project of furthering scientific education and supporting research and development, which eventually led to the creation of NASA in 1958. As Lynn Spigel has pointed out, the Sputnik crisis was part of a larger moment of American disillusionment, one in which the promises of the immediate postwar period were put into question. By the end of the decade, "Americans were looking backward at the great white hopes that had somehow led them down a blind alley. The utopian dreams for technological supremacy, consumer prosperity, and domestic bliss were revealing their limits in ways that could no longer be pushed aside," she writes, noting that due to a series of public relations scandals rocking the television industry during the late 1950s, television too (at least in terms of the ethics of the industry) became "another fallen idol."[7] In contrast to monochrome, color television was still being pushed as a *technological* wonder, a neglected advancement, finally perfected, and ready to be put to use not only in the service of education, but also in expanding television's reach around the globe and into space.

This chapter will explore the formulation of color television during the 1960s as a Cold War technology, extending both sight and culture on a global scale, promising to alter the electronic images transmitted and received around the world as well as the political landscape. This chapter will also detail the way color television was thought to illuminate not just the life and landscape of other countries but also other objects in our solar system, as color television was adapted for use on the Apollo missions starting in 1969. We will also see the purported darker side of color television during this period too, as it was said to harbor potential dangers for body and sight, as displayed in the color set radiation hazard scare that closed the decade.

COLOR GOES TO THE FAIR

RCA's color television display was one of the most popular sites at the American National Exhibition in Moscow. For eight hours a day over six weeks, visitors to Sokolniki Park could view programming meant to "represent a montage of American television without commercials" and visit a glass encased production studio in order to witness the behind-the-scenes workings of live television production. The programs, a mix of live and filmed, with contributions by Disney and others, aired through closed-circuit. The New York Stock Exchange contributed the animated "What Makes Us Tick" (1952) and the documentary "Your Share in Tomorrow" (1957), which were both propagandistic attempts to "explain the mechanics of capitalism to the Russian people."[8]

Live programs, which primarily utilized other exhibits at the fair, were said to be the most popular with visitors, especially a man-on-the-street style program centering on a Russian-speaking NBC production coordinator's spontaneous interviews with fairgoers. Also telecast were games and contests participated in by audience members (rounds of musical chairs for kids, best beard competitions for men). Fairgoers likely enjoyed both the participatory aspect of these live events at the studio and the effect of seeing themselves, or their fellow citizens, on color television, a service that was still only in the planning stage in the USSR. James Schwoch, however, has argued that these live color events demonstrate one of the unspoken political functions of the fair: "ob-

F O R T U N E

October 1962

Kennedy's Economics   R.C.A.'s Plunge into Color   A Second Look at Stock Options

FIGURE 6.2 The cover of *Fortune Magazine,* October 1962, an issue containing a profile of RCA's color venture, consists of an abstract color television image at its center and U.S. politicians at the White House at its border.

FIGURE 6.3 Screenshot of "What Makes Us Tick," produced by the New York Stock Exchange, 1952.

servation and surveillance of ordinary Soviet citizens interacting with simulations of American consumer society, as well as ordinary Soviets interacting with the Soviet bureaucracy."[9] The information gathered by observers—both human and technological—at the fair provided the United States and the USSR with data on the behavior and psychology of the Soviet citizenry, resulting, according to Schwoch, in the "ultimate Cold War social science experimental research project aimed at a target group."[10] In addition to serving as an opportunity for behavioral research, the color programming at the exhibit functioned as one big commercial for American consumer goods and lifestyles. Fashion shows highlighted the latest styles in women's clothes, and cooking shows presented "quick and easy uses of frozen foods, an almost unknown commodity to the average Russian housewife," while another program on the latest advancements in hair dye demonstrated how quickly an American woman could change her hair color and style.[11]

FIGURE 6.4 The Color Television Communications Center at the 1964 World's Fair.
AUTHOR'S PRIVATE COLLECTION.

Back in the United States five years later, RCA's color television exhibit, the Color Television Communications Center, at the 1964 world's fair in New York involved very similar events, technologies, displays, and public relations strategies, including a working color studio behind glass providing visitors with a panoramic view of productions, a color mobile unit, and live programming consisting of "fashion shows, interviews, illustrations by nationally known cartoonists and entertainment from the other pavilions."[12] NBC also sent programming outside of the fair and across its network, most notably a ninety-minute special, "World's Fair Opening Night," sponsored by US Steel, hosted by Henry Fonda, and featuring, along with filmed segments, live appearances by Carol Channing, Lorne Greene, Marion Anderson, and Fred MacMurray. According to the show's producer, Albert Fisher, the program almost did not air, as civil rights activists—protesting discrimination in housing, jobs, and education in the city and voicing their anger that "while millions of dollars are being spent on the World's Fair, thousands of Black and Puerto Rican people are suffering"—were "taking axes and cutting the cables of our cameras prior to our going on the air live."[13]

A filmed NBC News documentary hosted by a wry and sometimes critical Edwin Newman, "A World's Fair Diary," aired later that summer, and programs such as *Candid Camera, Queen for a Day*, and the *Today Show* broadcasted from the fairgrounds for special episodes. Jonathan Winters was scheduled to do a segment at the fair for an upcoming special in December 1964, pretending to be a BBC reporter sent over to cover the fair without knowing it was closed for the winter. However, during the middle of the shoot, Robert Moses, president of the World's Fair Corporation, accused Winters of mocking the fair and kicked him and the NBC crew off the grounds—which only led Winters to use his opening monologue to lampoon Moses and bring attention to the low attendance, financial disappointments, and other problems that had beset the Flushing Meadows project.

Close to three hundred RCA color sets were stationed across the fairground, connected via closed-circuit and placed where people would be relaxing (in lounges, restaurants, and public areas) or waiting in line for exhibits or food. Yet the most popular part of the Color Television Communications Center was, once again, the site that provided the opportunity for people to see themselves on screen. At the pavilion entrance, visitors could "walk by a unique 'color carousel' and see themselves on color television twice, once 'live' as they pass the camera, and moments later on TV tape."[14] In a surviving fragment of videotape from the carousel, fairgoers are seen looking directly at the camera, laughing, primping, or playfully performing (see figures 6.5–6.7). RCA also heavily publicized that, as a public service, any lost children at the fair would be brought to the studio and their image broadcast on the color monitors across the fairgrounds in hopes of eventually reuniting them with their parents.

In an RCA press release, Moses praised the Color Television Communications Center for providing both fairgoers and exhibitors with an important service and for playing "a prime role in promoting the Fair's theme, 'Peace Through Understanding.'"[15] At the exhibit's dedication, David Sarnoff made a similar assertion about the technology's ability to help create what Marshall McLuhan dubbed the "global village":

FIGURES 6.5–6.7 Visitors could see themselves on color TV at RCA's Color Carousel at the 1964 World's Fair. Screenshots from https://www.youtube.com/watch?v=s9Vm_peHmKg.

Within the Fair itself, the RCA Exhibit will serve to further the medium's bright new promise for moving the world closer to civilized harmony. Our programs in color will be fed on a regular basis into the exhibits and pavilions of many foreign nations. These nations, in turn, will furnish people and programs to the RCA studio to be integrated with the domestic offerings on our closed-circuit broadcast service. In this World's Fair of today, we therefore have the foreshadowings of the television service of tomorrow. It will be a service to which all nations can contribute and from which all nations can benefit. It can give new meaning to the theme of this great international exposition: peace through understanding. We have added sight to sound, color to sight and now space to color. There is neither end nor limit to the capacities of this service, which began a quarter century ago here in Flushing Meadows.[16]

While these claims to global prosperity and peace through technology and American style consumerism by both corporate and political leaders signaled a promotional and institutional strategy revolving around the developing economy of global communications, it was not an altogether accurate representation of what would eventually develop in the global communications marketplace or of what was occurring at the fair. In terms of global communications, a vision of simultaneous live programming available to all television viewers across the world was upheld as an ideal, one that promised unity through shared experience and virtual presence, but that proved complicated in its implementation and was a relatively rare event. And in regard to the New York World's Fair, this exhibition did not necessarily represent "the world," as claimed. After publicly criticizing the Bureau International des Expositions (BIE) and their rules, the often brash and controversial Moses had not only failed to win endorsement from the BIE but had also succeeded in angering the organization's leaders to the point that they officially requested that member nations *not* participate in the New York fair. Consequently, a majority of the larger European nations, along with Australia, Canada, and the Soviet Union, all chose to participate in the BIE sanctioned Century 21 Exposition in Seattle and Montreal's Expo 67 instead of coming to Queens. In addition, there was an overall sense that Moses's version of a world's fair was far more commercial than many of those sanctioned by the BIE, and less nationally focused, even though organizers trumpeted the fact that television and radio crews from around the world were sent to cover the fair and that part of the opening day program was sent live to Europe via the *Relay* satellite.[17] Beyond the fair, however, Sarnoff was also referring to the expansion of U.S. television into global markets, the introduction of color television in other nations of the world, and the coming of commercial satellite use for global distribution of programming.

GLOBAL COLOR

By 1964, the first year of the New York World's Fair, the networks were becoming increasingly focused on foreign television markets and the role that color television would play in programs sold and broadcast overseas. RCA was especially interested, of course, in bringing color to new markets to heighten the perceived impact and profile of color programming and advertising, to increase set sales, and to reinforce RCA as the central figure in color television innovation. Accordingly, NBC took it upon itself mid-decade to offer color training classes to foreign broadcasters and production companies, thereby positioning the network as the expert and the standard setter when it came to electronic color. Reportedly, a number of foreign production and engineering teams, including delegations from Japan, Sweden, Italy, France, Australia, and Canada, were sent over to the United States to take NBC color courses from RCA engineers and color experts.[18]

Yet, while RCA and NBC were training foreign producers and engineers and network international programming sales were on the rise overall, color television programming did not yet represent a major portion of foreign syndication in the early to mid-1960s, as there had not yet been an accompanying global spread of color television systems or sets.[19] For example, *Broadcasting* reported that the summer of 1964 saw programming sales of $2 million for NBC International over a three-month period in parts of Europe, Australia, Japan, and Venezuela. However, of the shows listed as making up that sales boom, all but one (*Bonanza*) were in black and white.[20] This was, of course, due to the fact that at that point only three countries had color systems—the United States, Japan, and Mexico. There was also some skepticism and criticism circulating about what would eventually be referred to as cultural imperialism, as

FIGURE 6.8 A Canadian ad for RCA color television from 1966, the first year that color broadcasting was offered in that country.

much of the international television trade had been touted as being one way: *from* the United States *to* everywhere else. *Los Angeles Times* writer Hal Humphrey, an early critic of the anticipated lopsided nature of the global television market, called for a "trade pact guaranteeing American purchase" of shows from the nations that U.S. networks were doing business with in 1963. Calling out Sarnoff on his inflated claims about the impact that American programs could have on people from developing nations, Humphrey snidely wrote, "Ah, how right he is. Imagine the comfort and feeling of togetherness with the rest of the world that a Mau Mau tribesman will feel the first time he sees an episode of *The Untouchables*."[21]

While the establishment and dissemination of a national commercial color system was both vexed and sluggish in the United States, it was even more so across the rest of the world. Certainly, the idea that color sets were considered a luxury item in the United States, where consumer goods and appliances were plentiful and often affordable, would make owning one seem even more far-fetched to those in still developing nations. Israel proved to be a fascinating example in this regard, as even though it had a color system in place by the late 1960s, the Israeli Broadcasting Authority (IBA) required that all color from imported and satellite programs be erased with a technical instrument called a *mechikon* ("the eraser") so that all programming would be shown only in monochrome. As Oren Soffer argues, the IBA's insistence on eliminating color that they were equipped to transmit (which continued into the early 1980s) was a direct consequence of color television's luxury status. Even basic black and white technology was thought to be "unfit for the modest Israeli lifestyle in a time of economic distress."[22] Following that logic, color television was, of course, even more of a frivolous distraction. As Soffer asserts, taking a stand against the technology was also a way to position Israeli values in opposition to Western capitalist ones: "In the same way that television was described in the 1960s and 1970s as representing the consumption culture of the West, color television was perceived to be an even more potent symbol—one that carried dangerous cultural implications for Israeli society."[23] Yet there was also evidence that the IBA did not want locally produced black and white programming broadcast side by side with foreign color productions, since the IBA, while able to broadcast color, was not equipped to produce its own color programming. They worried, of course, that they would look inferior—"pale by comparison."[24] However, by 1977, a workaround was developed. If they could afford it, Israelis could (and did) purchase color sets containing a device called the anti-mechikon, or anti-eraser, which would cancel out the IBA's color eraser and allow the viewers to see foreign programs in color.[25] In India, a country that did not adopt color television until 1982, there was a similar debate over color television as a symbol of excess in a country that was both a large industrial economy and one of the world's poorest nations. Opponents of color argued that over half of the country's villages did not even have electricity, and less than 20 percent of its population, even in the early 1980s, was in range of television signals.[26] The other side of the argument was that India would look as though they were lagging behind in technological and economic advancement if they continued to offer only black and white and that they could better sell sports programming to neighboring countries if it were in color. Once again, color became symbolic of modernism and investment in the excesses of consumerism.

Color television was certainly considered a luxury item in Cuba in the 1950s, but it was also, to use Yeidy Rivero's phrase, a "spectacle of progress," a symbol of the nation's technological prowess and alignment with American consumerism and political interests. In 1957, color came to the island via Canal 12, owned by Gaspar Pumarejo, Cuba's "foremost radio and television personality" of the period.[27] Equipped with RCA color transmitters and cameras, and broadcasting from the top of the Havana Hilton Hotel, the local channel began its colorcasts on October 24, 1957. The moment was touted by the U.S. and Cuban press as a major achievement, since Cuba was the second nation after the United States to officially launch regular color broadcasting. Throughout the following year or so, the new channel broadcast roughly twenty hours a week of programming, much of it filmed rather than live. As *Broadcasting-Telecasting* reported in the month leading up to the station's color premiere, Pumarejo promised that a thousand color sets would be placed in homes, social clubs, and select public venues by the time the first color show went on the air, estimating that ten thousand color sets would be sold by the end of 1958, and that it would "take approximately 20,000 sets in use to enable Canal 12 to begin live programming."[28]

After the revolution, however, color television's expense and status as a luxury good would be reframed as indulgent and extravagant, a reminder of former president Fulgencio Batista's enmeshment with both American private and governmental interests and a symbol incongruent with the socialist values and goals of Fidel Castro's new government. Consequently, color transmissions were halted and wouldn't begin again until almost twenty years later. As Rivero's work so expertly shows, television itself was not banished from the country, but rather reborn during the first few years of the 1960s. As Rivero points out, this "entailed a revision of production practices, a retraining of media workers, and a reassessment of taste."[29] Among other things, this meant that "the excesses of the commercial era" (specific genres, aesthetics, forms of design, commercial appeals, and even color) would be expunged from revolutionary television along with any trace of American programming.[30]

Japan did not imbue color television with such potent political and cultural symbolism as we find in the examples of Cuba and Israel; however, there was an embrace of color television as another sign of technological superiority and the country's rising status as a producer of high-end electronics as well as a reluctance and resistance to what some considered a rush to color conversion. During public hearings held on the introduction of color television, representatives from the semi-governmental agency in charge of all television relays, the Japan Telegraph and Telephone Corporation, voiced strong opposition to the coming of color—mostly on the grounds that it was premature, as such an expensive venture needed more careful consideration. The Japanese correspondent for the British weekly *Stage and Television Today* also claimed in 1960 that Japan had been "bulldozed" into adopting the new technology by one or two powerful media companies, "primarily Matsutaro Shoriki, a newspaper proprietor" and founder of Nippon TV Network, because the market for monochrome sets was close to the point of saturation.[31]

Although there were experimental color broadcasts in Japan in the early 1950s, the country officially entered into the business of regular color broadcasting using the NTSC system toward the end of 1960. However, color programs and program segments were few and far between and aired primarily in the larger markets (such as Tokyo and Osaka). Much as in the early days of color in the United States, the price of color sets made them out of reach for most Japanese consumers and many complained that even when they were able to afford them, the receivers required too frequent servicing.[32] Color sets could be found, however, in the lobbies and lounges of all the major Tokyo hotels, as well as some "beer halls and other public spaces."[33] After set prices began to decline and a microwave network was set up to bring color to the vast majority of the country, set sales began to go up rather dramatically. In 1967, for instance, a total of 1.1 million Japanese sets were sold, with 750,000 going to the Japanese domestic market.

Color came to Mexico only a few years after it was introduced in Japan. Guillermo González Camarena—who first patented a type of field-sequential color television system in 1942—developed a new color system called the simplified bicolor system (sbs), which was used to experimentally broadcast a weekly children's program on xhgc-tv (the flagship of the Canal 5 network) in Mexico City starting in 1963. Color television wasn't available to the rest of the nation until a few years later, and full conversion of the network's schedule occurred in 1967. By the end of the decade, color systems had been adopted and deployed by most countries in Europe, the USSR, Canada, the U.K., Thailand, Taiwan, and the Philippines. The rest of Asia, Australia, and the majority of Africa, the Middle East, and South America didn't convert until the 1970s.

Recent scholarship by Andreas Fickers reveals many of the tensions and complications that came along with the adoption of national color standards in Europe during the 1950s and 1960s.[34] As Fickers recounts, there were three distinct color systems that were under consideration for the common European television standard, two of which had been developed in Europe. In the U.K., bbc engineers, who would work to adapt the American ntsc system to their already established 405-line system used for monochrome broadcasts, began experimental broadcasts in 1956. That same year, in France, Henri de France announced that he had developed a new color system, the *système électronique couleur a mémoire* (secam), which was free of some of the problems with color shifting and hue that beset the ntsc system and made it less than ideal for the geography and weather patterns of Europe. And finally, in 1962, Telefunken, the West German electronics company, patented their phase-alternating line (pal) system—which boasted, among other things, a higher frame rate, higher resolution, and automatic hue adjustment. All three systems, ntsc, secam, and pal, were under consideration as the European standard in a set of meetings in Oslo and Vienna held by the ccir (International Radio Consultative Commission, a division of the International Telecommunication Union) in 1965 and 1966. With adoption of the NTSC supported by the British, SECAM by the French and Soviets, and PAL by Germany, Italy, Austria, and Scandinavia, there was much debate and lobbying and little agreement at these meetings, even though a common system would arguably be advantageous for all. Ultimately, since the CCIR was able to function only in an advisory capacity and there were complicated economic and political interests behind the selection of a particular standard, the attempt to set a single European color standard was unsuccessful. In detailing these debates from a variety of vantage points, Fickers reminds us that standards are far from "neutral agreements" and are instead places where ideologies, allegiances, practices, and motives inform technological infrastructure.[35] And in this instance, Fickers argues, the "CCIR meetings turned into an arena for the staging of a drama on color diplomacy, turning technical experts into political actors and color television transmission systems into symbolic icons of technonationalism."[36]

The conversion to color and the adoption of a particular color standard or system was more than just a decision made by a private media company or industry. It carried with it nationalistic and political implications and had the potential to align a nation with the United States and its specific articulation of the connection between consumerism, capitalism, and democracy. It also could more firmly situate countries within modernity and technical progress and/or garish displays of excessive consumption. Despite the ambivalent response it often received and the political and industrial battles it could inspire, color television's association with ideas about the future, progress, and the modern global marketplace made it a technology difficult to ignore—especially as it was about to enter the space race in a manner that was not simply rhetorical (as it was in Nixon's 1959 comparison of the invention of color television to that of rocket thrusters), but quite literal.

"A TRAVELOGUE WITH NO ATMOSPHERE": COLOR TV IN SPACE

Color television would follow black and white television into space in two interrelated circumstances: first as transmissions carried by global satellites, and then as a system carried aboard Apollo missions (starting with *Apollo 10*).[37] The coupling of color television—the cutting edge of consumer electronics of its age—with space technology symbolized the ul-

A The 21"* Rupert Contemporary consolette B The Genoa 21"* Moorish lowboy C New 19"* Color TV:
the Cabot Colonial consolette with casters D The Bremanger 19"* Nordic consolette with casters
E The 21"* Karlstad with clean-lined Scandinavian styling

Now RCA Victor gives you Color TV that's custom-engineered the Space Age way—with dependable RCA solid copper circuits.

It's breathtaking: beautiful new RCA Victor Color TV. And *behind* that beautiful picture are two important things you *can't* see.

One is reliability—of RCA Solid Copper circuits (shown at left). They replace old-fashioned hand-wiring in over 200 possible trouble spots. They won't come loose. Won't short circuit. Won't go haywire.

Then there's experience. RCA Victor has more experience in Color TV than many manufacturers have in making black-and-white sets.

Cabinet styles? You'll see several beautiful examples of any you name.

See for yourself why more people own RCA Victor Color TV than any other kind. Soon.

*19-in. tube (overall diag.) 180-sq. in. picture/21-in. tube (overall diam.) 267-sq. in. picture.

The Most Trusted Name in Electronics

Tmk(s)®

FIGURE 6.9 A 1966 RCA ad promoting the "Space Age"
solid copper circuits used in their color sets.

timate engagement with the modern, the unexplored, and the scientific. It was a boon to color television at a time when the networks had fully converted to color and roughly 35 percent of all households owned color sets. It was also the culmination of the promise of color television's extended, immersive, and spectacular vision as well as its various points of convergence with Cold War technology, surveillance, and truth-telling. Color television would bring new vantage points on the globe and images of a new world back to international television audiences.

RCA was the prime contractor for NASA's communication satellite *Relay*, the first satellite to broadcast a television transmission (which was the announcement of John F. Kennedy's assassination from the United States to Japan, to be precise). The first commercially available U.S. satellite, AT&T's Telstar, was launched in the summer of 1962 over the Atlantic, enabling live television transmissions between North America and Europe. The initial transmissions on July 23, 1962, were black and white and started off with a split screen of the Statue of Liberty on one side and the Eiffel Tower on the other. *Intelsat I* (popularly known as Early Bird), was launched by COMSTAT in 1965, providing nearly instantaneous contact across the Atlantic, while *Syncom III*, the first geostationary satellite, was positioned over the Pacific Ocean, bringing connection to and within East Asia starting in 1964. Live color global satellite transmission made its premiere through *Syncom III*, with the help of Project Relay as the U.S.–Europe link, and carried NBC's broadcast of the opening ceremonies of the 1964 Summer Olympics in Tokyo. Airing in the middle of the night in the United States meant that the event had a somewhat limited audience; consequently, all the rest of the Olympics coverage was taped and then shipped back to the United States for delayed broadcast (a delay that NBC hyped as never being more than eight hours).[38] In her book *Cultures in Orbit*, Lisa Parks argues that satellite programs during this time presented a fantasy of "global presence," a notion "predicated on an imagining of the TV studio as simultaneously connected to and detached from the world: It assumes an orbital position distant enough to visualize and construct the world as a 'whole sphere' while remaining instantly within reach of its most remote parts."[39] In her analysis of the satellite spectacular *Our World*—a 1967 program coordinated by the European Broadcast Union consisting of both live, on-location segments from multiple sites across the globe and prerecorded segments, broadcast simultaneously to twenty-four countries with a total audience around 500 million—Parks critiques the utopian and colonialist ideologies supporting the promise of the "global village."[40] *Our World* was put together in a way that was intended to answer the 1965 call of the United Nations in their program proposals envisioning ideal global space communications—a space for the global exchange of ideas and information, unfettered by ideology, economic, or social unrest or imbalance—without recognizing the hierarchical power relations already at work. Rhetorically, satellite television was promising to craft a sense of global citizenship and further the notion of color television's deep and extended vision that was at play in the travel and nature documentaries discussed in the previous chapter. Color television was now able to transmit live to and from space, delivering views from multiple points across the earth.

The meeting of satellites, global markets, and color television was understood to be representative not only of cutting-edge technologies and economic infrastructures but also of the peak of space age modernity and the international, technological, and scientific competition that was so much an American part of Cold War policy discourse. As such, while many of the early satellite programs were in black and white, network heads and other industry actors made public statements tying the technology to the expansion of color. As early as 1962, ABC's Leonard Goldenson announced to shareholders that the network would expand its color programming during the 1964–1965 season. In doing so, he immediately connected color with the future of global programming by stating, "With the tremendous strides being made in space and satellite technology, ABC International is continuing its activities to establish the internal associations and partnerships necessary to translate satellite transmissions from scientific curiosity into an effective and profitable world-wide television system."[41] As Schwoch notes, such descriptions and promises of satellite technology "demonstrate an articulation of satellites, space research, and the 'science = freedom' formula emergent in American global policy discourse at this phase of the Cold War."[42]

The launch of satellites by both the United States and the USSR in 1957 and 1958 were early volleys in the Cold War space race, as was the Russian cosmonaut Yuri Gagarin's 1961 achievement as the first human in space. It was, however, the first U.S. missions to the moon that would become the most iconic and visually moving achievement to Americans. Television's presence on the Apollo missions—first black and white and

FIGURE 6.10 A Westinghouse color television camera captures images
of the crew of Apollo 16. NASA IMAGES.

then color—would become an essential part of the selling of the space
program as well as the promotion of color television and the branding of
particular television manufacturers (RCA and Westinghouse) as technological pioneers through their association with the space program (see
figures 6.10 and 6.11).

Before a color camera came aboard *Apollo 10* in 1969, a black and
white RCA camera was taken on *Apollo 7* and *Apollo 8*, and a Westinghouse lunar surface camera traveled on *Apollo 9*. However, in the buildup
to these early missions, there was some reticence on NASA's behalf about
the television's presence on board, even though the agency had readily
established overtly commercial relationships with other corporations,
agreeing to use and promote products such as Tang—the fruit flavored
powdered drink formulated by General Foods—and Fisher Space Pens,
a ballpoint that could be used in zero gravity. As David Meerman Scott,
Richard Jurek, and Eugene A. Cernan argue in their book *Marketing the*

Moon, even though television was essential to the success of the Apollo missions, reluctant NASA engineers and higher-ups with military backgrounds had to be convinced that live television would not prove to be a physical burden, a distraction, a waste of resources, or an invasion of astronaut privacy, but was rather the very point of the mission. As Joshua Rothman of the *New Yorker* reflected recently, "Without television, the moon landing would have been a merely impressive achievement—an expensive stunt, to the cynical. Instead, seen live, unedited, and everywhere, it became a genuine experience of global intimacy."[43]

By the time color television was included in the Apollo missions, however, the astronauts on board seemed to be more enthusiastic about and playful with their cameras and they were recording not just their view on space but also their interactions with one another and their more mundane routines, such as shaving and eating. The head of the *Apollo 10* mission, Commander Tom Stafford, stood out as especially keen and was quite forceful both in vocalizing his belief in the importance of television's role in space and in stimulating public interest in the space program. The press took note of this enthusiasm, referring to Stafford and his fellow astronaut Eugene Cernan as "TV bugs at heart" who both contributed to the live transmissions "a light-hearted narration that was amusing and appealing."[44] Walter Cronkite remarked on it too during the broadcast of a transmission, speculating that this new fervor might have something to do with the addition of color, saying, "The crew of *Apollo 10* have shown a great deal more interest in television from outer space than earlier crews, which seemed to be a little bit reluctant in spending time with television. They only had the black and white RCA camera with which to work, but there was that reluctance, notably, it seemed to me, in the earlier flights."[45]

RCA and Westinghouse produced and developed their lunar television technology according to NASA's specifications. A number of issues had to be taken into account, however, in order to modify existing television technology to suit the particular needs and environment of space exploration. The cameras had to be light, small in size, and highly reliable, and able to withstand substantial shock and vibration, consume little power, capture clear images in very low light and, in the case of the lunar module camera, endure extreme heat. The camera's scan rate also had to be fairly low to fit the bandwidth required to radio the images to ground

FIGURE 6.11 Two of Westinghouse's Apollo television cameras: the field-sequential color camera (*left*) and the monochrome lunar surface camera (*right*).
PHOTO BY NASA. LICENSED UNDER PUBLIC DOMAIN VIA COMMONS.

stations. Consequently, the black and white camera designed and manufactured by RCA was a slow-scanned camera, which meant that instead of the standard 525 scanned lines interlaced at 30 frames per second that was used for broadcast, the cameras made for Apollo scanned at a rate of 320 lines at 10 frames per second—just acceptable enough for the slow moving objects that would be the focus of the broadcasts (astronauts at work in the modules, the earth from afar, the relatively barren but pock-marked surface of the moon, etc.). The moving images were fuzzy and often indistinct, but nonetheless they provided Americans back home with the excitement and wonder of joining the astronauts on their unprecedented exploration.

This low scan rate did present a problem for live transmission, however, as the scanning rates of the Apollo cameras were not compatible with the NTSC broadcast standard. The solution developed by NASA and RCA led to further degradation of the broadcast image, as it was dependent on a process of real-time scan conversion, not altogether unlike the kinescope recording process of early television. During live broadcasts from space, the raw broadcast signal was sent down to the ground stations (two in Australia and one in the Mojave Desert in California) and was then split into two separate signal branches. By means of one branch, the transmission was recorded on analog videotape, and via the other, the transmission was sent through the NTSC conversion process. The conversion method was simply a conventional camera recording the raw transmission off a ten-inch monitor as it came in. This converted transmission was sent from the ground stations to Houston, Texas, then traveled via microwave relay to the network pool in New York, and finally went out as a "live" (but slightly delayed) broadcast to the television audience. The low bandwidth requirements would pose an even more significant problem for color transmissions on the Apollo missions, of course, as color requires more data.[46] If this is the case, one might ask, why even attempt color broadcasting on the missions?

Color, as we have heard throughout this book, promised to add depth and veracity—two qualities that a mission to the moon would find extremely useful. While the monochrome broadcasts of the earth from space were spectacular because they allowed ordinary citizens to witness a historic and almost unfathomable event in real time, the images were grainy and sometimes even difficult to decipher. Color had the potential to offer more to viewers—to provide them with more legible and vibrant images than black and white cameras could provide. Two of the *Apollo 10* astronauts gave voice to the promises of color television in space in interviews. Eugene Cernan was quoted as saying,

> I could sit here and try to tell you what the colors look like on sunrise and sunset and you could attempt to picture them in your mind. Until you've seen them, until you've been able to feel them with your own eyes, you can't transmit it to another person. With this color television, we hope it will be able to do something that I think all of us in the program have wanted to do for a long time and that's share some of the experiences and the things that are happening.[47]

Stafford put it in more practical terms: "The view from space is too terrific not to share with the people footing the bill."[48]

Claiming that color television was a gift of virtual transportation to taxpayers in appreciation for their support of the reported $25 billion dollar Apollo Project was a strategic public relations move that ultimately benefited NASA, the U.S. government, and the manufacturers of color television. Beyond this, however, the challenge of adapting color television for space travel also presented the television industry with an opportunity to display their investment and success in technological and scientific experimentation. Specifically, they sought to achieve a more accurate depiction of colors, hues, and gradations of the earth from space and of the moon's surface during lunar landings, which could assist in further study of the moon and its atmosphere. The first use of color cameras in space seemed to support the claim of improved legibility that accompanied the coming of color (see figure 6.12). *Broadcasting* reported that the new miniaturized color cameras "provided both black and white and color pictures of far greater clarity and resolution than those of the slow-scan RCA vidicon camera used on the *Apollo 8* flight. . . . Network technicians reported the pictures provided by color conversion were slightly clearer than the black-and-white pictures."[49] And when the first color moving images were seen on television sets in May 1969 during the *Apollo 10* flight, the press described the footage as dazzling, calling it the "highest color travelogue ever" and noting that the "earth showed up as a ball streaked with blue, white, green and brown against a background of cold and fathomless black."[50]

What has existed as only a footnote to the achievement of color television during this mission, however, was the extended period in which the color cameras were broadcasting the "first color TV pictures from space." While viewers and on-air reporters were expecting to see an image of the earth or the moon from the color camera in the command module, what was really being captured by that camera was a detached part of the spacecraft called the S-IVB. As anchor of the CBS special report promising color footage of the earth for the first time in history, Cronkite narrates the action as a round, white-looking object comes into view. "There it is, there it is! There's the moon in color!" he exclaims. "There is the earth in color. . . . Look at that! Isn't that something? Ten thousand miles and there we are."[51] A few minutes pass as we listen to the exchange between the astronauts and mission control before Cronkite

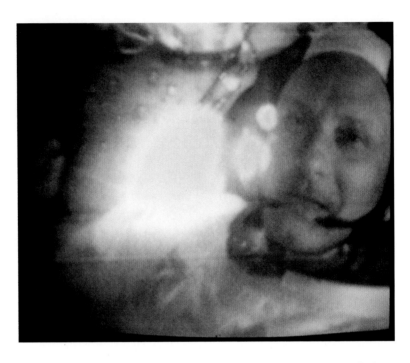

FIGURE 6.12 Image from the Apollo 10 broadcast of Commander Tom Stafford, May 18, 1969. NASA IMAGES, 569-33999.

begins to speak again: "Now, is that the earth? Or is that the . . . oh yeah, that's the SIVB. I'm afraid our excitement about seeing the earth was a little bit premature. That's not the earth at all. From that long distance it looked like you could make out the North American and South American continents. That's how your imagination can run riot. This is the SIVB." As the transmissions from the spacecraft continued, the television audience kept watching the fairly still and seemingly somewhat monochrome object in space while listening to the astronauts, mission control, and Cronkite's commentary. At one point, they heard the following exchange:

ASTRONAUT 1: Houston, you can't believe the picture we're getting; the resolution is fantastic.

ASTRONAUT 2: I'll say; this monitor makes it great.

ASTRONAUT I: How's the color?

HOUSTON: Hey, it's really beautiful; you've got it framed beautifully.

ASTRONAUT I: I think the color will be beautiful once we can show you the earth.

Cronkite continues to promise the view of the earth for the entire thirty to forty minutes leading up to its airing, building a sense of anticipation while also making viewers aware that what they were seeing was only an opening act. When the camera finally moves to the earth, the view really is far more impressive than the SIVB and docking footage in both the amount of detail and subtlety of color presented. However, while the electronic color images of the SIVB being transmitted (and as seen by the astronauts on their monitor) were being described as high fidelity, the images on sets at home seemed to be telling a slightly different story, as colors on television sets were pale or nonexistent, and the picture would sometimes break up or be filled with distortion or streaks of RGB. Even given such problems, the color transmissions were carrying more detailed and richer images and, since the color camera used the NTSC scan rate, they were not further degraded by the conversion process that the slow-scan transmission had to go through.

That was not the case, however, for the now iconic footage of Neil Armstrong's first steps on the moon in the following mission, *Apollo 11*. The camera that would capture that moment was not the color one on the command module, but rather a Westinghouse slow-scan S-band black and white camera deployed from the modularized equipment stowage assembly (MESA) compartment on the lunar module.[52] After the camera was lowered to record the first steps on the moon, it was detached from the lunar module (although still connected via a 100-foot cable) and placed on a tripod to follow the astronauts for two hours as they "raised the American flag, unveiled a commemorative plaque, took a phone call from President Nixon seated in the Oval Office, deployed a small array of scientific experiments, and collected soil and rock samples."[53] The color images that were disseminated from that mission over the summer of 1969 in the form of color films and photographs, however, were criticized for not being calibrated properly, while their overall accuracy was called into question. Apparently, the surface of the moon in the films was covered in a green overtone, while the photographs had both green and red distortions. Since viewers had no frame of reference for what the surface of the moon was supposed to look like and the color coming through each individual receiver could vary, the images left a confused impression of the "true" color of the moon. Jack Gould complained,

> As a public service in the case of color pictures from space, where the registration of hues is of some historical importance, couldn't the networks and individual stations run a couple of test patterns from Houston? Each of the varying color bars could be distinctly labeled as to its proper hue, whether white, yellow, blue, green, magenta or red. Then at the very least, for the specific transmission in which there is such wide interest, the set owner could have at least a few seconds to adjust the hue control as closely as possible.[54]

Apollo 12 was the first mission to bring a live color camera onto the surface of the moon; however, due to a mishap, the transmission was relatively brief. In attempting to better position the camera an hour after the broadcast began, an astronaut pointed the camera directly at the sun, thereby burning out the image processer and putting an end to all transmissions from the lunar surface during that mission.

Although for obvious reasons RCA wished to be selected as the developer of the first color television camera for Apollo, the design of their color camera—the large size, their use of multiple tubes, and the involvement of multiple mirrors—made its use impossible given the vibrations and temperature intensity and variation in space. Instead, Westinghouse engineers working for NASA developed a color camera that was based on Peter Goldmark's design for CBS in the 1940s—a field-sequential system involving a small rotating mechanical color wheel. A 1969 *New York Times* article began, "In an ironic footnote to the history of visual communications, a color TV system once deemed too crude for use on the ground has now been adopted as the sophisticated tool for relaying tinted images from space."[55] The camera also maintained a number of unique features, including its compact size, its own "mini monitor," and a special SEC (secondary electron conduction) imaging tube that could produce light at very low levels. And in order to get around the compatibility issue, the system transmitted each red, green, and blue image separately to the receiving stations and they were then combined together to "produce a single live color picture" at a rate compatible with the NTSC standard without much degradation.[56]

RCA did eventually succeed in getting one of their color cameras on the moon—the "RCA Sequential Color Wheel System." Stanley Lebar, a Westinghouse engineer who became manager of the Apollo television program, recalled how Robert Sarnoff had "cashed in all his chips to get the RCA logo on the moon" in the 1971 *Apollo 15* mission. However, while the camera performed "extremely well," unfortunately for the company, "the public interest in Apollo missions had waned by then, and whatever public relationship battle Sarnoff was fighting he had already lost in the earlier Apollo flights."[57]

AT DECADE'S CLOSE

Certainly color television's use in the Apollo missions was a high point for the industry. It signaled a grand achievement in the extension of vision and the centrality of the technology in the creation of the "global village." However, there was also a low point for the industry around that same time, which came in the form of a rather significant radiation scare. While the scare was likely exaggerated in its scope and potential dangers, it succeeded in bringing to the surface anxieties about the connection between vision problems and television screens, a more general concern over the possibility of radiation leaks from everyday technological objects, a growing mistrust in science toward the decade's end, and an underlying fear of nuclear war. As *Broadcasting* magazine noted, there had been long-standing concerns about radiation leaks from black and white tubes since 1946; however, it wasn't until routine testing revealed that specific models of GE color sets were meeting "X-radiation in excess of desirable levels" in May 1967 that there seemed to be any real evidence of such a risk. It was speculated that the high voltage required by color sets was at least partially to blame.[58]

Initially, the radiation concern was limited to a single type of set: "The unknown owners of some 90,000 large-screen color television sets were told by the government Friday to disconnect them immediately pending a check on possible radioactivity. The television sets involved are large-screen color consoles and tall models made by the General Electric Co. and purchased between Sept. 1, 1966 and May 31, 1967," the *Boston Globe* reported.[59] However, the number of sets with problematic readings had gone up to 112,000 by mid-August, and by February 1968, the sets involved were not just produced by GE but by almost all television manufacturers.

The response to the recall was relatively swift. The industry was brought before a congressional committee in late July, and the committee eventually proposed a federal radiation regulation bill. Further testing and evaluation was done by the National Center for Radiological Health and the Public Health Service throughout the rest of 1967 and into early 1968. The surgeon general eventually came out with a statement saying that testing showed that this low level of radiation posed only a small risk to any one set owner's health as long as he or she was watching a set in "normal viewing" conditions, which were understood to be "6 to 10 feet from the front of the set and avoiding any prolonged exposure to the set's rear and sides."[60] According to James Terrill Jr., director of the National Center for Radiological Health, the leakage beam in most of the problematic sets was directed downward "in a thin crescent pattern," and therefore did not pose a direct line of contact with the body of the viewer as long as the set was placed on the floor and not a high shelf.[61] Color set owners were also instructed to keep their distance from the set at all times and were warned against tinkering with it beyond the control panels so as to avoid being in direct contact with the radiation beam. As we have seen in earlier chapters, television's supposed effect on the body, most specifically the eye, had been part of the discourse surrounding the domestic technology since its inception and had been managed by theories of vision and distance. And yet the idea that a set could present a health hazard if watched too closely never seemed so real or so menacing than when it was said to be leaking radiation.

Although the public was well aware of the potential for death or devastating health effects (referred to as "atomic bomb disease" in the years immediately after Hiroshima and Nagasaki) that sudden and intense exposure to radiation could have on populations through the dropping of an atomic bomb or another nuclear catastrophe, the longer lasting and slower to develop effects that might result from lower levels of radiation were less well known to the public. Much of the discussion in the press and in congressional hearings was about what could happen from exposure over time to low-level radiation leaks like the ones from color television and was focused on damage to reproductive organs and/or genetic mutation of future generations—a lurking and terrifying dark side to scientific advancement. The anxieties and dread attached to radioactive materials and the role that nuclear weapons played in the Cold War would certainly have given a weight and complexity to the image of a slow and possibly deadly leak coming out of the home appliance your family gathered around regularly; so too would the notion of such a hidden danger lurking within the known and familiar. Color television in this instance was not just bringing images of the contemporary world into the home, it was also physically manifesting one of the world's most pressing and feared perils.

Although the radioactive color sets continued to make headlines through the end of the decade, there was also acknowledgment that the threat of potential harm had likely been exaggerated. W. Roger Ney, executive director of the National Council on Radiation Protection, came out and said in mid-1969 that the amounts of radiation coming from the sets "are too little to have a measurable effect on human beings." He went on to dismiss the proposal by two New York congressmen to have manufacturers "go into homes to test all of the nation's 15,000,000 color sets and to install radiation devices in them," adding, "I'd sure like to see that amount of effort put into things that are more clearly dangerous."[62] Nevertheless, by the end of that year, color television tube makers announced that the glass of all new color tube glass plates would be made with the compound strontium carbonate, which promised to contain a good portion of the excess radiation. Another consequence of the color television radiation scare was the enaction of the 1968 Radiation Control for Health and Safety Act, which had authorized the Food and Drug Administration to establish performance standards and monitoring procedures and initiate and support research, training, and development in order to better control, contain, and ultimately minimize the radiation emissions from electronic products (such as television sets, medical X-ray devices, and electronic heating devices).

Even with the radiation scare that closed out the 1960s, by 1970 color sets were outselling monochrome ones for the first time, and all new programming (with a few exceptions, of course) was being produced and shown in color on all three networks. Color was no longer the point of difference in American television but was well on its way to becoming the norm. The routinization of color viewing would have the effect of eventually altering some of the framing around the technology as the experience of spectacle was muted over time. Yet some of the discourses of immersion and extension of vision remained, especially as the technology was improved upon and the quality of the image increased.

Conclusion

Color television sets some day will range from huge, but mirror thin, units hung on the wall to tiny portables tailored to fit a lady's purse or a gentleman's pocket, industry executives predict.

—Chicago Tribune, 1967

In the late 1960s, the television receiver industry was beginning to imagine innovation beyond the postwar color set. While still funding color television research, manufacturers had begun investing in other technologies—such as LCD and solid-state components (the latter of which were put to use in portable color sets)—as potential areas of profit growth that promised to make television sets seem new again to consumers by revamping their size, look, and screen quality.[1] Although all networks had fully transitioned to color in the 1960s, by the mid-1970s, when dissemination had reached a saturation point and set sales began to drop off, cathode ray tube color television had been marketed as state-of-the-art for some twenty-five years, and the claim was wearing thin.

Complicating matters for RCA and Westinghouse, more manufacturers, both domestic and international, were competing in the cathode ray tube market, and Japanese companies were poised to dominate it (the Japanese controlled 35 percent of the market by 1976).[2] Consequently, U.S. manufacturers were feeling the pressure to find a successor to traditional color television sets. RCA engineers were given such a mandate, specifically to develop "low cost, thin, lightweight displays with high brightness, contrast, resolution and speed," a type of device that had been referred to as "mural television" because it was imagined that it would hang on the wall like a painting.[3] As Benjamin Gross's research has shown, although RCA was exploring a range of alternatives, a number of their executives and engineers were principally focused on liquid crystal screen technology as the most likely successor to cathode ray tubes.[4] The advantages of an LCD screen would include energy efficiency, color stability, and the ability to retain its vivid color even in bright light. An LCD television display would also be lightweight and could be housed in a thin box, a benefit pointed out in RCA's 1968 announcement of their developments in the use of liquid crystals, which included prototypes not just of television screens but also of electronic clocks and watches.[5] However, a few years after this announcement, RCA began to pull back from such research, primarily due to pressure from top management, who ultimately found LCD development a costly challenge to their relatively stable cathode ray tube business.[6] In 1976, the company sold off their lcd operation to Timex, and flat-screen displays would not be heralded again as the new form of television until the Japanese company Sharp announced in 1988 that it had developed a fourteen-inch color wall-mounted one-inch-thick color set.[7] However, it would take another decade for such flat-screen technologies to become viable options for consumers.

Computers were also being hailed as the answer to a number of color television's lingering technical inconsistencies and, as early as the 1970s, it was being predicted that the two technologies would merge, at least partially, at some point in the future.[8] In looking at a series of RCA ads in 1969–1970 (see figure C.1), we see how the company worked to directly bind computers with color television in the mind of the consumer, even before it was possible for television to claim digital technology, in order to make color television once again seem cutting-edge. The 1970 model was not digital; it was produced using computer *designed* and *tested* parts, which, at least according to the ad, promised to finally discipline electronic color into uniformity and predictability. Truly digital television, meaning systems and sets employing digital signals, was not in use until the 1990s, a point in time in which black and white television had all but disappeared. In fact, a 1992 Associated Press article noted that all of the major retailers had stopped selling regular sized black and white sets by that time and that the only real market left for them was for use in prisons.[9] (There had initially been a backlash when prisoners were given color sets as late as the 1980s due to their historical reputation as a luxury item.) Just as it had in film, black and white replaced color as the aberration, its use in the production of television programs now serving mostly to signal gravitas, reference history, mobilize

nostalgia, or connote artistry or artistic intent. Even the phrase "color television" eventually disappears as we begin to refer only to "television."

In recent years, digital television has brought stability, higher resolution, and increased depth to the color screen (which now comes in a variety of options, including LCD, LED, plasma, and OLED), but it has also introduced new complexities and contradictions at the level of standardization, technical specifications, color management, and the type of viewing experiences these technologies promise and engender. One area of complexity has to do with standards that required regular revisiting. Even though there was a proposal before the FCC to change the U.S. television standards in light of "advanced television technologies" in the late 1980s, the NTSC standard was not replaced until 2009, when the digital television standards—regulating data broadcasting, satellite direct television, and multichannel surround sound audio, along with standard definition and high-definition television—formulated by the Advanced Television Systems Committee (ATSC) were instituted.[10] Because of the rapid development of digital technologies, the ATSC has had to upgrade its standards every few years (the latest being ATSC 3.0), and in setting them, there are multiple extended international industrial debates and discussions over what might be considered the best color calibrations and processes. Beyond technical calibration, color management in contemporary film and television has elements that are part of traditional color practice, including incorporating tools of color harmony and color experts in the production process. Yet digital film in particular has brought with it advancements in color correction during postproduction that allow for an entirely new level of granularity in color use. This initially occurred during a stage described over a decade ago as the "digital intermediate" (DI), a point in the postproduction process when editing, color correction, and effects would occur, between the time when images were captured on film and when they were released, as in a final digital cut. The digital editing process enables colorists to alter saturation, hue, lighting, or skin tone in one tiny isolated area of a shot, thereby doing much of the work in the editing room that used to have to be done on set.[11] More recently, the DI stage has been redefined, as most productions are no longer shot on film before they are digitized. Consequently, the DI stage is, as a digital post-production VP explains, "the bridge between [the] offline creative edit and [the] final high-resolution, high-fidelity output," and DI itself carries on really "as a term of color correcting."[12] Digital colorists work with digital video as well, using editing software that facilitates everything from wide scale color alterations (such as adjusting all the frames in a sequence or in the entire program simultaneously) to spot color correcting. Beyond being able to create a consistency in color calibration and harmony that hadn't been possible before, these digital technologies contribute to the growing sense that television programs with high production values and Hollywood films are sharing more and more in terms of their aesthetics, or "look."

While watching programs on our current models of flat-panel display television sets, color instability and consumer set tinkering appear to exist as far-off notions for the average viewer. There is no fiddling with dials, no fussing with rabbit ears or questioning a particular network's choice of color palette. Digital screen color can now often *appear* to be seamless, since it can be difficult for an untrained eye to distinguish between colors produced by various systems and technologies. There is also not the same opportunity for interference in digital signals that there was in analog television, so the digital color image does not degrade or distort through bleeding or ghosting; but it can on occasion experience complete failure or macroblocking (the image on the screen looks like it has been broken into chunks of color) from an overload of information, weak signal strength, or malfunctioning equipment. Moreover, when viewing a standard definition color image on a smartphone, computer screen, or television, we have the impression of the quality of image being very much the same on all screen sizes.[13] Pixels have replaced beams of electrons, and while utter consistency is a fallacy in digital color (since there is variation in systems of color production and device displays, and picture defects do exist), digital television offers protection against interference and significantly higher resolution and takes up less bandwidth, even if it can be argued, as digital color historian Carolyn Kane does, that LCD technologies might maintain a "'colder' and 'flat' digital aesthetic."[14]

The history detailed in this book reveals the ways that color television altered not only the production practices and economics of the industry, but also how we understand seeing *through* and *with* color technology up to the current moment. While the claims made by the networks, inventors, and manufacturers about the perceptual abilities of color television in the postwar years were often inflated and packaged in promotional rhetoric, they succeeded in constructing a clear set of expectations for color viewing. Early viewers were promised an enhanced sensory experience that would allow them to more readily and actively surveil and be a part of nature, art, history, and foreign countries and planets, increasing their knowledge of the world and its attendant truths. It would bring them grand spectacles of entertainment intended to inspire awe and wonder and to engender a sense of immersion and transportation.

These beliefs about color's potential to reveal and transform are still at work in digital color to some degree but are now at play at in a dematerialized space in which color is organized through algorithm. Certainly, in respect to television specifically, these discursive constructions now frame high-definition and 3D television technologies even more so than color, since the latter has been naturalized into a system of daily viewing, and 3D and high-definition are considered to represent the most recent and advanced enhancements of electronic vision. That said, in her historically and theoretically rich book *Chromatic Algorithms*, Kane argues that digital color today is more highly standardized and restrictive than it was in the late 1960s period of experimentation with video and digital art, which has led to a subsequent diminishment of subjectivity, experimentation, and creativity.[15] Along similar lines, Sean Cubitt argues that largely due to the way color and texture have been standardized into "statistically averaged units," they have "become bound historically to the emergent database economy through a history of enumeration, averaging, and commodification."[16] Digital color may appear more seamless than analog electronic color, but this is at the cost, these scholars argue, of color's spontaneity, freedom, and range of expression. Digital color is in an almost constant process of revision and upgrade, and its engagement and intersection with industry, new practices and standards, artists and practitioners, and audiences' increasing expectations for color, depth, and fidelity is the legacy of electronic color, and this is where future histories and theories will be developed. Readers would be well-advised to pick up the work of scholars such as Cubitt and Kane to begin to trace the unique strands and qualities of digital color and how it ties in to the broader history of color media and color theory.

Before the transition to digital, color was the most significant technological development in television. However, as we have seen, even though the technology's discursive positioning in relation to spectacular realism succeeded in selling it as a new and unique perceptual experience, the road to color's acceptance and dissemination was complex and rather arduous, especially for RCA/NBC, the industrial actor arguably most invested in seeing it succeed. Electronic color represented transformation, modernity, and media sensory integrity, which means that its history is one not only of industry, but also of a larger perceptual shift corresponding with cultural and political changes occurring during this period. Overall, the history of color television reminds us to look more closely at those structuring elements that have become naturalized to our experience of popular mediums, whose histories we think we are already familiar with, and to ultimately discover previously untold facets of media transformations and new technologies.

NOTES

INTRODUCTION

1 Simon Brown, Sarah Street, and Liz Watkins, eds., *Color and the Moving Image* (New York: Routledge, 2013); Angela Vacche Dalle and Brian Price, eds., *Color: The Film Reader* (New York: Routledge, 2006); Tom Gunning, Joshua Yumibe, Giovanna Fossati, and Jonathan Rosen, *Fantasia of Color in Early Cinema* (Amsterdam: Amsterdam University Press, 2015); Scott Higgins, *Harnessing the Technicolor Rainbow: Color Design in the 1930s* (Austin: University of Texas Press, 2007); James Layton and David Pierce, *The Dawn of Technicolor: 1915–1935* (Rochester, NY: George Eastman House, 2015); Richard Misek, *Chromatic Cinema: A History of Screen Color* (New York: Wiley-Blackwell, 2010); Steven Peacock, *Colour* (Manchester: Manchester University Press, 2010); Sarah Street, *Colour Films in Britain: The Negotiation of Innovation 1900–55* (London: BFI, 2012); and Joshua Yumibe, *Moving Color: Early Film, Mass Culture, Modernism* (New Brunswick, NJ: Rutgers University Press, 2012).

2 See, for example, Regina Lee Blaszczyk, *The Color Revolution* (Cambridge, MA: MIT Press, 2012); and Carolyn Kane, *Chromatic Algorithms: Synthetic Color, Computer Art and Aesthetics after Code* (Chicago: University of Chicago Press, 2014).

3 Albert Abramson, *The History of Television*, 2 vols. (Jefferson, NC: McFarland, 1987), and *Electronic Motion Pictures: A History of the Television Camera* (Los Angeles: University of California Press, 1955); Raymond Fielding, *A Technological History of Motion Pictures and Television* (Berkeley: University of California Press, 1967); George Shiers, *Technical Development of Television* (Stratford, NH: Ayer, 2010); and Edwin Howard Reitan, website for the history of early color television, last updated January 30, 2007; available at https://web.archive.org/web/20160206062925/http://www.novia.net/~ereitan.

4 Brad Chisholm wrote a fantastically detailed dissertation in 1987 about CBS's development of a color system as well as a book chapter on the relationship between color film production and color television. See Chisholm,

"The CBS Color Television Venture: A Study of Failed Innovation in the Broadcasting Industry" (PhD diss., University of Wisconsin–Madison, 1987), and "Red, Blue and Lots of Green: The Impact of Color Television on Feature Film Production," in *Hollywood in the Age of Television*, ed. Tino Balio (Boston: Unwin Hyman, 1990).

5 Jonathan Sterne and Dylan Mulvin, "The Low Acuity for Blue: Perceptual Technics and American Color Television," *Journal of Visual Culture* 13, no. 2 (2014): 118–38; and Mulvin and Sterne, "Scenes from an Imaginary Country: Test Images and the American Color Television Standard," *Television and New Media* 17, no. 1 (January 2016): 21–43.

6 Jack Gould, "Tinted TV Shows Its Colors," *New York Times*, November 29, 1964, X17.

7 *Vericolor Television Studio Equipment Instruction Manual* (n.p.: Remington Rand, 1952), p. F. Available at www.earlytelevision.org/pdf/vericolor_manual .pdf.

8 Initially, Ravdin and SKF worked exclusively with Goldmark and CBS after RCA had turned the pharmaceutical company away when approached about a color system. (The color system RCA had developed was not at an especially advanced stage in 1949.) However, not long after the company's system became the color broadcast standard in 1953, RCA began to invest in medical color television too, eventually producing a camera in 1956 that claimed to be a significant improvement on previous models such as the ones produced by CBS. Weighing two hundred pounds and operated by remote control, the cameras would be installed on runners above operating tables on the same overhead fixtures that housed surgical lamps. Walter Reed Army Medical Center in Washington, DC, SKF in Philadelphia, and the University of Michigan Medical School in Ann Arbor were the first to order these new cameras. Walter Reed Army Medical Center developed a close working relationship with RCA after the hospital committed to installing three complete RCA color broadcast studios, replete with color microscopic mounts and a six-by-four-foot projector screen, within their medical system and promising to purchase more as they began to build out a "medical network for exchange of information and services." SKF, "Color Television at Medical Conventions," spring program pamphlet, 1950, Ravdin Papers, University of Pennsylvania Medical School archives, "Admin," box 44, folder 4.

9 "Color Television at Medical Conventions."

CHAPTER 1

1 Maurice le Blanc in 1880 and Jan Czczepanik in 1897 both described proposals for color television, although these did not result in practical, working models. For Bronk, see George Shiers, *Early Television: A Bibliographic Guide to 1940* (New York: Garland, 1977), 43.

2 W. E. Bijker, *Of Bicycles, Bakelites, and Bulbs: Toward a Theory of Sociotechnical Change* (Cambridge, MA: MIT Press, 1997), 6.

3 Elmer Engstrom, "Color Television—A Case History in Industrial Research," paper presented at the spring meeting of the Industrial Research Institute, San Francisco, April 21–23, 1954, p. 2, RCA press release, Sarnoff Library Collection, box M&A 1, file 33, Hagley Museum and Library, Wilmington, DE.

4 "Remarks by Mr. Frank Stanton, President of the Columbia Broadcasting System at CBS Color Television Demonstration," March 1, 1946, Frank Stanton Collection, Library of Congress, box 1, folder 10.

5 Doron Galili, "Seeing by Electricity: Television and the Modern Mediascape, 1878–1939" (PhD diss., University of Chicago, 2011). "Technological imaginary" is a concept developed by Patrice Flichy in *The Internet Imaginaire* (Cambridge, MA: MIT Press, 2007). See also Philip Sewell, *Television in the Age of Radio: Modernity, Imagination, and the Making of a Medium* (New Brunswick, NJ: Rutgers University Press, 2013).

6 Galili, "Seeing by Electricity," 86; see also John Durham Peters, "Helmholtz, Edison, and Sound History," in *Memory Bytes: History, Technology, and Digital Culture*, ed. Lauren Rabinovitz and Abraham Geil (Durham, NC: Duke University Press, 2004); and Jonathan Crary, *Suspension of Perception* (Cambridge, MA: MIT Press, 1999).

7 "Eye Taken from Boy Aided Television," *New York Times*, February 11, 1928.

8 Anne-Katrin Weber, "Recording on Film, Transmitting by Signals: The Intermediate Film System and Television's Hybridity in the Interwar Period," *Grey Room* 56 (Summer 2014): 21.

9 However, cone and rod cells, two types of photoreceptor nerve cells in the eye that make color vision possible, were missing elements in the early proposals for and prototypes of the electronic eye.

10 Herbert E. Ives and A. L. Johnsrud, "Scanning in Colors from a Beam Scanning Method," *Journal of the Optical Society of America* 20, no. 1 (1930): 11.

11 The title of this section is taken from "Painting Telepictures: Colors Are Seen on Television Screen as Radio Performs Its New Magic," *New York Times*, September 8, 1940.

12 "Colour and Daylight Television," *Manchester Guardian*, July 7, 1928.

13 Baird had been working on a concept of television since 1923, when he produced "shadowgraphs"—very basic images of lights and darks transmitted via a scanning apparatus.

14 J. C. Wilson, "Trichromatic Reproduction in Television," *Journal of the Royal Society of Arts* 82, no. 4258 (June 29, 1934): 855.

15 Herbert E. Ives, "Radio's Flickering 'Eyes' Now Sensitive to Color," *New York Times*, July 7, 1929.

16 Charles B. Rubinstein, "Optics at Bell Laboratories–General Optics, Television, and Vision," *Applied Optics* 11, no. 11 (November 1972): 2401–2411.

17 "Color Television," *Science*, July 5, 1929.

18 Ives and Johnsrud, "Scanning in Colors," 11.

19 "Color Television," *Western Electric News*, August 1929, 18.

20 "Colors Carried by Television for First Time," *Chicago Daily Tribune*, June 18, 1929.

21 "Colors Carried by Television for First Time."

22 Robert D. Heinl, "Television Reproduces Real Color," *Washington Post*, July 8, 1929.

23 Anne-Katrin Weber, "Television before TV: A Transnational History of an Experimental Medium on Display, 1928–39," PhD diss., University of Lausanne, 2014.

24 Weber, "Television before TV," 67.

25 Amy Louise Wood, *Lynching and Spectacle: Witnessing Racial Violence in America, 1890–1940* (Chapel Hill: University of North Carolina Press, 2011), 122.

26 Benjamin Gross, "Crystallizing Innovation: The Emergence of the LCD at RCA, 1951–1976" (PhD diss., Princeton University, 2011).

27 Russell Burns describes it this way: "With this method, the same colours do not overlap in alternate complete 600-line pictures; instead, in the first picture a red 200-line frame is interlaced with a blue-green frame and a red frame, while in the second picture a blue-green frame is interlaced with a red frame and a blue-green frame; that is, the red lines of the first picture are covered by the blue-green lines of the second picture and vice versa." *John Logie Baird: Television Pioneer* (London: Institution of Engineering and Technology, 2001), 365.

28 H. G. Kennard, "Television in Color Achieved by Baird Sets in England," *Christian Science Monitor*, January 18, 1941, 5.

29 "Report," *Wireless World*, April 1941.

30 "Painting Telepictures," *New York Times*, September 8, 1940.

CHAPTER 2

1 Regina Lee Blaszczyk, *The Color Revolution* (Cambridge, MA: MIT Press, 2012), 18.

2 Blaszczyk, *The Color Revolution*, 264.

3 Penny Sparke, *As Long as It's Pink: The Sexual Politics of Taste* (Halifax, Nova Scotia: Nova Scotia College of Design, 2010), 128.

4 John Gage, *Color and Meaning: Art, Science and Symbolism* (Berkeley: University of California Press, 1999).

5 For a succinct description of this type of work, see Paul Kay and Willett Kempton, "What Is the Sapir-Whorf Hypothesis?," *American Anthropologist* 86, no. 1 (March 1984): 64–79.

6 Isaac Newton, *Opticks: Or a Treatise of the Reflections, Refractions, Inflections and Colours of Light* (1704).

7 See René Descartes, *Principles of Philosophy* (1644); and John Locke, *An Essay Concerning Human Understanding* (1689).

8 Johann Wolfgang von Goethe, *Theory of Colors* (1810). Page numbers refer to *Goethe's Theory of Colours* (London: John Murray, 1840), reprinted in 2006 by Dover.

9 Ludwig Wittgenstein, *Remarks on Colour*, ed. G. E. M. Anscombe, trans. Linda L. McAlister and Margaret Schattle (Berkeley: University of California Press, 1978), 11.

10 Jonathan Crary, *Techniques of the Observer: On Vision and Modernity in the Nineteenth Century* (Cambridge, MA: MIT Press, 2001), 69. Italics in the original.

11 Goethe, *Theory of Colors*, 31, 110.

12 For more on this, see George Stahl's introduction to Schopenhauer's *On Vision and Colors* (New York: Princeton Architectural Press, 2012), 15.

13 Schopenhauer, *On Vision and Colors*, 15.

14 Schopenhauer, *On the Fourfold Root of the Principle of Sufficient Reason*, trans. E. F. J. Payne (LaSalle, IL: Open Court, 1974), 78. See also Schopenhauer, *The World as Will and Representation*, trans. E. F. J. Payne (New York: Dover, 1969).

15 Stahl, introduction to Schopenhauer, *On Vision and Colors*, 17.

16 Stahl, introduction to Schopenhauer, *On Vision and Colors*, 16.

17 Crary, *Techniques of the Observer*, 97.

18 Although, as Mary Ann Doane points out, there was an "insistent vocabulary of deception and failure" when it came to describing afterimages, or "persistence of vision," in the nineteenth and early twentieth century. Doane, *The Emergence of Cinematic Time* (Cambridge, MA: Harvard University Press, 2002), 80.

19 Goethe, *Theory of Colors*, 14.

20 Doane, *Emergence of Cinematic Time*, 80.

21 The "persistence of vision" theory was replaced by theories of "phi phenomenon, masking, and critical flicker fusion." Doane writes, "The assumptions underlying the theory of persistence of vision—retinal retention, the physiological duration of images—have been rejected in favor of the notion of critical thresholds beyond which the human eye is incapable of perceiving difference." See Doane, *Emergence of Cinematic Time*, 71.

22 Doane, *Emergence of Cinematic Time*, 79.

23 Joshua Yumibe, *Moving Color: Early Film, Mass Culture, Modernism* (New Brunswick, NJ: Rutgers University Press, 2012), 24.

24 Yumibe, *Moving Color*, 24.

25 The development of the interlaced scanning technique has upped that rate

to 60 frames per second, providing less disturbance in the perception of the image.

26 A. L. Sweet and N. R. Bartlett, "An Illusory Rotating Sweep," *American Journal of Psychology* 61, no. 3 (July 1948): 400–404.

27 G. H. Mowbray and J. W. Gebard, "The Purkinje After-Image on Screens of Cathode Ray Tubes," *American Journal of Psychology* 64, no. 4 (October 1951): 508–520.

28 Sean F. Johnston, "The Construction of Colorimetry by Committee," *Science in Context* 9, no. 4 (winter 1996): 390.

29 Johnston, "The Construction of Colorimetry by Committee," 390.

30 John Durham Peters refers to Helmholtz as "perhaps the last great universal genius of science," who "played a key role in the externalization and instrumentalization of the senses, which forms a crucial but largely forgotten backdrop for modern media." "Helmholtz, Edison and Sound History," in *Memory Bytes: History, Technology, and Digital Culture*, ed. Lauren Rabinovitz and Abraham Geil (Durham, NC: Duke University Press, 2004), 205–258. See also Richard L. Kremer, "Innovation through Synthesis: Helmholtz and Color Research," in *Hermann von Helmholtz and the Foundations of Nineteenth-Century Science*, ed. David Cahan (Berkeley: University of California Press, 1993), 229.

31 Kremer, "Innovation," in *Hermann von Helmholtz*, 229.

32 See Munsell's published works: *A Color Notation* (Boston: GH Ellis, 1905); and "A Pigment Color System and Notation," *American Journal of Psychology* 23, no. 2 (1912): 236–244; and *Atlas of the Munsell Color System* (Wadsworth-Howland, 1915).

33 Blaszczyk, *Color Revolution*, 46.

34 See Michel Eugéne Chevreul, *Principles of Harmony and Contrast of Colors: And Their Applications to the Arts*, trans. Charles Martel, 1855; Ogden N. Rood, *Modern Chromatics: With Applications to Art and Industry* (Chicago: New York: D. Appleton and Company, 1879); and Blaszczyk's description of the work of Bradley and Prang in color education during the 1880s, *Color Revolution*, 46.

35 Blaszczyk, *Color Revolution*, 64.

36 For more on the development of standards organizations and institutions during this period, see David Noble, *America by Design: Science, Technology and the Rise of Corporate Capitalism* (New York: Knopf, 1982).

37 Johnston, "The Construction of Colorimetry by Committee," 393.

38 Johnston, "The Construction of Colorimetry by Committee," 394.

39 Nickerson, "History of the Munsell Color System, Company, and Foundation: Its Scientific Application," *Color Research and Application* 1, no. 2 (summer 1976): 72–73.

40 Johnston, "The Construction of Colorimetry by Committee," 394.

41 Johnston, "The Construction of Colorimetry by Committee," 395.

42 Nickerson, "Fifty Years of the Inter-Society Color Council: Formation and Early Years," *Color Research and Application* 7, no. 1 (spring 1982): 5.

43 Johnston, "The Construction of Colorimetry by Committee," 402.

44 See also Johnston's discussion of the establishment of the CIE in 1919, which worked to set international lighting standards, consequently investing much of its effort in the measurement of the relationship between color and light. "The Construction of Colorimetry by Committee," 396–401.

45 Blaszczyk refers to how non-standardized color is considered "color chaos." See *Color Revolution*, 70.

46 Blaszczyk, *Color Revolution*, 73.

47 See Nickerson, "Fifty Years of the Inter-Society Color Council."

48 H. P. Gage, "Color Theories and the Color Council," SMPTE *Motion Image Journal* 35, no. 10 (October 1, 1940): 361–387.

49 Gage, "Color Theories and the Color Council," 378.

50 Noble, *America by Design*, 284.

51 Blaszczyk, *Color Revolution*, 116.

52 For more on this, see Sparke, *As Long as It's Pink*.

53 Blaszczyk, *Color Revolution*, 146.

54 Sarah Street, "Color Consciousness: Natalie Kalmus and Technicolor in Britain," *Screen* 50, no. 2 (summer 2009): 191–215.

55 Gage, *Color and Meaning*, 257–260.

56 Blaszczyk, *Color Revolution*, 8.

57 Blaszczyk, *Color Revolution*, 1.

58 For more, see Blaszczyk, *Color Revolution*, 141.

59 Blaszczyk, *Color Revolution*, 19.

60 David Bordwell, "Color, Shape, Movement . . . and Talk," David Bordwell's Website on Cinema, April 22, 2009, www.davidbordwell.net/blog/2009/04/22/color-shape-movement-and-talk.

61 Bordwell, "Color, Shape, Movement . . . and Talk."

62 Kinemacolor was only a two-color system (using red and green filters) and therefore wasn't able to reproduce the entire color spectrum.

63 Street, "Color Consciousness," 13.

64 Street, "Color Consciousness," 16.

65 David Bordwell, Janet Staiger, and Kristin Thompson, *The Classical Hollywood Cinema: Film Style and Mode of Production to 1960* (New York: Columbia University Press, 1985).

66 Bordwell, Staiger, and Thompson, *Classical Hollywood Cinema*, 355.

67 Natalie M. Kalmus, "Color Consciousness," *Journal of the Society of Motion Picture Engineers* (August 1935): 145. https://eastman.org/sites/default/files/technicolor/pdfs/ColorConsultants_ColorConsciousness.pdf.

68 Bordwell, Thompson, and Staiger, *Classical Hollywood Cinema*, 256.

69 Bordwell, Thompson, and Staiger, *Classical Hollywood Cinema*, 254.

70 Bordwell, Thompson, and Staiger, *Classical Hollywood Cinema*, 255.

71 Liora Salter defines voluntary standardization as intrinsically centered on and driven by industry. "The Housework of Capitalism: Standardization in the Communications and Information Technology Sectors," *International Journal of Political Economy* 23, no. 4 (winter 1993/94): 110.

72 Donald Fink, "Perspectives on Television: The Role Played by the Two NTSC's in Preparing Television Service for the American Public," *Proceedings of the IEEE* 64, no. 9 (September 1976): 1323.

73 Fink, "Perspectives on Television," 1323.

74 *Proceedings of the IRE* (1929), 1585.

75 *Proceedings of the IRE* (1929), 1585.

76 "Engineers are striving for a type of service which will satisfy moderate entertainment requirements and not require channels thousands of kilocycles in width or an apparatus which is as yet unknown." *Proceedings of the IRE* (1929), 1586.

77 The FCC began holding hearings on allocations in 1936.

78 They had proposed a system of 441 lines; 24 x 3 aspect ratio; and interlaced scanning at 20 frames per second.

79 Fink, "Perspectives on Television," 1326.

80 William Boddy, *Fifties Television: The Industry and Its Critics* (Urbana: University of Illinois Press, 1992), 33.

81 Boddy, *Fifties Television*, 33.

82 Fink, "Perspectives on Television," 1326–1327.

83 Boddy, *Fifties Television*, 35.

84 During the May 1941 FCC hearings, "CBS offered data on a mechanical color television system but was told by the commission that additional research and development of color television was necessary." Charles Kirshner, "The Color Television Controversy," *Pittsburgh Law Review* 13 (1951–1952): 71.

85 Bradley Chisholm, "The CBS Color Television Venture: A Study of Failed Innovation in the Broadcasting Industry" (PhD diss., University of Wisconsin–Madison, 1987), 203.

86 For more on this, see Chisholm, "The CBS Color Television Venture," 203.

87 Peter C. Goldmark, "Color Television—USA Standard." *Proceedings of the IRE*, October 1951, 1288.

88 Chisholm, "The CBS Color Television Venture," 262.

89 Holcomb B. Noble, "Frank Stanton, Broadcast Pioneer, Dies at 98," *New York Times*, December 26, 2006.

90 "Report of the Commission," FCC docket 7896, March 18, 1947, 3.

91 Hugh Slotten, *Radio and Television Regulation: Broadcast Technology in the United States, 1920–1960* (Baltimore: Johns Hopkins University Press, 2000), 26.

92 "RCA Lays Off-Color Egg, Verdict on D.C. Demonstration vs. CBS; But All Agree It Tops Black and White," *Variety*, October 12, 1949.

93 For more on CBS, UHF, and color, see Boddy, *Fifties Television*, 42–62.

94 The Senate advisory committee—headed up by E. U. Condon, director of NBS—seems to have been set up by Edwin Johnson, Democratic senator and chair of the Senate Interstate and Foreign Commerce Committee; Johnson was critical of and frustrated with the FCC and, more pointedly, its chairman, Wayne Coy, who Johnson believed was conspiring with powerful agents of the television industry to keep color television from the public. See Advisory Committee on Color Television, "Present Status of Color Television," report to the Committee on Interstate and Foreign Commerce (Washington, DC: Government Printing Office, 1950), iii.

95 Slotten, *Radio and Television Regulation*, 218.

96 Advisory Committee on Color Television, "Present Status of Color Television," 1.

97 As Slotten points out, while the Advisory Committee on Color Television did not recommend the adoption of a particular system, it did suggest that CBS's system had "progressed further toward full realization of its potential" within the confines of the suggested standards for scanning lines. Slotten, *Radio and Television Regulation*, 219.

98 Advisory Committee on Color Television, "Present Status of Color Television," 53.

99 Advisory Committee on Color Television, "Present Status of Color Television," 53.

100 Fink, "Alternative Approaches to Color Television," *Proceedings of the IRE*, 1951, 18–19.

101 Chisholm, "The CBS Color Television Venture," 357.

102 "Supreme Court to Review CBS Color TV Order," *Chicago Tribune*, March 6, 1951.

103 For more on RCA's public interest claim, see Kirshner, "Color Television Controversy."

104 Ed Reitan, "CBS Color Television System Chronology," last updated November 24, 2006, available at https://web.archive.org/web/20160101224814/http://www.novia.net/~ereitan/CBS_Chronology_rev_h_edit.htm.

105 Chisholm, "The CBS Color Television Venture," 428. It seems from a number of sources that Goldmark was pushing for this deal in an effort to keep color moving forward at CBS and had failed to disclose (or at least had minimized) the problems with Hytron. See also William Paley, *As It Happened: A Memoir* (New York: Doubleday, 1979), 221.

106 Fink, "Alternative Approaches to Color Television," 26.

107 Mara Mills, in her work on the vocoder and telephone technology, discusses the way that perception can and has been built into particular com-

munication technologies. "Media and Prosthesis: The Vocoder, the Artificial Larynx, and the History of Signal Processing," *Qui Parle: Critical Humanities and Social Sciences* 21, no. 1 (fall/winter 2012): 136.

108 Jonathan Sterne and Dylan Mulvin, "The Low Acuity for Blue: Perceptual Technics and American Color Television," *Journal of Visual Culture* 13, no. 2 (August 2014): 121. See also Carolyn Kane on this in *Chromatic Algorithms: Synthetic Color, Computer Art and Aesthetics after Code* (Chicago: University of Chicago Press, 2014), 67.

109 See T. Smith and J. Guild, "The CIE Colorimetric Standards and Their Use," *Transactions of the Optical Society* 33, no. 3 (1931–1932): 5–134.

110 Richard Sewall Hunter, *The Measurement of Appearance*, 2nd ed. (New York: John Wiley and Sons, 1991), 97.

111 W. T. Wintringham, "Color Television and Colorimetry," *Proceedings of the IRE*, October 1951, 1135–1172.

112 Donald G. Fink, *Television Standards and Practice: Selected Papers from the National Television System Committee and Its Panels* (New York, NY: McGraw-Hill, 1943), 371.

113 There were some "real viewers" asked to participate in field testing, although they did not participate in the psychophysical tests.

114 Chisholm, "The CBS Color Television Venture," 376. Chisholm also noted that this was done in Washington, DC, Saint Louis, and Baltimore, but nowhere outside the Eastern Seaboard.

115 Donald Fink, *Color Television Standards: Selected Papers and Records of the National Television System Committee* (New York: McGraw-Hill, 1955), 64.

116 Fink, *Color Television Standards*, 64.

117 Dylan Mulvin and Jonathan Sterne, "Scenes from an Imaginary Country: Test Images and the American Color Television Standard," *Television and New Media* 17, no. 1 (January 2016): 21–43.

118 Also note how Mulvin and Sterne conclude that "interpretations of white skin tones were directly encoded in the color standard." "Scenes from an Imaginary Country," 16.

119 See Sterne and Mulvin's discussion of the Weber-Fechner law of just-noticeable difference, a "logarithmic relationship between measurable stimulus and sensation," which is used in arguments for signal compression. "Low Acuity for Blue," 126.

120 Sterne and Mulvin, "Low Acuity for Blue," 122.

121 Yet in CBS's color system, unlike monochrome television, in order to include information about color, other details in the image had to be dropped.

122 Sterne and Mulvin point out that "since psychophysical theories of the eye suggested that human sensitivity was normally much higher for green than for red, and even more so for blue, the image only needed to transmit

a small amount of the blue signal and slightly more for red to achieve an image that was adequately sharp." "Low Acuity for Blue," 127.

123 See Peters, "Helmholtz, Edison, and Sound History," 183.

124 Peters, "Helmholtz, Edison, and Sound History," 187.

125 Mills, "Media and Prosthesis."

126 Mills, "Media and Prosthesis," 135.

127 Mills, "Media and Prosthesis," 107–49.

128 See Sterne and Mulvin, "Low Acuity for Blue."

129 The American NTSC system has been considered inferior to other color systems developed and standardized elsewhere (PAL, another international standard, for example).

130 "Device dependent" is a term used currently in the context of digital technologies, but here it refers to the idea that each brand, model, and even unit of a color receiver may display the RGB color signals in a unique way.

131 National Television System Committee (1951–1953), Report and Reports of Panel No. 11, 11-A, 12–19, with Some supplementary references cited in the Reports, and the Petition for adoption of transmission standards for color television before the Federal Communications Commission, n.p., 1953, 83.

132 Fink, "Alternative Approaches to Color Television," 1126.

133 Fink, "Alternative Approaches to Color Television," 1126.

134 As Mulvin and Sterne show, this language of "pleasing" images stems from postwar hedonic testing methods, which involve subjects being asked to rate the sensory experience on a scale representing a degree of acceptability. "Scenes from an Imaginary Country."

135 Fink, "Alternative Approaches to Color Television," 1126.

136 Advisory Committee on Color Television, "Present Status of Color Television," 7.

137 See Sterne and Mulvin, "Low Acuity for Blue"; and Boddy, *Fifties Television*.

138 RCA was the parent company of NBC, but RCA manufactured television and radio receivers while NBC was the network that provides programming. They worked together on the color television project but also often had separate roles in that mission.

139 Chisholm, "The CBS Color Television Venture," 439.

140 John T. Cahill, Robert L. Werner, Ray B. Houston, Eugene E. Beyer, "Petition of Radio Corporation of America and National Broadcasting Company, Inc. for Approval of Color Standards for the RCA Color Television System," June 25, 1953, 399–400.

141 Cahill, Werner, Houston, Beyer, "Petition of Radio Corporation of America," June 25, 1953.

142 Fink, *Color Television Standards*, 37.

143 Eugene Lyons, *David Sarnoff* (New York: Harper and Row, 1966), 304.

1   A version of this chapter was published as "'Never Twice the Same Colour': Standardizing, Calibrating and Harmonizing NTSC Colour Television in the Early 1950s," *Screen* 56, no. 4 (winter 2015): 415–435.

2   Ace Goodman, "The Hue and the Cry," *Saturday Review*, June 10, 1951, 24.

3   Robert Metz, *CBS: Reflections in a Bloodshot Eye* (New York: Playboy Press, 1975). CBS, for example, came under especially intense scrutiny, as their 1946 proposal for color was thought to be primarily a move to delay all television approval and operation, since they did not have enough stations at that point to compete effectively with NBC. In May 1950, CTI charged RCA and CBS with pushing ahead too hard and too quickly with the technology and therefore "trying to dominate television with control of color rights," while the RMA was also accused of having too much power in the standards process and possibly biasing the various committees. See "'Interests' Found Delaying Color TV," *New York Times*, May 9, 1950; and "RCA, CBS Charged with Trying to Control Television Color Rights," *Wall Street Journal*, May 19, 1950.

4   See Robert Lewis Shayon, "2591 Years of 'Progress': Thales, Paley and Sarnoff," *Saturday Review of Literature* 34 (July 28, 1951), 26, 83; Jack Gould, "The Hidden Costs of Color," *New York Times*, May 1, 1966; and Saul Carson, "On the Air: Color for What?" *New Republic* 121 (October 31, 1949), 20–21.

5   Neil Harris, "Color and Media: Some Comparisons and Speculations," *Prospects* 11 (1986), 7–27.

6   CBS had a number of color programs on the air from June to October 1951, the period immediately after its initial FCC approval. However, when the FCC reversed its decision and established the NTSC system as the standard, CBS stopped investing in and promoting color broadcasting to any great degree until the mid-1960s.

7   "Faded Rainbow," *Time*, October 22, 1956.

8   William Paley, *As It Happened: A Memoir* (New York: Doubleday, 1979), 208.

9   "Colorvision in 1954 Is Aim of Video Industry," *Chicago Daily News*, October 4, 1953.

10 John Crosby, "And Now—Color," *New York Herald Tribune*, June 3, 1951.

11 A compatible system is one in which existing monochrome sets could still pick up color broadcasts. CBS's system was an adaptable system, which required consumers to buy an adapter to receive any programming that broadcast through the color system.

12 Joseph Roizen, "Universal Color Television: An Electronic Fantasia," *IEEE Spectrum*, March 1967, 112–114. Some of the problems with the system

during this period were attributed to the receiver phosphors specified by the FCC, as many engineers noted that they were low in efficiency, leading to low screen luminances and trailing colors, with red and green in particular often leaving yellow trails behind moving objects.

13 See Bernard Grob, *Basic Television* (New York: Maple Press, 1954), 595–612, 647–652; and Robert L. Goodman, *Color TV Case Histories Illustrated* (Summit, PA: Tab Books, 1975).

14 Advisory Committee on Color Television, "Present Status of Color Television," report to the Committee on Interstate and Foreign Commerce (Washington, DC: Government Printing Office, 1950).

15 Advisory Committee on Color Television, "Present Status of Color Television," 59.

16 A number of the color troubles described here have to do with flicker rate. Flicker fusion rate or threshold is a concept of psychophysics, related to the notion of persistence of vision, which describes the frequency at which the human eye perceives a seamless moving image when confronted by an intermittent light stimulus—such as the scanning process in television reception. In film and television, the threshold is described as occurring at around 24 frames per second; however, at this speed, there might be problems with visual disturbances and irritations related to brightness. As RCA's Elmer Engstrom describes: "For black and white it was understood that it would require picture repetition rate of 60 per second. Actually in black and white television, 30 complete pictures are transmitted each second. A method called line interlace fools the eye into thinking it is seeing 60 pictures per second. Since television transmission is accomplished by scanning the picture in lines, we scan the even numbered lines of the picture across the entire picture area and then go back and scan the odd numbered lines. These odd lines are, of course, 'interlaced' with the even lines. Thus we complete a total picture scanning 30 times per second, but we pass over the picture area 60 times per second." "Color Television—A Case History in Industrial Research," Paper presented at the spring meeting of the Industrial Research Institute, San Francisco, April 21–23, 1954, 8, RCA press release files, Sarnoff Library Collection, box M & A, file 33, Hagley Museum and Library, Wilmington, DE. See also National Television System Committee (1951–1953), "Reports of Panel No. 11, 11-A, 12–19," vol. 1, 96–97.

17 For more on this, see the discussion of theories of failure in vision related to movement and color in Doane, *The Emergence of Cinematic Time: Modernity, Contingency, the Archive* (Cambridge, MA: Harvard University Press, 2002), 76–78. One such failure of vision was mentioned in a 1950 *Time* article: "Some viewers of the CBS complain of 'color flash' when they look away from the screen. . . . CBS officials point out that the eye quickly

becomes adjusted and that color flash (caused by the persistence in the eye of the last one-color picture seen) soon disappears." "Color Climax," *Time*, October 23, 1950, 68.

18 The advisory committee's 1950 report also contained a detailed discussion of ideal placement of the television viewer in front of the color screen. Advisory Committee on Color Television, "Present Status of Color Television," 7.

19 Elmer Engstrom, head of television research at RCA Labs, explained that one of the ways that his lab took advantage of the "properties of the human eye" to conserve spectrum space was to apply "a plan of mixed highs and transmit no color in the very small areas" because "the eye responds to brightness in the fine detail, but is insensitive to hue changes in the fine detail." "Color Television," 11.

20 See Mulvin and Sterne, "Low Acuity for Blue."

21 W. T. Wintringham, "Color Television and Colorimetry," *Proceedings of the IRE*, October 1951, 1135–1172; and Jack Gould, "New Age of Color," *New York Times*, November 8, 1953.

22 "Upheaval, Markets to Come for a Still-Infant Industry," *Life*, January 4, 1954, 58.

23 In 1953, NBC provided the comparison of $19,200 for a black and white and $28,900 for a color program. "Color Television Workshop for the Members of the Radio and Television Executives Society," December 10, 1953, 14–15, box 395, folder 2, National Broadcasting Company Archive, Wisconsin Historical Society.

24 Memo from Judy-Schwerin Research Corp., March 10, 1953, box 395, folder 7, National Broadcasting Company Archive, Wisconsin Historical Society. This warning against "color for color's sake" was a common one in discourse around color film too. For more on this, see Scott Higgins, *Harnessing the Technicolor Rainbow: Color Design in the 1930s* (Austin: University of Texas Press, 2007).

25 Gould, "New Age of Color."

26 For more on the implications of CBS's failed color venture, see Bradley Chisholm, "The CBS Color Television Venture: A Study of Failed Innovation in the Broadcasting Industry" (PhD diss., University of Wisconsin–Madison, 1987).

27 David Batchelor, *Chromophobia* (London: Reaktion Books, 2000).

28 Batchelor, *Chromophobia*, 22–23.

29 John Gage, *Color and Culture: Practice and Meaning from Antiquity to Abstraction* (Boston: Bullfinch Press, 1993), 204–209.

30 Stephen Melville, "Color Has Not Yet Been Named: Objectivity in Deconstruction," in *Deconstruction and the Visual Arts*, ed. P. Brunnette and D. Wills (Cambridge: Cambridge University Press, 1993), 451.

31　Memo from Alfred N. Goldsmith to David Sarnoff, December 7, 1950, National Broadcasting Company Archive, box 118, folder 51, Wisconsin Historical Society.

32　"The Importance of Color," memo, September 1951, National Broadcasting Company Archive, box 119, folder 71, Wisconsin Historical Society.

33　"The Importance of Color," memo.

34　See Engstrom, "Color Television."

35　In August 1954, for example, a series of color clinics for around 1,500 representatives for agencies and advertisers were held in twelve sessions over a week in the lounge of the Center Theatre, in Rockefeller Center, and featured a live color showing of "Products in Color." Memo, National Broadcasting Company Archive, box 122, folder 75, Wisconsin Historical Society.

36　"Products, Commercials and Agencies Presented on Color Clinics," October 27, 1953, memo, National Broadcasting Company Archive, box 395, folder 4, Wisconsin Historical Society.

37　"Agencymen See Color Backstage," *Broadcasting-Telecasting*, November 29, 1954, 34–36, 59.

38　Howard Ketcham, *Color Planning for Business and Industry* (New York: Harper and Brothers, 1958), 167. Charles A. Riley called Ketcham "one of the great authorities on color in this century," in *Color Codes* (Lebanon, NH: University Press of New England, 1995), 312.

39　Riley, *Color Codes*, 312.

40　Karal Ann Marling, *As Seen on TV: The Visual Culture of Everyday Life in the 1950s* (Cambridge, MA: Harvard University Press, 1996), 221.

41　Marling, *As Seen on TV*, 168.

42　"Special Color Report," *Television Magazine*, April 1954, 31.

43　Memo from the Judy-Scherwin Research Corp., March 10, 1953.

44　Ketcham, *Color Planning for Business and Industry*, 174.

45　"Color Television Workshop," December 10, 1953, 14–15.

46　"Color Television Workshop," December 10, 1953, 14–15.

47　David Bordwell, Janet Staiger, and Kristin Thompson, *The Classical Hollywood Cinema: Film Style and Mode of Production to 1960* (New York: Routledge, 1985), 354.

48　Higgins, *Harnessing the Technicolor Rainbow*, 126.

49　Bordwell, Staiger, and Thompson, *Classical Hollywood Cinema*, 355.

50　Sarah Street, "Color Consciousness: Natalie Kalmus and Technicolor in Britain," *Screen* 50, no. 2 (summer 2009): 192.

51　Street is quoting Kay Harrison, the U.K. manager of Technicolor at the time. See Street, "Color Consciousness," 213.

52　"Lighting Can Change the Color of a Product Considerably, and Color TV Will Demand Rigid Light Control," "Special Color Report," *Television Magazine*, April 1954.

53 See Ketcham, *Color Planning for Business and Industry*, 171–172.

54 "Color Television Workshop," December 10, 1953, 14–15.

55 "Special Color Report," *Television Magazine*, April 1954.

56 "The Importance of Color," memo.

57 "The Importance of Color," memo.

58 "The Importance of Color," memo.

59 Institute for Motivational Research, "Psy-color-gy: A Motivational Study of the Impact of Color Television" (1966), box 132, folder 1, Ernest Dichter Papers, Hagley Museum and Library, Wilmington, DE.

60 Regina Lee Blaszczyk, *The Color Revolution* (Cambridge, MA: MIT Press, 2012), 221.

61 Blaszczyk, *Color Revolution*, 221.

62 "After Years of Experiments, NBC Plans Spectacular Color Shows," *Buffalo Courier*, May 2, 1953.

63 "After Years of Experiments, NBC Plans Spectacular Color Shows."

64 John Crosby, "Want Some Confusion? Ask Nets about Color TV," *Washington Post*, October 27, 1953.

65 "The Current Upsurge in Color Television," press release (1960), box 1, file 4, RCA Publicity Files, David Sarnoff Research Center Records (unprocessed), Hagley Museum and Library, Wilmington, DE.

66 "Special Color Report" *Television Magazine*, April 1954.

67 Advisory Committee on Color Television, "Present Status of Color Television," 7.

68 E. Carlton Winckler, "Lighting the Network TV Program," *Journal of the SMPTE* 65 (September 1956), 495.

69 "Miss Color," *New Yorker*, August 11, 1951, 20.

70 Val Adams, "Marie: Red-Headed Test Pattern," *New York Times*, November 8, 1953. Actress Leslie Parrish was also an NBC color girl starting in 1954 under her birth name, Marjorie Hellen, and working at the network until 1959, and Nanette Fabray was used in many NBC color demonstrations and experimental broadcasts in the first couple of years of the 1950s.

71 Joseph Pugliese, "Biometrics, Infrastructural Whiteness, and the Racialized Zero Degree of Nonrepresentation," *Boundary* 34, no. 2 (2007).

72 See Richard Dyer, *White: Essays on Race and Culture* (New York: Routledge, 1997), 92–94; Brian Winston, "A Whole Technology of Dyeing: A Note on Ideology and the Apparatus of the Chromatic Moving Image," *Daedalus* 114, no. 4 (fall 1985): 105–123; Brian Winston, *Technologies of Seeing: Photography, Cinematography and Television*, (London: British Film Institute, 1997), 39–57; and Lorna Roth, "Looking at Shirley, the Ultimate Norm: Color Balance, Image Technologies, and Cognitive Equity," *Canadian Journal of Communication* 34 (2009): 111–136.

73 Dylan Mulvin and Jonathan Sterne, "Scenes from an Imaginary Country:

Test Images and the American Color Television Standard," *Television and New Media* 17, no. 1 (January 2016): 16.

74 Dyer, *White*, 94.

75 Winston, *Technologies of Seeing*, 56.

76 "The Current Upsurge in Color Television," 5–6.

77 Jesse C. Beesley, "What You Should Know about Color TV," *Los Angeles Times*, May 16, 1954.

78 Alfred R. Zipser, Jr., "Costs of Color TV Delay Mass Sales," *New York Times*, February 12, 1955, 23.

79 Crosby, "Want Some Confusion?," 31.

80 Crosby, "Want Some Confusion?," 31.

81 In 1966, Philco introduced a "color tuning eye," and in 1967, Westinghouse introduced an "on-screen tuning bar," which allowed set owners to make adjustments with a tuning knob in relation to two parallel lines on the right side of the screen that would come together once the image was "perfectly tuned." In 1968, Philco announced "auto-lock channel tuning" that would work with their color tuning eye. "Westinghouse Feature—a Picture in Ten Seconds," *Chicago Tribune*, November 12, 1967.

82 However, as late as 1960, journalists were noting problems with color reception (through weather disruptions, interference, etc.). As Joan Walker wrote for the *Washington Post* that year, "With all the elements with you, and all the dialing at your command, you can still end up with two performers side by side—one a man with normal skin color face and purple hands, the other an ashen faced chap waving yellow-green digits." "Living with Living Color," *Washington Post*, December 25, 1960.

83 Tom Gunning, "Colorful Metaphors: The Attraction of Color in Early Silent Cinema," *Fotogenia* 1, 1994: 249–255.

84 Steve Neale, *Cinema and Technology: Sound, Image, Colour* (London: Macmillan, 1985), 147.

85 Edward Buscombe, "Sound and Color," *Jump Cut* 17 (April 1978): 23–25.

86 "Color Television Workshop," December 10, 1953.

87 Frank Stanton, FCC testimony, March 22, 1950, folder 10, Stanton Files, Library of Congress. The proposal was for three hours per day, five days per week, before 6:00 PM; one half-hour per day, five days per week, between 6:00 and 8:00 PM; one half-hour per day, five days per week, at close of regular black and white transmissions, or at such earlier time after 9:00 PM as the network chose.

88 Frank Stanton, FCC testimony, March 22, 1950.

89 George Rosen, "Television Review: CBS's 'Premiere' Colorcast Historic but Lacking in Sock Showmanship," *Variety*, June 27, 1951.

90 "Tinted TV Debut," *Wall Street Journal*, June 26, 1951.

91 "CBS Color Football," *Billboard*, October 13, 1951.

92 Richard Lewine, "It's Been a Colorful Year," *Variety*, July 28, 1954.

93 Mark Schubin, "The Fandom of the Opera: How Opera Has Helped Create the Modern Media World," lecture at the Library of Congress, Washington, DC, October 6, 2011. PowerPoint and audio of the talk can be downloaded from http://www.schubincafe.com/tag/opera-history.

94 Sarnoff letter to station managers, July 1, 1954, National Broadcasting Company Archive, box 395, folder 2, Wisconsin Historical Society.

95 "Color Programming 1956," remarks by Richard Pinkham, February 1, 1956, National Broadcasting Company Archive, box 172, folder 19, Wisconsin Historical Society.

96 "ANA Color TV Demonstration from the Colonial Theatre," memo, September 21, 1953, National Broadcasting Company Archive, box 133, folder 12, Wisconsin Historical Society.

97 See memo from John Herbert to Pat Weaver, August 1953, National Broadcasting Company Archive, box 392, folder 27, Wisconsin Historical Society; "Color Television Workshop," December 10, 1953.

98 Memo from Joseph A. McDonald to Pat Weaver, Robert Sarnoff, et al., January 22, 1954, National Broadcasting Company Archive, box 166, folder 16, Wisconsin Historical Society.

99 "Five-fold Expansion of Color TV Program Schedule Announced by NBC," press release, August 1, 1955, National Broadcasting Company Archive, box 169, folder 34, Wisconsin Historical Society.

100 James L. Baughman, "'Show Business in the Living Room': Management Expectations for American Television, 1947–56," *Business and Economic History* 26, no. 2 (winter 1997): 718–726.

101 "BT Interview: Weaver Scans the Way Ahead," *Broadcasting-Telecasting* 48, no. 9 (February 28, 1955): 35, 38–40.

102 Baughman, "'Show Business in the Living Room'," 721.

103 "Networks: NBC-TV Announces 'Greatest Season' with 75 Spectaculars and Specials," *Broadcasting-Telecasting* 49, no. 2 (July 11, 1955): 94.

104 "Grey Agency Advises on Packaging and Color TV," *Broadcasting-Telecasting*, August 23, 1954, 32.

105 John Crosby, "Television's Peter Pan Is Pure Enchantment," *Hartford Courant*, March 8, 1955.

106 John Beaufort, "'Peter Pan' Afterglow; 'A Connecticut Yankee': Radio-TV," *Christian Science Monitor*, March 15, 1955.

107 Ray Oviatt, "Jackie Gleason Starts 'Living Again,'" *Toledo Blade*, October 3, 1956.

108 "TV Station Owners Cogitate Future of Color Programming," *Billboard*, May 29, 1954.

109 Furman Hebb, "Color TV Today," *Popular Electronics*, September 1959.

1 "NBC-RCA Cutting Some Fancy Chi Capers for All-Time Station Bow," *Variety*, April 4, 1956. "All-color" meant that both local and network programming were produced in color—not that the entire programming schedule was in color.

2 Robert Sarnoff would become known for streamlining financing, production, and programming at the network with the help of Robert Kinter, who became president in 1958. As opposed to Weaver, whose programming theories were geared toward experimentation and cultural uplift alongside network branding, Kinter and Sarnoff (referred to as "the Bob and Bob show") produced a steady stream of mass-appeal programming.

3 "Additional Exploitation at NARTB Convention," NBC Memo, March 12, 1956, National Broadcasting Company Archive, box 172, folder 17, Wisconsin Historical Society,

4 "Color Round-the-Clock at WNBQ (TV) Chicago," *Broadcasting-Telecasting*, April 9, 1956, 69–72.

5 "Color Round-the-Clock," 71.

6 Color set sales were relatively flat until the early 1960s, when RCA saw a modest sales jump.

7 Alan Brinkley, "The Fifties," Gilder Lehrman Institute of American History website, www.gilderlehrman.org/history-by-era/fifties/essays/fifties, accessed January 10, 2017.

8 Regina Lee Blaszczyk, *The Color Revolution* (Cambridge, MA: MIT Press, 2012), 256.

9 Lynn Spigel, *Make Room for TV: Television and the Family Ideal in Postwar America* (Chicago: University of Chicago Press, 1992).

10 Ray E. Barfield, *A Word from Our Viewers: Reflections from Early Television Audiences* (Westport, CT: Greenwood Press, 2008), 29.

11 Herbert Pfister, "TV Color Sampler Costs only $8," *Popular Mechanics*, September 1951, 165.

12 Furman Hebb, "Color TV Today," *Popular Electronics*, September 1959, 41.

13 "A Profile of Today's Color Owners," NBC memo, National Broadcasting Company Archive, box 11, folder 9, "Mass Communication Ephemera," Wisconsin Historical Society.

14 Thomas E. Coffin, "Preliminary Report on Colortown," memo, November 29, 1956, National Broadcasting Company Archive, box 140, folder 16, Wisconsin Historical Society.

15 In 1961, the president of Crosley wrote, "The phenomenal growth of color receivers in this area is due in large part to the cooperation of Ohio Appliances, Inc., the RCA distributor in Cincinnati, Dayton and Columbus, Ohio, with Crosley Broadcasting," and described how WLW-T, the local color

station, also worked out payment plans with tavern owners to display (and thus promote) color receivers in the town. He also described a related focus on sports through WLW-T's purchase of a color mobile unit. "RE: Dunville, Cincinnati-'Colortown U.S.A' in Television Daily 'Impact of Color Television,'" NBC pamphlet, 1960, National Broadcasting Company Archive, box 11, folder 9, "Mass Communication Ephemera," Wisconsin Historical Society.

16 Coffin, "Preliminary Report on Colortown."

17 Mark Alvey, "'Too Many Kids and Old Ladies': Quality Demographics and 1960s U.S. Television," *Screen* 45, no. 1 (2004): 40–62; Lizabeth Cohen, *A Consumers' Republic: The Politics of Mass Consumption in Postwar America* (New York: Vintage, 2003); Wendell Smith, "Product Differentiation and Market Segmentation as Alternative Marketing Strategies," *Journal of Marketing* 21, no. 1 (July 1965): 3–8.

18 Cohen, *A Consumers' Republic*, 295.

19 Pierre Martineau, "The Personality of the Retail Store," *Harvard Business Review* 36 (1958): 47–55.

20 Thomas E. Coffin and Sam Tuchman, "The Impact of Color," in *Television: The Business of Colorcasting*, ed. Howard W. Coleman (New York: Hastings House, 1968), 121–123.

21 Coffin and Tuchman, "The Impact of Color," 121–122.

22 Coffin and Tuchman, "The Impact of Color," 121–122.

23 "They're Selling Color TV Today," *Electrical Merchandising*, March 1956, box 1, file 48, Vladimir Zworykin Files, David Sarnoff Research Center Records (unprocessed), Hagley Museum and Library, Wilmington, DE.

24 "They're Selling Color TV Today."

25 See, for example, "Color Television: A Rating Survey in Color vs. Black & White TV Homes and an Attitude Study among Color TV Set Owners," Burke Marketing Research (Cleveland: AVCO Broadcasting Corporation, 1959). NBC claimed in 1962 that six major surveys of color audiences had occurred at that point.

Six major surveys so far (1962):

(1) Colortown study conducted in 1956 by NBC and Batten, Barton, Durstine & Osborn, Inc.

(2) the Cincinnati study conducted in 1959 by the Crosley Broadcasting Corp and Crosley's WLW, Cincinnati.

(3) the "Trendex five-city study" conducted in 1959 by NBC.

(4) the "impact study" conducted in 1960 by the Crosley Broadcasting Corp and WLW.

(5) "the impact of color commercials in black and white programs" conducted in 1961 by NBC and William Esty company.

(6) "Omaha-ARB study" completed in May 1962.

Impact study, 1960, wlw-Crossley, section 3, "The Broadcaster," 1962, box 9, folder 19, RCA Public Relations Files, David Sarnoff Research Center Records (unprocessed), Hagley Museum and Library, Wilmington, DE.

26 Eric Schaps and Lester Guest, "Some Pros and Cons of Color TV," *Journal of Advertising Research* 8, no. 2 (1968): 28–39.

27 Impact study, 1960 wlw-Crosley, section 3, "The Broadcaster," 1962, box 9, folder 19, RCA Public Relations Files, David Sarnoff Research Center Records (unprocessed), Hagley Museum and Library, Wilmington, DE.

28 Joshua Yumibe, *Moving Color: Early Film, Mass Culture, Modernism* (New Brunswick, NJ: Rutgers University Press, 2012), 108–109.

29 Stefan Schwarzkopf and Rainer Gries, eds., *Ernest Dichter and Motivation Research* (New York: Palgrave, 2010), 4.

30 Institute for Motivational Research, "Psy-color-gy: A Motivational Research Study on Television Commercials in Color," Submitted to: Television Advertising Representatives, Inc., New York, NY, October 1966.

31 "Psy-color-gy."

32 "Psy-color-gy."

33 "Psy-color-gy."

34 "Psy-color-gy," xxi–xxx.

35 "Additional NBC Color Programming," memo, April 27, 1955, National Broadcasting Company Archive, box 405, folder 3, Wisconsin Historical Society.

36 "Additional NBC Color Programming."

37 "Additional NBC Color Programming."

38 Kenyon and Eckhardt promotion department, "RCA Victor Color Television Promotion Plans," report to RCA Victor, July 18, 1955, National Broadcasting Company Archive, box 69, folder 21, Wisconsin Historical Society.

39 Kenyon and Eckhardt, "RCA Victor Color Television Promotion Plans."

40 Anna McCarthy, *Ambient Television: Visual Culture and Public Space* (Durham, NC: Duke University Press, 2001).

41 Kenyon and Eckardt promotion department, "RCA Victor Color Television Promotion Plans."

42 Kenyon and Eckhardt promotion department, "RCA Victor Color Television Promotion Plans."

43 Cohen, *A Consumers' Republic*, 264.

44 McCarthy, *Ambient Television*, 69. See also Malcolm Gladwell, "The Terrazzo Jungle," *New Yorker,* March 15, 2004, www.newyorker.com/magazine/2004/03/15/the-terrazzo-jungle.

45 McCarthy, *Ambient Television*, 63.

46 Radio dealer Brunio and Krish-Radisco installed twenty-one-inch color receivers in supermarkets in December 1956. "RCA's Master Plan to Sell Color TV," *Time,* January 14, 1956.

47 There were limitations to these units. Describing this time as the "novelty

days" of TV mobile units—both monochrome and color—Allen A. Walsh wrote, "In almost every instance, once the equipment was installed and tested, it was painfully realized that there was barely enough room for technical personnel and none for program personnel and client representatives." "Color Television Mobile Units," *Journal of the SMPTE* 81 (November 1972): 846.

48 "Color TV Meets the People," RCA *Radio Age*, January 1955, 11.

49 "RCA, NBC Accelerate Color TV Drive," RCA *Radio Age*, October 1955, 7.

50 See Charles Musser and Carol Nelson, *High-Class Moving Pictures: Lyman H. Howe and the Forgotten Era of Traveling Exhibition, 1880–1920* (Princeton, NJ: Princeton University Press, 1991); John Plunkett, "Selling Stereoscopy: Automatic Machines and American Salesmen, 1890–1915," *Early Popular Visual Culture* 6, no. 3 (November 2008): 239–255; Dawn Larsen, "The Canvas Cathedral: Toby Shows as Nativistic Social Movements," *Theatre History Studies* 21 (June 2001), 87–101; and Solveig Jülich, "Media as Modern Magic: Early X-Ray Imaging and Cinematography in Sweden," *Early Popular Visual Culture* 6, no. 1 (April 2008): 1934.

51 Gregory A. Waller, "Robert Southard and the History of Traveling Film Exhibition," *Film Quarterly* 57, no. 2 (winter 2003–2004): 11.

52 Waller, "Robert Southad and the History of Traveling Film Exhibition."

53 "Now! For Your Closed-Circuit Show . . . RCA TV COLOR CARAVAN," pamphlet, 1956, National Broadcasting Company Archive, box 230, folder 1, Wisconsin Historical Society.

54 "Now! For Your Closed-Circuit Show."

55 See "Color Status Report," February 7, 1957, National Broadcasting Company Archive, box 176, folder 10, Wisconsin Historical Society.

56 O. B. Hanson, "Expansion of AT&T Color Television Network Circuits," memo to Robert Sarnoff, March 2, 1954, National Broadcasting Company Archive, box 122, folder 75, Wisconsin Historical Society.

57 Hanson, "Expansion of AT&T Color Television Network Circuits."

58 Roy Bacus, "The Local Station and Color," in Coleman, *Television*, 176.

59 In a 1966 study by Katz Agency Research, the average amount spent by stations to convert was $293,000. See Bacus, "The Local Station and Color," 190.

60 "The Broadcaster," RCA publicity files. WCCO-TV in Minneapolis was also an early color broadcaster, producing *Country Holiday* in December 1954. "Twin City Milestones," Pavek Museum website, http://www.pavekmuseum .org/tctvchron.html, accessed September 4, 2017. See also Ed Reitan, "The Color Pioneers: Local Television Stations with Early Live Color Capability," last updated November 21, 2006. Available at https://web.archive.org /web/20151222080454/www.novia.net/~ereitan/PION_6m.htm.

61 "City to Get First Full-Time TV Color Station," *Chicago Daily Tribune*, November 4, 1955.

62 Christopher Anderson and Michael Curtin, "Mapping the Ethereal City: Chicago Television, the FCC, and the Politics of Place," *Quarterly Review of Film and Video* 16, no. 3–4 (1997): 289–305.

63 See, for example, Harriet van Horne, "The Chicago Touch," *Theatre Arts*, July 1951; and "The Chicago School with Special Emphasis on Dave Garroway," *Time*, September 11, 1950.

64 "Garroway," *Time*, September 11, 1950.

65 "Garroway," *Time*, September 11, 1950, 60.

66 "Garroway," *Time*, September 11, 1950, 60.

67 "Closed-Circuit Color Television Press Conference," Colonial Theatre, New York City, November 3, 1955, National Broadcasting Company Archive, box 169, folder 31, Wisconsin Historical Society.

68 "Color at WNBQ (TV) Three Months Later," *Broadcasting-Telecasting*, July 16, 1956, 66.

69 "Color at WNBQ (TV) Three Months Later," 67.

70 "Color at WNBQ (TV) Three Months Later," 66.

71 "Color House," *RCA* 112 (December 1961): 36.

72 "Color House."

73 "Dedication Day—NBC Washington—May 22, 1958," Internet Archive, https://archive.org/details/DedicationDay-Nbc-washington-May221958 colorVideotape.

74 "Dedication Day—NBC Washington—May 22, 1958."

75 "Dedication Day—NBC Washington—May 22, 1958."

76 Lynn Spigel, *TV by Design: Modern Art and the Rise of Network Television* (Chicago: University of Chicago Press, 2009), 112.

77 Ed Reitan, "Early Color Television Studio Facilities," last updated July 26, 2005. Available at https://web.archive.org/web/20151017172613/http://www.novia.net/~ereitan/studios.html.

78 Joshua Gleich, "The Lost Studio of Atlantis: Norman Bel Geddes's Failed Revolution in Television Form," *Velvet Light Trap* 70 (fall 2012): 3–17.

79 Gleich, "The Lost Studio of Atlantis," 14.

80 John M. Clifford, "Color City," memo to S. L. Weaver and R. A. W. Sarnoff, November 8, 1954, National Broadcasting Company Archive, box 122, folder 75, Wisconsin Historical Society.

81 Clifford, "Color City," 1.

82 Savings from centralization of all operations in Color City were at about $1 to $1.5 million a year. Clifford, "Color City," 2.

83 Pat Weaver, *The Best Seat in the House: The Golden Years of Radio and Television* (New York: Alfred A. Knopf, 1993), 206.

84 "NBC's $3,176,00 Color TV Facility Will Open," *Los Angeles Times*, March 20, 1955.

85 "NBC-TV's Color City in Burbank to Start Operations with Facilities Unmatched in Industry," NBC press release, March 18, 1955, National Broadcasting Company Archive, box 169, folder 38, Wisconsin Historical Society.

86 "NBC-TV's Color City in Burbank to Start Operations." The same press release mentions that when not in use, the audience pit was "covered up to become part of the studio floor."

87 "Entertainment 1955, Spectacular Dedicating NBC's Color City to Offer Gala Salute to Showbusiness by Top Performers on NBC Colorcast of Sunday, March 27, 7:30 to 9 PM, EST," NBC press release, March, 9 1955, National Broadcasting Company Archive, box 169, folder 32, Wisconsin Historical Society.

88 Spigel, *TV by Design*, 299.

89 See Spigel, *TV by Design*, 317.

90 RCA would sometimes cross-promote or cobrand with NBC sponsors in magazine ads, as was the case with ads in 1956 that headlined "Compatible Color" and matched plaid dress shirts from Arrow with images on color RCA-Victor sets. In a similar but seemingly misguided campaign to cross-promote ABC's popular *Stop the Music* program with Van Heusen's "TV Spectacolor" line of shirts, one ad centers on Bert Parks dressed in bright pink and gray, script in hand, apparently directing a segment of the show, as the headline copy reads "Van Heusen stars you in TV Spectacolors." Since ABC didn't air its first color program until at least five years after the ad appeared, and "TV Spectacolors" evokes "spectaculars," which were most strongly associated with NBC, this campaign is a bit of an oddity.

91 Spigel, *TV by Design*, 85.

92 Spigel, *TV by Design*, 86.

93 Bacus, "The Local Station and Color,"in Coleman, *Television*, 185–186.

94 Joan Walker, "Living with Living Color," *Washington Post*, December 25, 1960.

95 CBS also began airing the occasional color episode in some of their anthology programs. One of the most striking, a 1957 episode of *US Steel Hour*, has been discussed in some detail by Spigel in her analysis of the ways in which jazz and blues inspired modern costume and set design during this period. "Drum as a Woman" was a highly promoted experimental drama conceived, written, and performed by Duke Ellington that explored the history of jazz primarily through dance and music. See Spigel, *TV by Design*, 52–58.

96 Ed Reitan, "RCA-NBC Firsts in Color Television," last updated March 8, 2004. Available at https://web.archive.org/web/20160113001124/http://www.novia.net/~ereitan/rca-nbc_firsts.html.

97 In January 1957, NBC was left with an extra thirty minutes for the program

when Dean Martin and Jerry Lewis agreed only to fulfill an hour of the time slot. Ernie Kovacs agreed to fill the extra time, and the resulting "The Silent Show," a series of skits Kovacs performed without dialogue as the character Eugene, was a hit with critics at the time and remains one of Kovacs's most admired works.

98 Street, *Colour Films in Britain: The Negotiation of Innovation, 1900–55* (London: British Film Institute, 2012), 163.

99 Robin Pogrebin, "Magical Find Excites tv Historians; 'Cinderella' Film Reflects an Emerging Medium," *New York Times*, June 20, 2012, www.ny times.com/2002/06/20/arts/magical-find-excites-tv-historians-cinderella -film-reflects-an-emerging-medium.html.

100 Robin Pogrebin, "Magical Find Excites tv Historians."

101 Ilka Chase, "As I Was Saying: How Television Brings an Ancient Fairytale to Glowing Life Tonight," *Chicago Tribune*, March 31, 1957.

102 See ad for color videotape and a discussion of Ampex and rca's use of the word "tape." "Broadcasters, tv Tape Services, Producers of Tape Commercials and Programs Gain a Big, New Dimension in Color," Color Television History blog, King of the Road, www.kingoftheroad.net/colorTV/TVtape1 .html.

103 Spigel, *tv by Design*, 49–50.

104 June Bundy, "Reviews: Ageless Fred Astaire Clicks in Memorable Video Special," *Billboard,* October 27, 1958, 5.

105 Jack Gould, "Score One for Color tv: Art Masterpieces Shown on Van Gogh Program," *New York Times*, November 26, 1961.

106 Jack Gould, "Criteria for Buying a Color tv Set," *New York Times*, September 27, 1965.

107 Scott Higgins, *Harnessing the Technicolor Rainbow: Color Design in the 1930s* (Austin: University of Texas Press, 2007), 11–12.

108 Leo Burnett, "Review: An Evening with Fred Astaire," *Variety*, October 22, 1958, 35.

CHAPTER 5

1 J. P. Telotte, *Disney tv* (Detroit: Wayne State University Press, 2004), 16.

2 J. P. Telotte. *The Mouse Machine: Disney and Technology* (Champaign: University of Illinois Press, 2008), 54.

3 Cecil Smith, "tv's Call to Color: Television Appears on Threshold of Age of Color," *Los Angeles Times*, March 25, 1962.

4 Warren Abbot, "What Color Means to Chicago Stars," *Chicago Tribune*, November 10, 1968.

5 Erik Barnouw, *Tube of Plenty: The Evolution of American Television* (New York: Oxford University Press, 1990), 301.

6 See Joshua Yumibe, *Moving Color: Early Film, Mass Culture, Modernism*

(New Brunswick, NJ: Rutgers University Press, 2012), 9–11; and Trond Lundemo, "The Colors of Haptic Space: Black, Blue and White in Moving Images," in *The Color Film Reader*, ed. Angela Dalle Vacche and Brian Price (New York: Routledge, 2006), 88–101.

7 Yumibe, *Moving Color*, 10–11.

8 Gunning, "Colorful Metaphors: The Attraction of Color in Early Silent Cinema," in *Fotogenia 1*, ed. Richard Abel (Bologna: Editrice Club, 1995), 249.

9 See André Bazin, *What Is Cinema?* trans. and ed. Hugh Gray (Berkeley: University of California Press, 1967), 2:23–27.

10 Gunning, "Colorful Metaphors," 251.

11 Richard Misek, *Chromatic Cinema: A History of Screen Color* (New York: Wiley-Blackwell, 2010), 40–43.

12 Michele Hilmes, *Only Connect*, 4th ed. (Belmont, CA: Wadsworth Publishing, 2013), 256.

13 All of these manufacturers' products used the RCA twenty-one-inch picture tube.

14 "Color on the Networks: Well on the Way to 100%," *Broadcasting*, January 3, 1966, 75–80; "Full Color on Networks Seems Certain in 1967," *Broadcasting*, January 2, 1967, 84–86; and "Color Homes Push TV Viewing to Record High," *Broadcasting*, January 15, 1968, 62.

15 See "Westinghouse Feature—a Picture in Ten Seconds," *Chicago Tribune*, November 12, 1967; and "Better and Easier Tuning Featured by Philco-Ford," *Chicago Tribune*, November 10, 1968.

16 Jack Gould, "TV: Color Breakthrough," *New York Times*, October 14, 1965.

17 Cynthia Lowry, "Owners of Tinted TV Sets—Color Them Blue," *Los Angeles Times*, November 26, 1965, D28.

18 NBC continued to argue throughout the 1960s that color gave them a "ratings boost," as shows in color—even if seen by most people in black and white—got a ratings advantage. According to a 1965 report, "The ratings of NBC color programs were 77% higher in color homes than in black and white homes, while CBS' color programs enjoyed an 18% ratings advantage in color homes and ABC's a 35% advantage." "NBC Again Reports Color Boosts Ratings," *Broadcasting*, November 1, 1965, 30, 32.

19 "Bonanza's Lorne Greene Lauded as No. 1 Salesman for Color TV," *Los Angeles Times*, September 11, 1966.

20 "Ray Evans and Jay Livingston Interview, pt. 2 of 3," Archive of American Television, undated. http://www.emmytvlegends.org/interviews/shows/bonanza#.

21 "Bonanza's Lorne Greene Lauded as No. 1 Salesman for Color TV," *Los Angeles Times*, September 11, 1966.

22 Lawrence Laurent, "Bonanza's Sleek Enough to Slide By," *Washington Post*, October 24, 1961.

23 "Color Expert of 'Bonanza' Has Problems," *Los Angeles Times*, October 20, 1963.

24 For example, in all of 1963, CBS broadcast only "one special and five episodes of *Lassie* in color." Sandford Brown, "Color Catches Fire," *Saturday Evening Post*, August 17, 1963.

25 NBC was at 100 percent color programming by November 1966; CBS did not reach 100 percent until later, in 1967. "Full Color on Networks Seems Certain in 1967," *Broadcasting*, January, 2, 1967, 84–86.

26 Smith, "TV's Call to Color: Television Appears on Threshold of Age of Color."

27 Surprisingly, Screen Gems's *I Dream of Jeannie*, a fantastical sitcom that begins with an astronaut finding a beautiful genie in a bottle when his small space capsule lands on a deserted island in the South Pacific, aired on NBC in black and white its first season (1965–1966). However, the program seemed like an ideal match for color, with its fantastical contexts enhanced by the bright, saturated hues of the mise-en-scène—especially when it came to Jeannie's pink and purple costume and the matching decor inside her plushly outfitted bottle—and it was converted to color for its second season.

28 Maurice Berger and Lynn Spigel, *Revolution of the Eye: Modern Art and the Birth of American Television* (New Haven, CT: Yale University Press, 2014), xiv.

29 Michael Curtin, *Redeeming the Wasteland: Television Documentary and Cold War Politics* (London: Routledge, 1995).

30 Curtin, *Redeeming the Wasteland*, 8.

31 "Color Sparks Travel-Adventure," *Broadcasting*, May 31, 1965, 40.

32 Barbara Delatiner, "An Art Program Needs Tinted TV," *Newsday*, January 20, 1964; Jack Gould, "Score One for Color TV: Art Masterpieces Shown on Van Gogh Programs," *New York Times*, November 26, 1961.

33 "Public Served Better through Color TV: Documentaries in Tint Have Broader Appeal Stations Discover," *Broadcasting*, January 2, 1967, 50, 52, 54, 56, 58, 64, 66.

34 Curtin, *Redeeming the Wasteland*, 61.

35 Curtin, *Redeeming the Wasteland*, 220.

36 "Television Reviews: Elizabeth Taylor in London," *Variety*, October 9, 1963, 29.

37 Jack Gould, "Sophia Loren Guides Roman Tour," *New York Times*, November 13, 1964. Two somewhat more down-market iterations of the D'Antoni/Baer star-returns-to-birthplace format were *Inger Stevens in Sweden* and *Melina Mercouri's Greece*, both of which aired on ABC in 1965.

38 "Jacqueline Kennedy's Journey," in Tele- Follow-up Comment, *Variety*, April 4, 1962, 42.

39 "ABC Will Repeat First Lady's Show," *New York Times*, March 14, 1966, 63.

40 Lisa Parks, "As the Earth Spins: NBC's *Wide Wide World* and Live Global Television in the 1950s," *Screen* 48 (January 2001): 337–338.

41 Davison Taylor, "Re: Color Show," memo to Sylvester Weaver, June 18, 1954, box 405, file 3, NBC Collection, Wisconsin Historical Society. This show does not seem to have had the same format as the Sunday news program *Kaleidoscope* that aired on NBC later in the decade with Charles van Doren as host.

42 Jennifer Lynn Petersen, "Travelogues and Early Nonfiction Film: Education in the School of Dreams," in *American Cinema's Transitional Years: Audience, Institution, Practices*, ed. Charlie Keil and Shelley Stamp (Berkeley: University of California Press, 2004), 191–213.

43 Petersen, "Travelogues and Early Nonfiction Film," 197.

44 Petersen, "Travelogues and Early Nonfiction Film," 208.

45 "Ganges—Sacred River," *Variety*, September 23, 1964, 78.

46 Lynn Spigel, *TV by Design: Modern Art and the Rise of Network Television* (Chicago: University of Chicago Press, 2009).

47 "Historical Met Art Museum Colorcast," *Variety*, May 12, 1954, 31.

48 Spigel, *TV by Design*, 166.

49 "NBC Special Will Show U.S. through Eyes of Its Arts," *Los Angeles Times*, July 26, 1966.

50 Sanka Knox, "Sarnoff Couples Art and Color TV: NBC Head Tells Whitney Friends of Glowing Future," *New York Times*, May 21, 1965.

51 David Sarnoff, *Looking Ahead: The Papers of David Sarnoff* (New York: McGraw-Hill, 1968), 131.

52 Walt Dutton, "Picasso Auction Artistic Triumph for NBC Staff," *Los Angeles Times*, February 7, 1967.

53 Harry Gilroy, "TV: George Washington, More Than Just a Portrait," *New York Times*, April 25, 1969.

54 Delatiner, "An Art Program Needs Tinted TV."

55 Barbara Delatiner, "NBC Fails to Put Michelangelo on Pedestal," *Newsday*, December 23, 1965.

56 William Wilson, "Few Quibbles Follow Michelangelo Special," *Los Angeles Times*, December 23, 1965.

57 Lawrence Laurent, "Michelangelo Program Proves Hazam is Television Giant," *Washington Post*, December 23, 1965. (Laurent estimated that viewers missed "90% of the impact" if they watched in black and white.)

58 "Awe Inspiring Michelangelo," *Boston Globe*, December 23, 1965.

59 Larry Wolters, "Color TV Test: Tour of the Louvre," *Chicago Tribune*, November 8, 1964.

60 See, for example, Barbara Delatiner, "Visit to Louvre Was Too Short," *Newsday*, November 18, 1964.

61 MoMA was one of the first to have a dedicated department of photography, starting in 1947 under the direction of Edward Steichen, who curated the famous Family of Man exhibit, which was on display at MoMA in 1955 before beginning an eight-year world tour.

62 Gerald Thompson, interview by Christopher Parsons, Wild Film History, March 9, 1998, www.wildfilmhistory.org/oh/21/Gerald+Thompson.html.

63 Cynthia Chris, *Watching Wildlife* (Minneapolis: University of Minnesota Press, 2006), 64.

64 "Color Helps Sell National Geographic Series," *Broadcasting*, January 2 1967, 34.

65 By no coincidence, the subscriber of *National Geographic* magazine was largely the same as the imagined color television viewer—wealthier and more educated than average—with a substantial portion of this audience being in the upper middle and upper classes.

66 Catherine A. Lutz and Jane L. Collins, *Reading National Geographic* (Chicago: University of Chicago Press, 1993), 31.

67 Grace Glueck, "Gallery View; Photojournalism That Colors the News in Many Ways," *New York Times*, May 4, 1986, www.nytimes.com/1986/05/04 /arts/gallery-view-photojournalism-that-colors-the-news-in-many-ways.html.

68 Lutz and Collins, *Reading National Geographic*, 19.

69 Lutz and Collins, *Reading National Geographic*, 32.

70 Chris, *Watching Wildlife*, 48.

71 Chris, *Watching Wildlife*, 56.

72 Brad Matsen, *Jacques Cousteau: The Sea King* (New York: Vintage, 2010), 169.

73 Louise Sweeney, "Undersea World of Jacques Cousteau Tonight on ABC-TV," *Christian Science Monitor*, January 8, 1968, 6.

74 Alexander Wilson, *The Culture of Nature: North American Landscape from Disney to the Exxon Valdez* (Toronto: Between the Lines, 1991), 137.

75 Alexander Wilson, *The Culture of Nature*, 137.

76 Jack Gaver, "Undersea Pictures Are Hard to Take," *Washington Post*, April 15, 1966.

77 Cynthia Lowry, "Cousteau Opens Sea to All," *Washington Post*, December 10, 1970.

CHAPTER 6

1 "CBS News Presents the Nixon–Khrushchev Moscow Debate," aired July 25, 1959. Available at the Internet Archive, https://archive.org/details/Nixon-KhrushchevMoscowDebatejuly251959.

2 "CBS News Presents the Nixon–Khrushchev Moscow Debate."

3 "CBS News Presents the Nixon–Khrushchev Moscow Debate."

4 Eduard Ivanyan, quoted by Gregory Feifer, "Fifty Years Ago, American Exhibition Stunned Soviets in Cold War," Radio Free Europe, July 23, 2009,

www.rferl.org/content/Fifty_Years_Ago_American_Exhibition_Stunned _Soviets_in_Cold_War/1783913.html.

5 "Dedication Day, NBC-Washington," May 22, 1958, available at the Internet Archive, https://archive.org/details/DedicationDay-Nbc-washington-May22 1958colorVideotape.

6 In 1955, General Sarnoff published and distributed a pamphlet called "Program for a Political Offensive against World Communism," in which he outlined a plan to win the Cold War and prevent a "hot" war. There was much focus on the efficacy and power of propaganda, and he suggested that television mobile units be used in order to bring an "anti-Communist voice" to Eastern Bloc regions. He wrote, "Mobile big-screen television units in black-and-white and in color carry our message. Their very novelty will guarantee large and attentive audiences." "Program for a Political Offensive against World Communism," April 5, 1955, M&A 29, folder 8, 30–33. David Sarnoff Papers, Hagley Museum and Library, Wilmington, DE.

7 Lynn Spigel, *Welcome to the Dreamhouse: Popular Media and Postwar Suburbs* (Durham, NC: Duke University Press, 2001), 109.

8 Sam Kaplan, "Color Television on a Journey to Moscow," *New York Times*, June 21, 1959.

9 James Schwoch, *Global TV: New Media and the Cold War, 1946–69* (Champaign: University of Illinois Press, 2009), 107.

10 Schwoch, *Global TV*, 107.

11 Schwoch, *Global TV*, 107.

12 "Radio, TV Goes to the World's Fair," *Broadcasting*, April 6, 1964, 140–141.

13 These activists were part of CORE, the Congress of Racial Equality. See Albert Fisher, "New York World's Fair Memories," December 2003, New York World's Fair 1964/1965 website, www.nywf64.com/fisher02.shtml; and Joseph Tirella, "'A Gun to the Heart of the City,'" April 22, 2014, Slate, www .slate.com/articles/news_and_politics/history/2014/04/core_s_1964 _stall_in_the_planned_civil_rights_protest_that_kept_thousands.html. For more details on the actions that occurred at the fair and their relation to the broader civil rights movement, see also Joseph Tirella's book *Tomorrow-Land: The 1964–65 World's Fair and the Transformation of America* (New York: Lyons Press, 2014).

14 Description in the 1965 Official Guide to the World's Fair. See "RCA," New York World's Fair 1964/1965 website, www.nywf64.com/rca01.shtml.

15 "RCA Exhibit to Serve as Official Color Television Communications Center," RCA press release, April 11, 1963, p.1, New York World's Fair 1964/1965 website, www.nywf64.com/rca02.shtml.

16 Sarnoff's remarks at the dedication and preview of the RCA exhibit, New York World's Fair, April 2, 1964, as quoted in David Sarnoff, *Looking Ahead: The Papers of David Sarnoff* (New York: McGraw-Hill, 1968), 146–147.

17   "Radio, TV Goes to the World's Fair," 140–141.

18   "Color Classes," *Variety*, December 15, 1965, 52.

19   This was not the case for domestic first-run and off-network syndicators who saw color as a moment to sell innovation and for local stations who may be new to color, to broadcast old programs in color for the first time.

20   The black and white shows listed included *Dinah Shore Show*, *Profiles in Courage*, and *Kentucky Jones*. "International Sales by NBC Tops $2 million," *Broadcasting*, August 31, 1964, 9.

21   Hal Humphrey, "Just How 'Awesome' Is Global TV?," *Los Angeles Times*, November 3, 1963.

22   Oren Soffer, "The Eraser and the Anti-Eraser: The Battle over Color Television in Israel," *Media, Culture and Society* 30, no. 6 (November 2008): 764.

23   Soffer, "The Eraser and the Anti-Eraser," 765.

24   Soffer, "The Eraser and the Anti-Eraser," 763.

25   Soffer writes, "After only two years on the market, about 10,000 anti-erasers were sold at a cost of approximately 40 million liras. Over the next two years, Israelis would spend a further 400 million liras to purchase anti-eraser devices." "The Eraser and the Anti-Eraser," 772.

26   Carol Honsa, "India Tunes Eye to Color TV, Discovers It's Not a Black and White Issue," *Christian Science Monitor*, February 24, 1982. Available at www.csmonitor.com/1982/0224/022437.html.

27   Joe Cohen, "Cuba's New Channel 10 Just as Yanks Like It," *Variety*, August 6, 1958, 39.

28   "Canal 12, Cuban Color Outlet Plans to Go on Air October 24," *Broadcasting-Telecasting*, September 9, 1957, 110.

29   Yeidy Rivero, *Broadcasting Modernity: Cuban Commercial Television, 1960–1960* (Durham, NC: Duke University Press, 2015), 168.

30   Rivero, *Broadcasting Modernity*, 168–169.

31   Peter Robinson, "Colour TV: It Was 'Forced' on Japan," *Stage and Television Today*, August 11, 1960, 22.

32   Yuzo Takahashi, "A Network of Tinkerers: The Advent of the Radio and Television Receiver Industry in Japan," *Technology and Culture* 41, no. 3 (July 2000): 476.

33   Takahashi, "A Network of Tinkerers."

34   Andreas Fickers, "The Techno-politics of Colour: Britain and the European Struggle for a Colour Television Standard," *Journal of British Cinema and Television* 7, no. 1 (April 2010): 95–114.

35   Fickers, "The Techno-politics of Colour," 96.

36   Fickers, "The Techno-politics of Colour," 111.

37   The title of this section is taken from a report by Westinghouse researchers: Stanley Lebar and Charles P. Hoffman, "TV Show of the Century: A Travelogue with No Atmosphere," *Electronics*, March 6, 1967.

38 The closing ceremonies were also broadcast live. "Land of the Rising Hurdlers," display ad *New York Times*, October 4, 1964.

39 Lisa Parks, *Cultures in Orbit: Satellites and the Televisual* (Durham, NC: Duke University Press, 2005), 37.

40 Parks, *Cultures in Orbit*, 22.

41 Clare Reckert, "A.B.-Paramount Theatres Plans to Offer Color Television Shows," *New York Times*, May 16, 1962.

42 Schwoch, *Global TV*, 122.

43 Joshua Rothman, "Live from the Moon," *New Yorker*, August 23, 2014. Available at www.newyorker.com/books/joshua-rothman/live-moon.

44 "Earth Scene from Space Puts Viewer in Apollo Spacecraft," *Chicago Tribune*, May 19, 1969.

45 Apollo 10 CBS News coverage, May 19, 1969, www.youtube.com/watch?v=KbGHIQvObNo.

46 They had been considering a digital TV system but decided to go with analog. Among the reasons given was that "good-quality digital TV required impractically high information." See Paul P. Coan, "Apollo Experience Report—Television System," NASA, November 1973, https://ntrs.nasa.gov/archive/nasa/casi.ntrs.nasa.gov/19740002701.pdf 4.

47 "Quality Color Comes from Outer-Space Show," *Broadcasting*, May 26, 1969, 58.

48 "Quality Color Comes from Outer-Space Show," *Broadcasting*, May 26, 1969, 58.

49 "Quality Color Comes from Outer-Space Show," *Broadcasting*, May 26, 1969, 58.

50 "Apollo 10 Transmits TV Color Pictures," *Hartford Courant*, May 19, 1969, 5.

51 Apollo 10 CBS News coverage, May 19, 1969, https://www.youtube.com/watch?v=KbGHIQvObNo.

52 This camera did use the NTSC scan rate.

53 David Meerman Scott, Richard Jurek, and Eugene A. Cernan, *Marketing the Moon: The Selling of the Apollo Lunar Program* (Cambridge, MA: MIT Press, 2014), 68.

54 Jack Gould, "TV Pictures Raise Questions about Moon's Color," *New York Times*, July 30, 1969.

55 "'Outdated' Color System to Relay Space Images," *New York Times*, April 5, 1969.

56 "Westinghouse Builds Color TV Camera and 'Mini' Monitor for Apollo 10," Westinghouse Electric press release, May 16, 1969, 3, NASA.gov online archive.

57 Stanley Lebar, "The Color War Goes to the Moon," *Invention and Technology* (summer 1997): 52–54.

58 Gene Smith, "General Electric Will Modify 90,000 Large Color Television Sets against Possible X-Radiation Leaks," *New York Times*, May 19, 1967.

59 "Color TV Hunted as Radiation Hazard," *Boston Globe*, July 22, 1967.

60 "Excessive Radiation Found in U.S. Study of Color Sets," *New York Times*, March 15, 1968.

61 Smith, "General Electric Will Modify 90,000 Large Color Television Sets."

62 "TV Radiation Peril Called Exaggerated," *Newsday*, April 10, 1969.

CONCLUSION

Epigraph: "Coming: Wall and Pocket Size Color TV Sets, *Chicago Tribune*, November 12, 1967.

1 Albert Abramson, *The History of Television, 1942–2000* (Jefferson, NC: McFarland, 1987), 2:108. Solid-state technology (for example, microchips and transistors) takes up less space than parts such as vacuum tubes and allows for the apparatus to be much slimmer and smaller in size. The first solid-state imaging device was produced in 1965 by the aerospace division of Westinghouse. Two years later, RCA announced the release of a solid-state camera and, the year following, its first solid-state portable color receiver.

2 Tracy Dahlby, "Quality or Conspiracy in Color Television?" *New York Times*, January 30, 1977.

3 Benjamin Gross, "Crystallizing Innovation: The Emergence of the LCD at RCA, 1951–1976" (PhD diss., Princeton University, 2011), 94.

4 Gross, "Crystallizing Innovation," 94.

5 William K. Stevens, "Display Device Crystalizes for RCA," *New York Times*, May 29, 1968.

6 Hirohisa Kawamoto, "The History of Liquid-Crystal Displays," *Proceedings of the IEEE* 90, no. 4 (April 2002): 467.

7 Benjamin Gross, "How RCA Lost the LCD," *IEEE Spectrum*, November 1, 2012, http://spectrum.ieee.org/consumer-electronics/audiovideo/how-rca -lost-the-lcd.

8 See, for example, "Television Screen Future Video Terminal," *Hartford Courant*, October 17, 1976.

9 Jonathan Yenkin, "America Is Finally Pulling the Plug on Black-and-White Television Sets," *Los Angeles Times*, September 6, 1992. Available at http://articles.latimes.com/1992–09–06/news/mn-251_1_black-and-white -television.

10 The ATSC is an international body consisting of 140 member organizations, including IEEE, NAB, the Consumer Electronics Association, National Cable Television Association, and SMPTE. This sampling of members serves as a reminder of how television is no longer the relatively discrete medium

and industry that it once was, as it now involves a wide range of media forms, technologies, and interests.

11 For more on DI, see John Belton, "Painting by the Numbers: The Digital Intermediate," *Film Quarterly* 61, no. 3 (spring 2008): 58–65.

12 Linda Romanello and Marc Loftus, "The Evolution of the Digital Intermediate," Light Iron website, April 2, 2015, http://lightiron.com/about/news /evolution-digital-intermediate.

13 See Sean Cubbitt's discussion of digital color for more details on this. *The Practice of Light: A Genealogy of Visual Technologies from Prints to Pixels* (Cambridge, MA: MIT Press, 2014), 144–151.

14 Carolyn Kane, *Chromatic Algorithms: Synthetic Color, Computer Art and Aesthetics after Code* (Chicago: University of Chicago Press, 2014), 69.

15 Kane, *Chromatic Algorithms*.

16 Cubbitt, *The Practice of Light*, 151.

BIBLIOGRAPHY

Abramson, Albert. *Electronic Motion Pictures: A History of the Television Camera*. Los Angeles: University of California Press, 1955.

———. *The History of Television*. 2 vols. Jefferson, NC: McFarland, 1987.

———. "A Short History of Television Recording." *SMPTE Journal* 64 (1955): 72–76.

———. *Zworykin: Pioneer of Television*. Urbana: University of Illinois Press, 1995.

Advisory Committee on Color Television. "Present Status of Color Television." Report to the Committee on Interstate and Foreign Commerce. Washington, DC: Government Printing Office, 1950.

Anderson, Christopher, and Michael Curtin, "Mapping the Ethereal City: Chicago Television, the FCC, and the Politics of Place." *Quarterly Review of Film and Video* 16, no. 3–4 (1997): 289–305.

Alvey, Mark. "Too Many Kids and Old Ladies: Quality Demographics and 1960s U.S. Television." *Screen* 45, no. 1 (spring 2004): 40–62.

Baird, John Logie. *Television and Me*. Edinburgh: Mercat Press, 2004.

Barnouw, Erik. *Tube of Plenty: The Evolution of American Television*. New York: Oxford University Press, 1990.

Batchelor, David. *Chromophobia*. London: Reaktion Books, 2000.

Baughman, James L. "'Show Business in the Living Room': Management Expectations for American Television, 1947–56." *Business and Economic History* 26, no. 2 (winter 1997): 718–726.

Bazin, André. *What Is Cinema?* 2 vols. Translated and edited by Hugh Gray. Berkeley: University of California Press, 1967.

Belton, John. "Painting by the Numbers: The Digital Intermediate." *Film Quarterly* 61, no. 3 (spring 2008): 58–65.

Berger, Maurice, and Lynn Spigel. *Revolution of the Eye: Modern Art and the Birth of American Television*. New Haven, CT: Yale University Press, 2014.

Bijker, W. E. *Of Bicycles, Bakelites, and Bulbs: Toward a Theory of Sociotechnical Change*. Cambridge, MA: MIT Press, 1997.

Blaszczyk, Regina Lee. *The Color Revolution*. Cambridge, MA: MIT Press, 2012.

Boddy, William. *Fifties Television: The Industry and Its Critics*. Urbana: University of Illinois Press, 1992.

Bordwell, David, Janet Staiger, and Kristin Thompson. *The Classical Hollywood Cinema: Film Style and Mode of Production to 1960*. New York: Columbia University Press, 1985.

Brown, George H. *A Part of Which I Was: Recollections of a Research Engineer*. Princeton, NJ: Angus Cupar, 1982.

Brown, Simon, Sarah Street, and Liz Watkins, eds. *Color and the Moving Image*. New York: Routledge, 2013.

Burns, Russell W. *John Logie Baird: Television Pioneer*. London: Institution of Engineering and Technology, 2001.

Busch, Lawrence. *Standards: Recipes for Reality*. Cambridge, MA: MIT Press, 2011.

Buscombe, Edward. "Sound and Color." *Jump Cut* 17 (April 1978): 23–25.

Bussard, Katherine, and Lisa Hostetler. *Color Rush: American Color Photography from Stieglitz to Sherman*. New York: Aperture Books, 2013.

Cahan, David. *Hermann von Helmholtz and the Foundations of Nineteenth-Century Science*. Berkeley: University of California Press, 1993.

Chevreul, Michel Eugène. *Principles of Harmony and Contrast of Colors: And Their Applications to the Arts*. Translated by Charles Martel. Rev. ed. New York: Schiffer, 2007.

Chisholm, Bradley. "The CBS Color Television Venture: A Study of Failed Innovation in the Broadcasting Industry." PhD diss., University of Wisconsin–Madison, 1987.

———. "Red, Blue and Lots of Green: The Impact of Color Television on Feature Film Production." In *Hollywood in the Age of Television,* edited by Tino Balio, 213–234. Boston: Unwin Hyman, 1990.

Chris, Cynthia. *Watching Wildlife*. Minneapolis: University of Minnesota Press, 2006.

Coates, Paul. *Cinema and Colour: The Saturated Image*. London: British Film Institute, 2010.

Cohen, Jonathan, and Mohan Matthen, eds. *Color Ontology and Color Science*. New York: Bradford, 2010.

Cohen, Lizabeth. *A Consumers' Republic: The Politics of Mass Consumption in Postwar America*. New York: Vintage, 2003.

Coleman, Howard W., ed. *Television: The Business of Colorcasting*. New York: Hastings House, 1968.

Crary, Jonathan. *Suspension of Perception*. Cambridge, MA: MIT Press, 1999.

———. *Techniques of the Observer: On Vision and Modernity in the Nineteenth Century*. Cambridge, MA: MIT Press, 2001.

Cubbitt, Sean. *The Practice of Light: A Genealogy of Visual Technologies from Prints to Pixels*. Cambridge, MA: MIT Press, 2014.

Curtin, Michael. *Redeeming the Wasteland: Television Documentary and Cold War Politics*. London: Routledge, 1995.

Dalle Vacche, Angela, and Brian Price, eds. *Color: The Film Reader*. New York: Routledge, 2006.

DeMarsh, LeRoy. "TV Display Phosphors/Primaries—Some History." *SMPTE Journal* 102, no. 12 (December 1993): 1095–1098.

Descartes, René. *Extracts in Descartes: Philosophical Writings*. Translated and edited by E. Anscombe and P. T. Geach. Middlesex, England: Nelson, 1970.

———. *Principles of Philosophy*. 1644.

Doane, Mary Ann. *The Emergence of Cinematic Time: Modernity, Contingency, the Archive*. Cambridge, MA: Harvard University Press, 2002.

Dyer, Richard. *White: Essays on Race and Culture*. New York: Routledge, 1997.

Engstrom, Elmer. "Color Television—A Case History in Industrial Research." Paper presented at the spring meeting of the Industrial Research Institute, San Francisco, April 21–23, 1954, box 1, file 17. RCA Public Relations Files, David Sarnoff Research Center Records (unprocessed), Hagley Museum and Library, Wilmington, DE.

Fickers, Andreas. "The Techno-politics of Colour: Britain and the European Struggle for a Colour Television Standard." *Journal of British Cinema and Television* 7, no. 1 (April 2010): 95–114.

Fielding, Raymond. *A Technological History of Motion Pictures and Television*. Berkeley: University of California Press, 1967.

Fink, Donald. "Alternative Approaches to Color Television." *Proceedings of the IRE* 39, no. 10 (October 1951): 11–26.

———. *Color Television Standards: Selected Papers and Records of the National Television System Committee*. New York: McGraw-Hill, 1955.

———. "Perspectives on Television: The Role Played by the Two NTSC's in Preparing Television Service for the American Public." *Proceedings of the IEEE* 64, no. 9 (September 1976): 1322–1331.

Gage, H. P. "Color Theories and the Color Council." *SMPTE Journal* 35, no. 10 (October 1, 1940): 361–387.

Gage, John. *Color and Culture: Practice and Meaning from Antiquity to Abstraction*. Boston: Bullfinch Press, 1993.

———. *Color and Meaning: Art, Science and Symbolism*. Berkeley: University of California Press, 1999.

Galili, Doron. "Seeing by Electricity: Television and the Modern Mediascape, 1878–1939." PhD diss., University of Chicago, 2011.

Gleich, Joshua. "The Lost Studio of Atlantis: Norman Bel Geddes's Failed Revolution in Television Form." *Velvet Light Trap* 70 (fall 2012): 3–17.

Goethe, Johann Wolfgang von. *Theory of Colours*. 1810. New York: Dover, 2006. (Reprint of *Goethe's Theory of Colours*. London: John Murray, 1840.)

Goldmark, Peter C. "Color Television—USA Standard." *Proceedings of the IRE,* October 1951, 1288–1311.

Goldmark, Peter C., E. R. Piore, J. M. Hollywood, T. H. Chambers, and J. J. Reeves. "Color Television." *Proceedings of the IRE.* Part 1, March 1943, 465–478. Part 2, September 1943, 162–182.

Goodman, Robert L. *Color TV Case Histories Illustrated.* Summit, PA: Tab Books, 1975.

Grob, Bernard. *Basic Television.* New York: Maple Press, 1954.

Gross, Benjamin. "Crystallizing Innovation: The Emergence of the LCD at RCA, 1951–1976." PhD diss., Princeton University, 2011.

Gunning, Tom. "Colorful Metaphors: The Attraction of Color in Early Silent Cinema." *Fotogenia* 1 (1994): 249–255.

Gunning, Tom, Joshua Yumibe, Giovanna Fossati, and Jonathan Rosen. *Fantasia of Color in Early Cinema.* Amsterdam: Amsterdam University Press, 2015.

Harris, Neil. "Color and Media: Some Comparisons and Speculations." *Prospects* 11 (1986): 7–27.

Higgins, Scott. *Harnessing the Technicolor Rainbow: Color Design in the 1930s.* Austin: University of Texas Press, 2007.

Hunt, R. W. G. *The Reproduction of Colour in Photography, Printing and Television.* 4th ed. Tolworth, England: Fountain Press, 1987.

Hunter, Richard Sewall. *The Measurement of Appearance.* 2nd ed. New York: Wiley, 1991.

Ives, Herbert E., and A. L. Johnsrud. "Scanning in Colors from a Beam Scanning Method." *Journal of the Optical Society of America* 20, no. 1 (1930): 11.

Johnston, Sean F. "The Construction of Colorimetry by Committee." *Science in Context* 9, no. 4 (winter 1996): 387–420.

Kalmus, Natalie M. "Color Consciousness." *Journal of the Society of Motion Picture Engineers* (August 1935): 139–147.

Kane, Carolyn. *Chromatic Algorithms: Synthetic Color, Computer Art and Aesthetics after Code.* Chicago: University of Chicago Press, 2014.

Kay, Paul, and Willett Kempton. "What Is the Sapir-Whorf Hypothesis?" *American Anthropologist* 86, no. 1 (March 1984): 64–79.

Ketcham, Howard. *Color Planning for Business and Industry.* New York: Harper and Brothers, 1958.

Kirshner, Charles. "The Color Television Controversy." *Pittsburgh Law Review* 13 (1951–1952): 65–84.

Kisseloff, Jeff. *The Box: An Oral History of Television, 1920–1961.* New York: Penguin, 1995.

Kiver, Milton S. *Color Television Fundamentals.* New York: McGraw-Hill, 1955.

Kremer, Richard L. "Innovation through Synthesis: Helmholtz and Color

Research." In *Hermann von Helmholtz and the Foundations of Nineteenth-Century Science*, edited by David Cahan, 205–258. Berkeley: University of California Press, 1993.

Layton, James, and David Pierce. *The Dawn of Technicolor: 1915–1935*. Rochester, NY: George Eastman House, 2015.

Locke, John. *An Essay concerning Human Understanding*. 1689. Reprint, Oxford: Oxford University Press, 1970.

Lundemo, Trond. "The Colors of Haptic Space: Black, Blue and White in Moving Images." In *The Color Film Reader*, edited by Angela Dalle Vacche and Brian Price, 88–101. New York: Routledge, 2006.

Lupton, Ellen. *Mixed Messages: Graphic Design in Contemporary Culture*. Princeton, NJ: Princeton Architectural Press, 1996.

Lutz, Catherine A., and Jane L. Collins. *Reading National Geographic*. Chicago: University of Chicago Press, 1993.

Lyons, Eugene. *David Sarnoff*. New York: Harper and Row, 1966.

Marcus, George H. *Design in the Fifties: When Everyone Went Modern*. New York: Prestel, 1996.

Marling, Karal Ann. *As Seen on TV: The Visual Culture of Everyday Life in the 1950s*. Cambridge, MA: Harvard University Press, 1996.

Martineau, Pierre. "The Personality of the Retail Store." *Harvard Business Review* 36 (1958): 47–55.

Matsen, Brad. *Jacques Cousteau: The Sea King*. New York: Vintage, 2010.

McArthur, Tom. *Vision Warrior: The Hidden Achievements of John Logie Baird*. Kirkwall, Scotland: Orkney Press, 1990.

McCarthy, Anna. *Ambient Television: Visual Culture and Public Space*. Durham, NC: Duke University Press, 2001.

McLean, Donald. *Restoring Baird's Image*. London: Institution of Electrical Engineers, 2000.

Melville, Stephen. "Color Has Not Yet Been Named: Objectivity in Deconstruction." In *Deconstruction and the Visual Arts*, edited by P. Brunnette and D. Wills, 33–49. Cambridge: Cambridge University Press, 1993.

Mills, Mara. "Media and Prosthesis: The Vocoder, the Artificial Larynx, and the History of Signal Processing." *Qui Parle: Critical Humanities and Social Sciences* 21, no. 1 (fall/winter 2012): 107–149.

Misek, Richard. *Chromatic Cinema: A History of Screen Color*. New York: Wiley-Blackwell, 2010.

Mowbray, G. H., and J. W. Gebard. "The Purkinje After-Image on Screens of Cathode Ray Tubes." *American Journal of Psychology* 64, no. 4 (October 1951): 508–520.

Mulvin, Dylan, and Jonathan Sterne. "Scenes from an Imaginary Country: Test Images and the American Color Television Standard." *Television and New Media* 17, no. 1 (January 2016): 21–43.

Munsell, Albert. *Atlas of the Munsell Color System*. Malden, MA: Wadsworth-Howland, 1915.

———. *A Color Notation*. Boston: GH Ellis, 1905.

———. "A Pigment Color System and Notation." *American Journal of Psychology* 23, no. 2 (1912): 236–244.

Murray, Susan. "'Never Twice the Same Colour': Standardizing, Calibrating and Harmonizing NTSC Colour Television in the Early 1950s." *Screen* 56, no. 4 (winter 2015): 415–435.

———. "Reviving the Technical in Television Histories." In *Companion to the History of American Broadcasting*, edited by Aniko Bodroghkozy. New York: Blackwell, 2018.

Musser, Charles, and Carol Nelson. *High-Class Moving Pictures: Lyman H. Howe and the Forgotten Era of Traveling Exhibition, 1880–1920*. Princeton, NJ: Princeton University Press, 1991.

National Television System Committee (1951–1953). Report and Reports of Panel No. 11, 11-A, 12–19, with Some supplementary references cited in the Reports, and the Petition for adoption of transmission standards for color television before the Federal Communications Commission. N.p., 1953.

Neale, Steve. *Cinema and Technology: Sound, Image, Colour*. London: Macmillan, 1985.

Newton, Isaac. *Opticks: Or a Treatise of the Reflections, Refractions, Inflections and Colours of Light*. 1704.

Nickerson, Dorothy. "Fifty Years of the Inter-Society Color Council: Formation and Early Years." *Color Research and Application* 7, no. 1 (spring 1982): 1–11.

———. "History of the Munsell Color System, Company, and Foundation: Its Scientific Application." *Color Research and Application* 1, no. 2 (summer 1976): 69–77.

Noble, David. *America by Design: Science, Technology and the Rise of Corporate Capitalism*. New York: Knopf, 1982.

Paley, William. *As It Happened: A Memoir*. New York: Doubleday, 1979.

Parks, Lisa. "As the Earth Spins: NBC's Wide Wide World and Live Global Television in the 1950s." *Screen* 42, no. 4 (January 2001): 332–349.

———. *Cultures in Orbit: Satellites and the Televisual*. Durham, NC: Duke University Press, 2005.

Peacock, Steven. *Colour*. Manchester: Manchester University Press, 2010.

Peters, John Durham. "Helmholtz, Edison, and Sound History." In *Memory Bytes: History, Technology, and Digital Culture*, edited by Lauren Rabinovitz and Abraham Geil, 177–198. Durham, NC: Duke University Press, 2004.

Petersen, Jennifer Lynn. "Travelogues and Early Nonfiction Film: Education in the School of Dreams." In *American Cinema's Transitional Years: Au-*

dience, Institution, Practices, edited by Charlie Keil and Shelley Stamp, 191–213. Berkeley: University of California Press, 2004.

Riley, Charles A. *Color Codes.* Lebanon, NH: University Press of New England, 1995.

Rivero, Yeidy. *Broadcasting Modernity: Cuban Commercial Television, 1950–1960.* Durham, NC: Duke University Press, 2015.

Roizen, Joseph. "Universal Color TV: An Electronic Fantasia." *IEEE Spectrum* 4, no. 3 (March 1967): 112–114.

Rood, Ogden N. *Modern Chromatics: With Applications to Art and Industry.* New York: D. Appleton and Company, 1879.

Rorimer, Anne. *New Art in the 60s and 70s: Redefining Reality.* London: Thames and Hudson, 2001.

Roth, Lorna. "Looking at Shirley, the Ultimate Norm: Color Balance, Image Technologies, and Cognitive Equity." *Canadian Journal of Communication* 34 (2009): 111–136.

Salter, Liora. "The Housework of Capitalism: Standardization in the Communications and Information Technology Sectors." *International Journal of Political Economy* 23, no. 4 (winter 1993/94): 105–133.

Sarnoff, David. *Looking Ahead: The Papers of David Sarnoff.* New York: McGraw-Hill, 1968.

Schopenhauer, Arthur. *On the Fourfold Root of the Principle of Sufficient Reason.* Translated by E. F. J. Payne. LaSalle, IL: Open Court, 1974.

———. *The World as Will and Representation.* Translated by E. F. J. Payne. New York: Dover, 1969.

Schopenhauer, Arthur, *On Vision and Colors,* and Philipp Otto Runge, *Color Sphere.* Translated by Georg Stahl. New York: Princeton Architectural Press, 2010.

Schwarzkopf, Stefan, and Rainer Gries. "Ernest Dichter, Motivation Research and the 'Century of the Consumer'." In *Ernest Dichter and Motivation Research,* 3–40. New York: Palgrave, 2010.

Schwoch, James. *Global TV: New Media and the Cold War, 1946–69.* Champaign: University of Illinois Press, 2009.

Scott, David Meerman, Richard Jurek, and Eugene A. Cernan. *Marketing the Moon: The Selling of the Apollo Lunar Program.* Cambridge, MA: MIT Press, 2014.

Sewell, Phillip. *Television in the Age of Radio: Modernity, Imagination, and the Making of a Medium.* New Brunswick, NJ: Rutgers University Press, 2013.

Shiers, George. *Technical Development of Television.* Stratford, NH: Ayer, 2010.

Slotten, Hugh. *Radio and Television Regulation: Broadcast Technology in the United States, 1920–1960.* Baltimore: Johns Hopkins University Press, 2000.

Smith, T., and J. Guild. "The CIE Colorimetric Standards and Their Use." *Transactions of the Optical Society* 33, no. 3 (1931–1932): 5–134.

Soffer, Oren. "The Eraser and the Anti-Eraser: The Battle over Color Television in Israel." *Media, Culture and Society* 30, no. 6 (November 2008): 759–775.

Sparke, Penny. *As Long as It's Pink: The Sexual Politics of Taste.* Halifax: Nova Scotia College of Design, 2010.

Spigel, Lynn. *TV by Design: Modern Art and the Rise of Network Television.* Chicago: University of Chicago Press, 2009.

———. *Welcome to the Dreamhouse: Popular Media and Postwar Suburbs.* Durham, NC: Duke University Press, 2001.

Sterne, Jonathan. *MP3: The Meaning of a Format.* Durham, NC: Duke University Press, 2012.

Sterne, Jonathan, and Dylan Mulvin. "The Low Acuity for Blue: Perceptual Technics and American Color Television." *Journal of Visual Culture* 13, no. 2 (August 2014): 118–138.

Street, Sarah. "'Colour Consciousness': Natalie Kalmus and Technicolor in Britain." *Screen* 50, no. 2 (summer 2009): 191–215.

———. *Colour Films in Britain: The Negotiation of Innovation, 1900–55.* London: British Film Institute, 2012.

Sweet, A. L., and N. R. Bartlett. "An Illusory Rotating Sweep." *American Journal of Psychology* 61, no. 3 (July 1948): 400–404.

Telotte, J. P. *Disney TV.* Detroit: Wayne State University Press, 2004.

———. *The Mouse Machine: Disney and Technology.* Champaign: University of Illinois Press, 2008.

Tirella, Joseph. *Tomorrow-Land: The 1964–65 World's Fair and the Transformation of America.* Guilford, CT: Lyons Press, 2014.

Tyler, Kingdon S. *Telecasting in Color.* New York: Harcourt, 1946.

Wade, Robert J. *Designing for TV: The Arts and Crafts in Television Production.* New York: Pellegrini and Cudahy, 1952.

Waller, Gregory A. "Robert Southard and the History of Traveling Film Exhibition." *Film Quarterly* 57, no. 2 (winter 2003): 2–14.

Weaver, Pat. *The Best Seat in the House: The Golden Years of Radio and Television.* New York: Knopf, 1993.

Weber, Anne-Katrin. "Recording on Film, Transmitting by Signals: The Intermediate Film System and Television's Hybridity in the Interwar Period." *Grey Room* 56 (summer 2014): 6–33.

———. "Television before TV: A Transnational Medium on Display, 1928–1939." Ph.D. diss., University of Lausanne, 2014.

Wilson, J. C. "Trichromatic Reproduction in Television." *Journal of the Royal Society of Arts* 82, no. 4258 (June 29, 1934): 841–863.

Winston, Brian. *Technologies of Seeing: Photography, Cinematography and Television.* London: British Film Institute, 1997.

———. "A Whole Technology of Dyeing: A Note on Ideology and the Apparatus of the Chromatic Moving Image." *Daedalus* 114, no. 4 (fall 1985): 105–123.

Wintringham, W. T. "Color Television and Colorimetry." *Proceedings of the IRE,* October 1951, 1135–1172.

Wittgenstein, Ludwig. *Remarks on Colour.* Edited by G. E. M. Anscombe. Translated by Linda L. McAlister and Margaret Schattle. Berkeley: University of California Press, 1978.

Wood, Amy Louise. *Lynching and Spectacle: Witnessing Racial Violence in America, 1890–1940.* Chapel Hill: University of North Carolina Press, 2011.

Yumibe, Joshua. *Moving Color: Early Film, Mass Culture, Modernism.* New Brunswick, NJ: Rutgers University Press, 2012.

additive color mixing, 19–20, 42, 52–53

Adler, Hazel, 49

Advanced Television Systems Committee (ATSC), 254, 291n10

advertising, 101, 104–7, 136–37, 153

aesthetics, 159, 170–71, 173–74

afterimages, 39–41. *See also* persistence of vision

American Broadcasting Corporation (ABC): color, late investment in, 87, 125, 150; colorcasts, 185–86; logo, 165; *The New Alice in Wonderland*, 185–86; and satellite transmissions, 238; *Sophia Loren in Rome*, 193–94; *The Undersea World of Jacques Cousteau*, 213–14

American National Exhibition (Moscow), 222, 224

American Society of Cinematographers, 56–57

AMPEX color videotape, 218–19

animated color programs, 185–86

Apollo missions: camera technology, 240–43, 245–47; color benefits, 242–43; color difficulties, 245–46; live broadcasts, 242–45; moon landing, 245–46; television, importance to, 240; television, reluctant use of, 239–40

attentiveness studies, 136–38

Baird, John Logie: eye experiment, 15–16; first color demonstration, 17–19, 25–26; funding, 23; high defi-

nition color systems, 29–31; legacy, 30–31; monochrome demonstrations, 25, 261n13; stereoscopic television, 29–30; television variants, 18

bars, 143, 174

Bel Geddes, Norman, 156

"Bidwell's ghost," 40–41

Birren, Faber, 105–7

Bonanza (NBC), 183–85

British Broadcasting Corporation (BBC), 30–31, 234

calibration, in-home, 113–14

camera calibration, 107–8, 111–12

Caucasian skin (color reproduction), 108, 110–13

CBS. *See* Columbia Broadcasting System (CBS)

chapter overviews, 6–10

Chicago, 128, 141, 151–53

chromophobia, 95–96

chronochrome film process, 52–53

Cinderella (CBS), 168–69

close-ups, in demonstrations, 26

Cold War: American National Exhibition (Moscow), 222, 224; color television, as symbol, 6, 219–21; "the kitchen debate," 217–19; and space technology, 221, 237–38

color: as additional dimension, 179, 181, 255–56; business of, 36; education, 43–44; emotional responses to, 108–7;

color (*continued*)

Goethe's theory of, 37–39, 49; harmony (*see* color harmony); industrialization of, 43; mixing theories, 41–42; moods created by, 106; moral associations, 95–96; Newton's theory of, 37, 49; objective vs. subjective, 36–38; OSA definition, 45; perception of, 93; physiological, 38; rationalization of, 126; scholarship on, 2–3; Schopenhauer's theory of, 38–39; standardization (*see* standardization, of color); therapeutic, 49, 51, 106

colorcasts: CBS, 71, 84, 87–88, 90, 117, 119, 166, 187, 282n95; NBC, 116, 119–22, 140, 166–67, 183–84

Color City (NBC), 155–59

color film: chronochrome, 52–53; coloring techniques, early, 51; differentiation, studio, 53; and genre, 114–15, 167; haptic quality, 181; Kinemacolor, 53; meaning of, 181–82; "natural coloring" process, 51–52; scholarship on, 2; Technicolor, 53, 55–56, 103–4, 114–15; vs. videotape, 172–73

color harmony, 44, 47–49, 103–5

colorimetry, 34, 44, 74, 103

colorists, 48, 51, 254

color lighting, 171–74

color measurement. *See* colorimetry

color mixing, 19–20, 42, 52–53

color photography, 19–20, 80. *See also* Kromskop

color programming, difficulties of, 165–66

color revolution, 49–51

color spaces, 34

color standards, contexts of, 34, 36

color television: broadcasts (*see* colorcasts); criticism of, 86–87; demonstrations of (*see* demonstrations, early color); as failure, 87; histories of, 3, 12–14; inevitability of, 1, 14, 114, 126, 155, 177–78; instability of, 92, 96; introduction of, 129–30; as luxury item, 130–31, 135, 252; as new way of seeing, 4 (*see also* vision); poor public perception of, 88, 93–94, 126; production ban, 72; psychological effects, purported, 5–6, 136–38; resistance to, 88, 93–94, 126; responses to, early, 1–2, 93; as risky, 94; scholarship, lack of, 2–3; sets, in-home, 183; standardization (*see* standardization, of color television); successors to, 251–52, 254–56; as troublesome, 1–2, 16–17

Color Television Inc. (CTI), 66–67, 270n3

color test girls, 107–8, 110–12

Color TV Caravan (RCA/NBC), 145–46, 149–50

color videotape, 154, 166, 169–70, 172

Columbia Broadcasting System (CBS): color, ambivalence to, 186–87, 285n24; colorcasts, 71, 84, 87–88, 90, 117, 119, 166, 187, 282n95; color conversion, 151, 155; and color standardization, 64, 66–69; color studios, 155; color system, failure of, 84–85; color system, promotion of, 31, 60–64; color system, resistance to, 69–72; color test girls, 110; *Elizabeth Taylor in London*, 193; extravaganzas, 124; eye logo, 162, 164–65; FCC lawsuit, 69–70; Hyton Electronics purchase, 72; NTSC system support, 84; Patty Painter, 62, 64, 110; *Premiere*, 71, 88, 110, 117, 119; and production ban, 72; Quality Television campaign, 60, 62; specials, 167–69; Television City, 155; UHF support, 60, 62, 78

commercials, 101, 104–7, 136–37, 153

Commission Internationale de L'Eclairage (CIE) color system, 34

compression, of data, 76–79, 93

computers, 252–53, 255

Condon Committee, 67, 80, 267n94

consumer vision, 6

conversion to colorcasting, 150–53, 155–56, 163

Cousteau, Jacques, 213–16

Cuba, 232–33

cultural documentaries: art, 197–200; and cinema, early, 195–96; color, showcasing, 189; contexts of, 188; nature, 205–16; overview, 188–91; photography, 201; selected list of, 189–90; for selling color, 195–97; travel, 191–96; *Wide Wide World*, 194–95

cultural imperialism, 231

dark (passive) colors, 106

data compression, 76–79, 93

demonstrations, early color: Bell Labs, 19–22, 26; close-ups, 26; Goldmark's system, 31–33; Jolson and race, 26–27; in malls, 145; subject considerations, 25, 27–28

demonstrations, monochrome, 23–26

Dichter, Ernest, 107

digital film, 254

digital intermediate stage, 254–55

digital television, 254–56

DuMont, 64, 84, 120, 125, 153

Eastman Kodak Company, 55, 75–76, 112, 122, 169, 201

Eisenhower, Dwight D., 153–54

Elizabeth Taylor in London (CBS), 193

European color systems, 234–35

Evening with Fred Astaire, An (NBC), 170–72

experiments with color, early, 12–14, 16, 19–22. *See also* Baird, John Logie

eye fatigue, 73, 92

eyes, 14–16

Federal Communications Commission (FCC): color standardization, 1, 31, 60, 67–70, 77; hearings, on color systems, 64, 66–67, 75, 81, 266n84; lawsuits against, 69–70; monochrome stan-

dardization, 7, 58–60; 1950 decision (for CBS), 69–70, 108; 1953 reversal (to NTSC), 84–85, 87–88, 90, 270n6; and NTSC, 72, 84–85; reports, 68–69; UHF support, 62

fidelity, image, 79–80, 90

Fink, Donald G., 57–58

food, 99–101

foreign markets, 229, 231–35

functional color, 106–7

genre, 114–16, 165–67, 182

Goethe's color theory, 37–39, 49

Goldmark, Peter, 5, 17, 31, 60, 62, 64, 66, 246

Goodman, Ace, 86

Helmholtz, Hermann von, 41–42, 78

human perception, 78–80. *See also* psychophysical testing

I Dream of Jeannie (NBC), 285n27

immersion: Baird's goal of, 29–30; nature documentaries, 207; rhetoric of, 4–6, 30, 179, 181, 255–56

imperialism, cultural, 231

India, 232

Institute for Motivational Research (IMR) studies, 137–38

interior design, 48

Inter-Society Color Council (ISCC), 46

Israel, 231–32

Ives, Frederic E., 19, 42–43

Ives, Herbert E., 19–23, 25

Japan, 233–34

Jolson, Al, 21, 26–27

Kaleidoscope (NBC), 195

Kalmus, Natalie, 48, 55

Khrushchev, Nikita, 217–19

Kinemacolor, 53

kinescope, color, 99, 166, 169–70

"kitchen debate," 217–19

Kodak, 55, 75–76, 112, 122, 169, 201
Korean War, 71–72, 81, 90
Kromskop, 19, 42–43

light (active) colors, 106
lighting, 104–5, 110, 171–74
linguistic relativity, 37
liquid crystal displays (LCDS), 250–52
"local color" concept, 129–30

malls, 143, 145
marketing, of color television: and class,
    133–38; to consumers, 133–35, 140,
    142–43; NBC promotional events,
    127–29; segmentation, 133–35; to tele-
    vision industry, 96–97, 99, 126
market segmentation, 133–35
McNamara, Marie, 110–11
mechanical color converters, 131–32
medical education, 5, 66, 196–97,
    260n8
Mexico, 234
middle-class life, 130–31, 145
modernism, 159, 170–71, 173–74
mod style, 187
monochrome demonstrations, 23–25
monochrome television, 252, 254
Munsell, Albert, 34, 43–44, 68, 101, 103
Munsell Color Company, 44–45
musical programs, 121, 167, 170–74

National Broadcasting Company (NBC):
    An Evening with Fred Astaire, 170–72;
    art documentaries, 197–200; Bel Ged-
    des collaboration, 156–57; Bonanza,
    183–85; Caucasian skin, represent-
    ing, 108, 110; color, rationalization
    of, 125–26; colorcasts, 116, 119–22,
    140, 166–67, 183–84; Color City
    (Burbank), 155–59; color conversion,
    151, 155–56, 163; Color Corps, 98,
    105; color harmony, use of, 48–49,
    103; color test girls, 110–11; Color-
    town study, 133; Color TV Caravan,

145–46, 149–50; demonstrations, of
    color, 81, 98–99; I Dream of Jeannie,
    285n27; Kaleidoscope, 195; marketing,
    to consumers, 133–35, 140, 142–43;
    marketing, to television industry,
    96–97, 99, 126; musical programs,
    121; National Color TV Week, 142–43;
    National Geographic specials (see Na-
    tional Geographic); opera broadcasts,
    120–21; peacock logo, 159–64; Peter
    Pan, 124, 167–69; ratings boost, color,
    284n18; RCA partnership, 138, 140–42,
    282n90; specials, 166–67, 169; spec-
    taculars, 122–25; "spectrum spectac-
    ular" events, 127–29; and sponsors,
    97, 105, 122–23, 140–41; Sylvester
    "Pat" Weaver, 122–23, 127, 157, 277n2;
    testing, of color, 101, 103; Tommy Tint,
    128–29; WNBQ, 127–29, 151–53, 161,
    211; workshops, on color, 48–49, 98,
    104–5, 229; "The World of Jacques-
    Yves Cousteau," 214–16; World's
    Fair (1964), 225–26; xylophone logo,
    159–60
National Geographic: educational films,
    210; magazine, 209–10; television
    specials, 206–7, 209–10, 287n65;
    "The World of Jacques-Yves Cous-
    teau," 214–16
nationalism, 219–220
National Television System Committee
    (NTSC): and color standardization, 67,
    72–75, 79–81; color system, 81, 84–85,
    90–92, 108; creation of, 59–60; and
    the FCC, 72, 84–85; psychophysical
    testing, 73–76, 80; racial bias, in test-
    ing, 112; RCA system recommendation,
    81–84; reconstitution (1950), 72
nature documentaries, 205–16
network television, financial structure,
    182–83
New Alice in Wonderland, The (ABC),
    185–86
news reporting, 179, 181

Newtonian color theory, 37, 49
Nixon, Richard, 217–19

opera, 120–21, 158
Optical Society of America (OSA), 45
Ostwald's color system, 48–49, 101
overlay sheets, 131

Painter, Patty, 62, 64, 110, 117, 119
Paley, William, 62, 64, 66, 88, 119
Pathé Cinema, 51
peacock logo, NBC's, 159–64
persistence of vision, 40, 73, 263n21.
   See also afterimages
Peter Pan (NBC), 124, 167–69
Phillips color cameras, 183
photography, 201, 203–5, 287n61
physiological color, 38–39
pop art, 201
Premiere (CBS), 71, 88, 110, 117, 119
prestige programming, 173–74
psychophysical testing, 73–76, 80
"Psy-Color-gy" report, 107
Purkinje afterimages, 40–41

Quality Television campaign (CBS), 60,
   62

race and racism, 26–27, 108, 110–13
radiation scare, 247–49
Radio Corporation of America (RCA):
   American National Exhibition (Moscow), 222, 224; Color City (Burbank),
   155–59; color clinics, 113; color management techniques, 89; and color
   standardization, 64, 66–70, 81–84;
   color system, 90; Color TV Caravan,
   use of, 145–46, 149–50; FCC lawsuit,
   69–70; LCD development, 251–52;
   marketing, to consumers, 141–43,
   145–47, 149–50; and monochrome
   standardization, 59; NBC partnership,
   138, 140–42, 282n90; Relay satellite,
   237; roadshow, technological, 145–47,

149–50; single-gun system demonstrations, 81–84; space cameras,
   240–43, 247; television research,
   early, 28; WNBQ, 127–29, 151–53, 161,
   211; World's Fair (1964), 225–26, 228
Radio Manufacturers Association (RMA),
   59
realism, 79–80, 90, 114–16, 181
Relay (NASA satellite), 237
road shows, technological, 145–49

Sarnoff, David: business strategy, 121,
   198, 219, 229; Cold War, 220–21, 228;
   research focus, 28–29; standardization, push for, 59; WNBQ conversion,
   151–52, 154; World's Fair speech,
   228–29
Sarnoff, Robert, 127, 154, 197–98, 247,
   277n2
Sarnoff, Thomas, 184
satellites, 221, 237–38
scanning, definition of, 40
shopping malls, 143, 145
sight. See vision
skin tones, 30, 108, 110–13
Society of Motion Picture Engineers
   (SMPE), 56
Sophia Loren in Rome (ABC), 193–94
space technology, 221, 235, 237–38. See
   also Apollo missions
sports programming, 196
Sputnik, 221
Standard Color Card of America, 46
standardization, of color, 34, 36, 43–46,
   48. See also color harmony; colorimetry; Munsell Color Company
standardization, of color television:
   CBS's promotions, 60–64; contexts,
   34, 36; data compression, 76–78,
   93; FCC hearings, 64, 66–67, 75, 81,
   266n84; FCC 1950 decision, 69–70;
   FCC reports, 68–69; fidelity, 79–80;
   as limiting, 81; NTSC system, 81–84,
   90; political implications, 234;

standardization, of color television
(*continued*)
proposal evaluations, 67–68; proposals for (1949), 66–67. *See also* Federal Communications Commission (FCC); National Television System Committee (NTSC)
standardization, of film, 56–57
standardization, of monochrome television, 57–60
standardization movement, 44–46, 48
standard observer model, 74
subjectivity: of color, 36–38, 74, 126; and color standards, 73; and photographs, 80; Schopenhauer on, 38–39; of vision, 16, 37–40, 73, 80
subtractive color mixing, 42

Technicolor, 53, 55–56, 103–4, 114–15
television, 12, 14–16
three-color mixing theory, 41
Tommy Tint, 128–29

UHF standard, 60, 62
Undersea World of Jacques Cousteau, The, 213–14

veracity, 219–21
VHF standard, 60, 62
vision: anxieties about, 92; and color technology, 255–56; color variation, 93; failures of, 73; as ideal, 16; and satellites, 238; sensitivity of, 92–93; subjectivity of, 16, 37–40, 73

Walt Disney's Wonderful World of Color (WWOC), 176–79
Weaver, Sylvester "Pat," 122–23, 127, 157, 277n2
Westinghouse space camera, 246–47
WGN-TV (independent), 153
Wide Wide World (NBC), 194–95
WNBQ (NBC), 127–29, 151–53, 161, 211
women: as color specialists, 48; color test girls, 107–8, 110–11; marketing to, 135–36, 142–44
World's Fair (New York, 1964), 225–26, 228–29
WRC-TV (NBC), 153–54

Zoo Parade, The (NBC), 211
Zworykin, Vladimir, 28–29